2007 Legislative Changes Supplement

During its 2007 session, the General Assembly of North Carolina made changes in the laws affecting purchasing and contracting by local governments. The changes in this supplement apply specifically to *A Legal Guide to Purchasing and Contracting for North Carolina Local Governments*, second edition, by Frayda S. Bluestein. For a more detailed discussion of the legislation, please see Chapter 22, "Purchasing and Contracting," in the School of Government's publication *North Carolina Legislation 2007*, which is available online in PDF format at www.sog.unc.edu/pubs/nclegis/index.html.

Page 10. Question 13.

"Automobiles"* and "food service equipment" should be included in the list of items that local school units may purchase using lease-purchase or installment-purchase contracts. The quote from the statutes in the first and second paragraphs should read: "automobiles; school buses; mobile classroom units; food service equipment; photocopiers; and computers, computer hardware, computer software, and related support services."

Page 33. Question 41.

A new subsection 41.i(1) (see the text below) added between subsection 41.i and subsection 41.j reflects the 2007 legislative changes affecting federal contract purchases.

> *i(1). Federal (including GSA) contract purchases [143-129(e)(9a)].*
>
> The bidding statute contains an exception for purchases from federal contracts that is similar to the exception for state contracts (see Question 41.i). This exception allows local governments to purchase apparatus, supplies, materials, or equipment from contracts established by the United States government, including any federal agency, if the contractor is willing to extend to the local government the same or more favorable prices, terms, and conditions as established in the federal contract. Many federal contracts are awarded by the General Services Administration (GSA) and others are awarded by specific federal agencies, such as the Department of Transportation. Specific provisions of some federal contracts make them available to local governments. This exception is necessary for North Carolina local governments even when the contract itself is available to local governments since without the exception the local government would still be required to comply with state bidding requirements (either informal or

* "Automobiles" is added here to correct an omission in the original *Guide*. It does not reflect a change in legislation.

formal, depending upon the amount of the contract).

The wording of the exception allows a local government to contract with a vendor who has a federal contract even if the federal contract does not contain terms allowing local government participation. The absence of a provision in a federal contract extending its terms to local governments does not prevent the vendor from separately contracting for the same items and the same or better prices, terms, and conditions. Like the "piggybacking" (see Question 41.l and Appendix 3) and state contract exceptions, however, this exception does not create an obligation on the part of the federal contract vendor to extend the terms of the contract to local governments. Such an obligation would only exist if it is a part of the federal contract.

Like the exception for state contract purchases, this exception overlaps with the "piggybacking" exception, which authorizes purchases from suppliers who have contracted with another public agency. Under the more specific exception for federal contracts, however, the "piggybacking" exception's limitations on the time of the original contract award and its requirements for public notice and local governing board approval do not apply.

Page 37. Question 44.

The question and answer text as revised to reflect the 2007 legislation now reads:

> **44. Is bidding required when a local government purchases items from a state contract or federal (GSA) contract vendor?**
>
> Specific exceptions in the statute, G.S. 143-129(e)(9) (state contracts) and G.S. 143-129(e)(9a) (federal contracts), authorize local governments to purchase from state or federal contract vendors without bidding. For a more complete explanation of these exceptions, see Question 41.i and the new Question 41.i(1).

Page 105. Appendix 1: Dollar Thresholds in North Carolina Public Contracting Statutes.

The corrected chart included with this supplement replaces page 105.

Page 112. Appendix 2: G.S. 115C-528. Lease purchase and installment purchase contracts for certain equipment.

The 2007 legislation adds "food service equipment" to the list of items that local school units may purchase using lease-purchase or installment-purchase contracts. The first sentence of G.S. 115C-528(a) now reads:

> Local boards of education may purchase or finance the purchase of automobiles; school buses; mobile classroom units; food service equipment; photocopiers; and computers, computer hardware, computer software, and related support services by lease purchase contracts and installment purchase contracts as provided in this section.

Pages 119 and 120. Appendix 2: G.S. 142-129. Procedure for letting of public contracts.

The 2007 legislation adds the following new subparagraph (e)(9a) between subparagraphs (e)(9) and (e)(10).

> (9a) Purchases of apparatus, supplies, materials, or equipment from contracts established by the United States of America or any federal agency, if the contractor is willing to extend to a political subdivision of the State the same or more favorable prices, terms, and conditions as established in the federal contract.

Laminated Card: Dollar Thresholds in North Carolina Public Contracting Statutes.

The laminated card showing the Dollar Thresholds chart included with this supplement replaces the chart provided with the original *Guide*.

A Legal Guide TO Purchasing AND Contracting FOR North Carolina Local Governments

Second Edition

Frayda S. Bluestein

UNC
SCHOOL OF GOVERNMENT

School of Government, UNC Chapel Hill

Established in 1931, the Institute of Government provides training, advisory, and research services to public officials and others interested in the operation of state and local government in North Carolina. The Institute and the university's Master of Public Administration Program are the core activities of the School of Government at The University of North Carolina at Chapel Hill.

Each year approximately 14,000 public officials and others attend one or more of the more than 200 classes, seminars, and conferences offered by the Institute. Faculty members annually publish up to fifty books, bulletins, and other reference works related to state and local government. Each day that the General Assembly is in session, the Institute's *Daily Bulletin*, available in print and electronic format, reports on the day's activities for members of the legislature and others who need to follow the course of legislation. An extensive Web site (www.sog.unc.edu) provides access to publications and faculty research, course listings, program and service information, and links to other useful sites related to government.

Operating support for the School of Government's programs and activities comes from many sources, including state appropriations, local government membership dues, private contributions, publication sales, course fees, and service contracts. For more information about the School, the Institute, and the MPA program, visit the Web site or call (919) 966-5381.

First edition 1998. Second edition 2004

Printed in the United States of America

18 17 16 15 14 8 9 10 11 12

ISBN 1-56011-464-9

Contents

Introduction xi

Chapter I Local Government Contracts 1

The Law of Contracts 1

1. What is a contract? 1
2. What laws govern local government contracts, and are they different from the laws governing other types of contracts? 1
3. What are the essential requirements for a valid local government contract? 1
4. What is the common law of contracts? 2

Limitations on Local Government Contracting 3

5. What are the limitations on the purposes for which local governments may legally contract? 3
6. Can a local governing board enter into a contract that binds its discretion or the discretion of future governing boards? 5

Individual Authority to Contract 5

7. Who has authority to contract on behalf of a local government? 5
8. Is the authority to execute a contract the same as the authority to approve a contract? 6
9. Can a local government be liable on contracts under the doctrine of apparent authority? 7
10. Can an individual's lack of authority be cured by ratification? 7

Budgetary Authority 8

11. What does it mean to have proper budgetary authority for a contract? 8
12. Can local governments enter into contracts that extend beyond the current fiscal year? 9
13. Are there special procedures for lease-purchase or installment-purchase contracts? 9
14. What is a nonappropriation clause, and does its presence mean that the contract is not a continuing contract? 12
15. What is a nonsubstitution clause, and what is a deficiency judgment? 12

Contract Formalities 13

16. Do all contracts have to be in writing? 13
17. Does the written record of a resolution or ordinance adopted by a local government satisfy a writing requirement? 14
18. Can a faxed or other electronic document satisfy a writing requirement? 15
19. Who has the authority to sign contracts on behalf of a local government? 15
20. Is a witness or a corporate seal required when contracts are executed? 16

Chapter II Competitive Bidding Requirements 17

Underlying Purposes of Competitive Bidding 17

21. Why are there competitive bidding requirements for public contracts? 17
22. Is the main purpose of competitive bidding to get the lowest price? 17
23. What does fairness require in the context of public contracting? 17
24. Can a local government consider best value rather than just lowest price when bidding and awarding contracts? 18
25. Do the goals of fairness and value ever conflict? 18

Sources of Legal Requirements 19

26. Where can I find the competitive bidding requirements in the North Carolina General Statutes? 19

Entities Covered by Competitive Bidding Statutes 19

27. Which local governments are required to comply with competitive bidding requirements? 19
28. Are there any governmental units that are exempt from the competitive bidding requirements? 19
29. Do nonprofit organizations or other quasi-public organizations that receive public funds have to comply with the bidding laws? 20
30. Are volunteer fire departments required to comply with the competitive bidding laws? 21

Contracts Covered by Competitive Bidding Statutes 22

31. Do the competitive bidding procedures apply when the unit is spending money under federal or state grants or money from other outside sources? 22
32. What if funds are donated to the unit on condition that they must be used to purchase a particular item or to construct a facility using a specified contractor? 22
33. What types of contracts are covered by the bidding laws? 23
34. Are contracts for services subject to the competitive bidding laws? 23
35. What is the definition of a service contract, and what are some examples? 24
36. Do the competitive bidding requirements apply to contracts that are a mixture of goods and services? 24
37. How does the "predominant aspect" rule of interpretation apply to specific contracts, such as contracts for goods that include installation? 25
38. Are local governments required to bid computer software contracts? 25
39. Are contracts for demolition work covered by the competitive bidding statutes? 26
40. Are there special rules for the purchase of food or food services? 27
41. Which contracts are exempt from the competitive bidding requirements? 27
    a. Purchases from other units of government [143-129(e)(1)] 27
    b. Emergencies [143-129(e)(2)] 28
    c. Group purchasing programs [143-129(e)(3)] 29
    d. Change order work [143-129(e)(4)] 30
    e. Gas, fuel, and oil [143-129(e)(5)] 30
    f. Sole-source purchases [143-129(e)(6)] 30
    g. Information technology goods and services [143-129(e)(7); 143-129.8] 31
    h. Guaranteed energy savings contracts [143-129(e)(8)] 32
    i. State contract purchases [143-129(e)(9)] 32
    j. Purchase of used goods [143-129(e)(10)] 33
    k. Construction management at risk [143-129(e)(11)] 33
    l. Previously bid or "piggybacking" contracts [143-129(g)] 33
    m. Transportation authority purchases [143-129(h)] 34
    n. Solid waste management facilities [143-129.2] 35

o. Use of unit's own forces (force account work) [143-135] 35
p. Purchases of goods and services from nonprofit work centers for the blind and severely disabled [143-129.5] 36
q. Supplies and food for school food services [G.S. 115C-264] 36
42. Do lease contracts have to be bid? 36
43. Do sole-source items have to be bid? 37
44. Is bidding required when a local government purchases items from a state contract vendor? 37
45. What is the "request for proposals" procedure that is authorized for information technology goods and services? 37
46. What procedures apply to purchases from North Carolina Correction Enterprises? 38
47. Can a local government piggyback on another governmental unit's contract without going out for bids if a vendor who has a contract with the other unit is willing to provide the goods at the same price? 39

Application of Dollar Thresholds 39

48. What are the dollar thresholds for formal and informal procedures? 39
49. Do the dollar thresholds apply to the cost of each item or to the total contract amount? 39
50. Are local governments required to identify and consolidate all of their needs for particular items before going out for bids in order to avoid the statute's prohibition on dividing contracts? 39
51. How does a local government generate the estimated cost in order to determine the level of competition required? 40
52. What if a good faith estimate suggests that the informal bidding procedure should be used but one or more of the bids actually exceeds the informal bidding limit? 40
53. Are taxes and delivery costs included in the estimate when determining what level of bidding is required? 40
54. What if a change order or other modification made to an informally bid contract after it has been awarded and executed brings it above the formal limit? 40

Specifications 41

55. What are specifications, and what purposes do they serve? 41
56. Do the statutes contain specific requirements for how specifications should be prepared? 41
57. Where can local government officials find the information they need to prepare good specifications? 41
58. Are there any legal limitations on how specifications are prepared? 42
59. Is it legal to specify brand names? 42
60. Does the desire to standardize equipment justify specifying a particular brand? 43
61. What is an "approved products" or "qualified products" list? 43
62. Are there state rules requiring purchase of products with recycled content or purchase of remanufactured or reused materials? 44
63. What is a performance specification, and when should one be used? 44
64. What is the purpose of a pre-solicitation or pre-bid conference? 45
65. Can the local government make attendance at a pre-bid conference or site visit mandatory and reject the bids of contractors who do not attend? 45

Types of Contracts and Solicitations 46

66. What are the differences between an IFB or RFB, an RFP, and an IFQ or RFQ, and which of these are North Carolina local governments allowed to use? 46

67. Can a local government trade in surplus property as part of a competitive bidding process for the purchase of new equipment? 47
68. Can a local government solicit bids to lock in a price without committing to a particular quantity of items to be purchased, and, if so, how does the unit determine what level of bidding is required? 48
69. Can a local government include in a contract an option to renew the contract for additional terms or to purchase additional quantities at the unit's discretion? 48
70. Can a renewal or additional-quantities provision in a contract allow for a price adjustment? 49

Formal Bidding Procedures (Requirements Found in G.S. 143-129) **49**

***Advertisement* 49**

71. Where must bid opportunities be advertised? 49
72. When and for how long must the advertisement for a bid opportunity appear? 50
73. What information must be in the advertisement of a bid opportunity? 51
74. Can a local government change the date of a bid opening after the advertisement for the bid opportunity has appeared? 51
75. Are local governments required to maintain bidders lists and to send individual notice of bidding opportunities to bidders? 52
76. If a local government maintains a bidders list, is it required to list all suppliers who wish to be listed? Can the local government remove bidders from the list? 53
77. If a bidder is removed from the bidders list, does that mean that the bidder is disqualified from bidding? 53
78. Can a local government disqualify bidders based on prior poor performance or other factors? 53

***Bid Opening* 54**

79. Are sealed bids always required in the formal bidding process, and why are they used? 54
80. What should be done if a bid is erroneously opened by an employee of the unit prior to the bid opening? 54
81. Are local governments authorized to receive bids electronically? 55
82. Describe the "reverse auction" alternative to the formal bidding procedure that local governments are authorized to use. 56
83. Do bid openings have to be public meetings of the governing board? 56
84. Who can or must attend a bid opening, and how is a bid opening conducted? 56
85. Can members of the public, including the bidders present at the bid opening, look at the bids after they are opened but before the evaluation or award has been made? 57
86. Can a late bid be accepted if the bidder can show it was the fault of a delivery company or some other agent and not directly the fault of the bidder? 58

***Bid Bond or Bid Deposit* 58**

87. What is a bid bond or bid deposit, and when is one required? 58
88. Can a bid bond or bid deposit be accepted if it is submitted in a form other than the ones listed in the statute? 59
89. If a bid is not accompanied by a proper bid deposit, can the bid be accepted if the bidder can provide the proper bid deposit before the contract is awarded or soon after the bid opening? 60
90. How is the amount of the bid deposit calculated for contracts where the amount of work or quantity to be purchased is not specified? 60

91. If a bid is received without the proper bid deposit, can it be counted for purposes of the three-bid requirement? 60
92. Can a local government accept a faxed bid bond? 61

***Number and Form of Bids* 61**

93. How many bids must be received under the formal bidding procedure before a contract can be awarded? 61
94. Can a local government accept a faxed bid in a formal bidding procedure? 61
95. If a bid is submitted but is determined to be unacceptable (nonresponsive) after it has been reviewed and evaluated, does it count as a bid for purposes of the three-bid requirement? 62
96. What should be done if a bid solicitation for a construction or repair contract in the formal range generates fewer than three bids? 62
97. Can the unit make any changes in the specifications in the second round of bidding? 62
98. What should be done with bids already received if readvertisement of a bid opportunity is necessary? 63
99. What if a contract for construction or repair work was estimated to cost more than the formal threshold amount but the estimate was very close to the threshold and fewer than three bids were received? 63

***Evaluating Bids* 64**

100. Who is responsible for evaluating the bids and determining which bidder should receive the award of the contract? 64
101. What is the legal standard for evaluating bids, and under what circumstances may or must a bid be rejected? 64
102. What if there is an ambiguity or omission in a bid that makes it difficult to determine what is being bid? Can the local government contact the bidder to resolve the question? 65
103. What if there is a discrepancy in a bid between the unit price and the extension? 65
104. Is the local government required to reject a bid if it is not made on the proper bid form or if the form is not properly completed? 65

***Errors in Bids and Bid Withdrawal* 66**

105. What if a bidder discovers a mistake in his or her bid and wishes to withdraw the bid? 66
106. If a bid is withdrawn for a mistake, does it count for purposes of the three-bid requirement for construction or repair contracts? 66
107. What if a bidder who has made an error that affects the price can show that, even with an adjustment to correct the error, he or she is still the lowest responsible bidder? Can the appropriate adjustment legally be made? 67
108. What if the local government, rather than the bidder, discovers an error in a bid? Is the bidder required to withdraw? 67

***Negotiating with Bidders* 67**

109. Can the local government ever negotiate with a bidder after the bids are opened but before the contract is awarded? 67
110. If the local government is not successful in negotiating with the lowest responsible bidder, can it pursue negotiations with the next lowest responsible bidder? 68
111. What does "available funds" mean for purposes of this provision? Is the unit limited to the actual budgeted amount? 68
112. Can the local government negotiate with the lowest responsible bidder on price only, without making changes in specifications? 68

Awarding Contracts **69**

113. Who is legally authorized to award contracts on behalf of a local government under the formal bidding statute? 69
114. Must contract awards be made at a meeting, or at any particular kind of meeting, of the board; and what is the procedure for award when authority is delegated? 69
115. Are there any particular findings that must be made before a contract can be awarded? 69
116. Can a local government award a contract in one budget year for an item to be paid for out of the next year's budget? 70

Lowest Responsible Bidder Standard for Award **70**

117. Does a local government have the authority to award a contract to someone other than the lowest bidder? 70
118. Is the local government required to prove that the lowest bidder is not responsible in order to award to another bidder? 71
119. How much discretion does the local government have to award a purchase contract to a higher bidder? Can the award go to a higher bidder who offers a higher quality of equipment? 72
120. How much and what kind of documentation is required if the local government awards a contract to someone other than the low bidder? 72

Preferences **73**

121. Can a local government establish a preference for local bidders? 73
122. Doesn't state law establish a preference for minority-owned and women-owned businesses? 74

Post-Award Procedures **74**

123. Must a local government contract be approved by any entity other than the local governing board? 74
124. Is a binding contract created as of the moment the board or designated official awards the contract? 74
125. Can a local government rescind its award of a contract under the competitive bidding statutes? 75
126. Can a local government award a contract contingent upon obtaining necessary funding or some other condition? 76
127. Is the bidder relieved of his or her obligation if the local government takes too long to award or execute a contract? 76
128. How long must a local government retain bid and contract documents? 77

Performance and Payment Bonds **77**

129. When and why are performance and payment bonds required? 77

Informal Bidding Procedures (Requirement Found in G.S. 143-131) **78**

130. What is the dollar threshold for contracts that are subject to the informal bidding procedure? 78
131. What if the estimated cost of a contract is within the informal range but one or more of the bids actually received is within the formal range? 79
132. What does the informal procedure require? 79
133. What methods may be used to secure informal bids for contracts in the informal range? 79
134. During the process of soliciting informal bids, is the person obtaining the bids required to tell a vendor the prices he or she has already received? 79
135. How many bids are required under the informal procedure? 80

136. What is the standard for awarding contracts in the informal range? 80
137. What procedures are required for contracts costing less than the informal threshold amount? 80

Contract Issuance 81

138. What are the legal requirements that apply when a local government issues a contract? 81
139. Is a purchase order a contract, and what information should it contain? 81

Optional Procedures 81

140. How should local governments go about letting contracts that are not subject to the competitive bidding requirements? 81
141. Must a local government adhere to a bidding procedure it has undertaken even when the law didn't require bids in the first place? 82
142. Does the local government have to award contracts to the lowest responsible bidder when contracts are not subject to the competitive bidding statutes? 82

Legal Challenges and Protests 83

143. What are the legal and practical consequences of failing to comply with the competitive bidding statutes? 83
144. What are the procedures for protesting a local government bidding process or contract award decision? 84
145. What would be the basis of a legal claim arising out of a competitive bidding process? 84
146. Can a purchasing agent or other official be personally liable for failure to comply with a competitive bidding requirement? 86
147. Who may bring a legal claim arising out of a competitive bidding process? 87

Chapter III Purchasing Organization and Policies 89

148. How should the purchasing function be organized in a local government? 89
149. What is the best way to deal with small purchases? 90
150. Are local governments required to have a purchasing policy or procedures manual? 91
151. What is the purpose of a purchasing policy or procedures manual? 91
152. Does the governing board have to adopt or approve the purchasing manual or policy? 92
153. Is there a difference between a vendor manual and a purchasing manual? 93
154. What should be included in a purchasing policy or manual? 93
155. How should a local government or purchasing agent develop a purchasing policy? 94
156. Can local governments engage in cooperative or joint purchasing with other units of government? 95

Chapter IV Ethics and Conflicts of Interest 97

157. What are the sources of law that govern ethics and conflicts of interest in purchasing? 97
158. What does state law prohibit in the area of conflict of interest? 97
159. Is it illegal for the spouse or relative of a public official to benefit from a contract? 100
160. Does a contract create a conflict of interest if a governing board member who stands to benefit was not involved in making or voting on the contract? 101
161. Can a board member avoid liability under the statute by not voting on the contract? 102

162. What is the legal effect of a contract that violates G.S. 14-234? 102
163. Can the governing board ratify a contract that was made in violation of G.S. 14-234? 102
164. Is there a dollar figure that is used to determine when a gift is considered of nominal value? 102
165. Does a gift to the local government or to a department violate the gifts and favors statute? 103
166. Can local government officials or employees legally accept an invitation to a site visit to be paid for by a contractor or potential contractor? 103
167. Is it illegal for employees to purchase items for their personal use through local government contracts? 104

Appendix 1 Dollar Thresholds in North Carolina Public Contracting Statutes 105

Appendix 2 Selected Statutes 107

§ 14-234 Public officers or employees benefiting from public contracts; exceptions. 107
§ 14-234.1 Misuse of confidential information. 109
§ 115C-441 Budgetary accounting for appropriations. 110
§ 115C-522 Provision of equipment for buildings. 111
§ 115C-528 Lease purchase and installment purchase contracts for certain equipment. 112
§ 133-32 Gifts and favors regulated. 113
§ 133-33 Cost estimates; bidders' lists. 114
§ 143-128 Requirements for certain building contracts. 114
§ 143-129 Procedure for letting of public contracts. 117
§ 143-129.1 Withdrawal of bid. 121
§ 143-129.7 Purchase with trade-in of apparatus, supplies, materials, and equipment. 122
§ 143-129.8 Purchase of information technology goods and services. 122
§ 143-129.9 Alternative Competitive Bidding Methods. 123
§ 143-131 When counties, cities, towns and other subdivisions may let contracts on informal bids. 123
§ 143-132 Minimum number of bids for public contracts. 124
§ 143-133 No evasion permitted. 124
§ 143-135 Limitation of application of Article. 124
§ 153A-13 Continuing contracts. 125
§ 153A-449 Contracts with private entities. 125
§ 159-28 Budgetary accounting for appropriations. 125
§ 160A-16 Contracts to be in writing; exception. 127
§ 160A-17 Continuing contracts. 127
§ 160A-17.1 Grants from other governments. 127
§ 160A-20.1 Contracts with private entities. 128
§ 160A-461 Interlocal cooperation authorized. 128

Appendix 3 Interpretations of the "Piggybacking" Exception to North Carolina's Formal Bidding Requirements 129

Appendix 4 Understanding the Responsiveness Requirement in Competitive Bidding 137

Index 155

Introduction

Who should use this book?

This book is written for city, county, and school officials who are involved in contracting for goods and services. Most of the information will also apply to other types of local government entities, including special purpose authorities and districts of various kinds, although purchasing officials from these entities should check to make sure that statutory provisions that apply specifically to their forms of government do not conflict with the general principles or statutes discussed here.

What other books should be consulted for information on related subjects?

Several other books published by the School of Government address in more detail topics that are discussed in this book. For information on local government construction contracting, refer to *Construction Contracts with North Carolina Local Governments*, written by A. Fleming Bell, II. For further elaboration on matters involving local government finance, consult *Local Government Finance in North Carolina* and *Financing Capital Projects in North Carolina*, both written by David M. Lawrence. For a thorough treatment of legal issues involved in local government property transactions, including disposal of surplus property, see *Local Government Property Transactions in North Carolina*, also written by David M. Lawrence. Conflicts of interest and ethics issues are discussed in detail in *Ethics, Conflicts, and Offices: A Guide for Local Officials* by A. Fleming Bell, II.

Most of the state statutes governing purchasing are set forth in Appendix 2 of this *Legal Guide to Purchasing and Contracting.* For a complete compilation of statutes affecting local government finance and administration, a good resource is the single volume entitled *Administrative and Financial Laws for Local Government in North Carolina*, published by the LexisNexis Company of Charlottesville, Virginia, and available from the School of Government.

For additional information on the law of contracts in North Carolina, readers should consult *North Carolina Contract Law* by John N. Hutson Jr. and Scott A. Miskimon, which is available from LexisNexis.

The Council of State Governments, in collaboration with the National Association of State Purchasing Officials, has published a very informative book entitled *State and Local Government Purchasing*, which is currently in its fifth edition. This book surveys practices and laws dealing with public purchasing throughout the country and provides good background discussion of almost every significant issue in the public purchasing field.

Another excellent resource is *Service Contracting: A Local Government Guide*, written by Donald F. Haney and published by the International City/County Managers Association. This book contains thorough discussions of various types of solicitation methods (which may be used by North Carolina local governments when the mandatory competitive bidding laws do not apply) and contains definitions and contract terms that are extremely useful in drafting and understanding contracts.

A helpful overview can also be found in *An Elected Official's Guide to Procurement*, written by Patricia C. Watt and published by the Government Finance Officers Association. Although Watt does not discuss specific legal requirements applicable in North Carolina, her book provides a good introduction to many of the organizational and administrative issues in purchasing.

How can I make sure the information in this *Legal Guide to Purchasing and Contracting* is current, especially the dollar thresholds for statutory bidding requirements?

Readers of this and other School of Government publications on related subjects should contact the School, consult School of Government resources on the Internet, and monitor other sources of information in order to stay current on the law affecting purchasing. Appendix 1 of this *Legal Guide to Purchasing and Contracting* contains a "Dollar Thresholds in North Carolina Public Contracting Statutes" chart. This chart is also available on the purchasing and contracting section of the School of Government's Web site. Changes in thresholds that occur prior to revisions in this publication will be reflected on the Web site version.

Chapter I
Local Government Contracts

The Law of Contracts

1. What is a contract?

Courts have defined a contract as "an agreement, upon sufficient consideration, to do or not to do a particular thing."[1] Put another way, a contract is an agreement that a court will enforce; and a court will only enforce agreements that meet certain legal requirements. The legal requirements for local government contracts are discussed in this chapter. Not everything local governments do must be reflected in a contract. There are some agreements that do not meet certain legal requirements for court enforcement but which both parties are willing to perform. For example, an oral agreement may be sufficient if both parties perform and are satisfied with the result, even though a court would require a writing to enforce the obligation. A contract is only necessary if one or both parties want to have some legal way to enforce an agreement or if a statute specifically requires it.

2. What laws govern local government contracts, and are they different from the laws governing other types of contracts?

The best way to think about North Carolina local government contracts is that they are subject to the same basic requirements as all contracts, plus an additional layer of rules that apply only to public contracts and some requirements that apply only to North Carolina local governments. Each set of requirements must be met in order for the contract to be enforceable. The most important sources of law governing North Carolina local government contracts are the common law of contracts; state statutes affecting contracts generally, including the Uniform Commercial Code; and state statutes regarding local government contracting.

3. What are the essential requirements for a valid local government contract?

A contract must satisfy the common law requirements for enforceability, be for a legally authorized purpose, be entered into by a person with proper authority, be supported by proper budgetary authorization, satisfy applicable

---

1. Elliott Bldg. Co. v. City of Greensboro, 190 N.C. 501, 504, 130 S.E. 200, 202 (1925) (citing 2 William Blackstone, Commentaries *442; Mordecai's Law Lectures, 1104).

competitive bidding requirements, and be properly executed. This book discusses each of these requirements in more detail.

4. What is the common law of contracts?

Although many legal issues are addressed in laws enacted by state and federal legislatures (statutes), many cases involve issues that no statute directly addresses. Judges resolve these cases based on the "common law" that has developed over the course of many years using judicial decisions that have been rendered earlier and that deal with the same issues (precedent). The common law was originally drawn from law that existed in England and was adopted when courts were first established in this country. Most fundamental aspects of contract law are found in the common law, and more specific requirements contained in the statutes add to or modify the common law.

Several common law principles of contracting are familiar. Contracts are created when one party makes an *offer* and the party to whom the offer is made *accepts* the offer on the exact terms offered. If the offer is modified, the acceptance does not create a contract. Instead, it is viewed as a rejection and a counteroffer. The counteroffer must be accepted by the original offeror in order for the contract to be created. An example of how a statute modifies the common law is that under the Uniform Commercial Code (UCC), discussed in Question 16, an acceptance may modify an offer and still create a contract.[2]

Another common law rule for contracts is that there must be *consideration* passing between the parties or a court will not enforce the agreement. The courts define consideration as a benefit or advantage to the promisor or a loss or detriment to the promisee.[3] In other words, the courts will not enforce an agreement that amounts to a gift or in which one or more of the parties hasn't really promised to do anything for or give anything of value to the other. A court would not enforce my promise to buy you a car for your birthday since you have not agreed to do anything in return. A court would, however, enforce our agreement to trade cars on your next birthday, assuming all other formalities for contracting are met. The consideration is usually money, but it doesn't legally have to be. It can also be a promise to do something the promisor is not otherwise bound to do, or to refrain from doing something the promisor has a legal right to do. As noted in the section titled "Limitations on Local Government Contracting" in this chapter, there are some legal limitations on the kinds of promises local governments can make.

There are too many common law principles that affect contracting to discuss here. It is, however, important to mention the court's equitable jurisdiction and its application in the area of contracting.

Early in the development of our judicial system, there were two separate judicial forums: one in which matters of law were heard and one in which *equity* was the basis for the decision. If a party did not have a legal basis for a claim, he or she could raise the claim in the equity court and ask for relief based on fairness or prevention of severe hardship rather than on strictly legal argu-

2. N.C. GEN. STAT. § 25-2-207 (hereinafter G.S.).

3. Fawcett v. Fawcett, 191 N.C. 679, 681, 132 S.E. 796, 798 (1926).

ments. Later, the two court systems merged so that a single court could rule based on law or equity.

In contract cases there is one significant equitable remedy that courts still use: it is called *quantum meruit.* (*Quantum meruit* is Latin for "as much as he deserved.") If a court finds that a purported contract is unenforceable, because either a common law or statutory requirement has not been met, but one of the parties has performed his or her duties in good faith and the other party has the benefit of that performance, the court may order the benefiting party to pay the party who performed for the value of what was received. The court isn't really enforcing a contract, since none existed; and the amount received may be less than the contract amount would have been, since the party who performed is entitled only to the value of what was given, which does not include profit.

For example, in a North Carolina case, a contractor hired to do paving work for a town performed the work but was not paid. The town discovered that no bids were received on the project, even though the statute required bids. The contractor sued to recover payment, but there was no valid contract, due to the town's failure to bid. (See Question 143.) The court required the town to pay the value of the work done by the contractor under *quantum meruit,* since failure to do so would leave the town unjustly enriched and the contractor without any remedy.[4]

The validity of cases that allowed *quantum meruit* recovery under government contracts is in doubt, however, in light of more recent decisions holding that such recovery is barred by sovereign immunity. The North Carolina appellate courts have ruled in several cases that the doctrine of sovereign immunity, which shields governments from monetary liability, bars a claim under an implied or quasi contract theory.[5] Courts had previously held that a governmental entity waives sovereign immunity when it enters into a contract, since by doing so it has agreed to be liable for a breach of the contract.[6] The recent cases, however, refused to extend the concept of waiver to cases where no legally enforceable contract was entered into. Under this line of cases, sovereign immunity would be a defense to any claim for *quantum meruit* recovery under a local government contract.

Limitations on Local Government Contracting

5. What are the limitations on the purposes for which local governments may legally contract?

In order for a local government contract to be valid, the subject or purpose of the contract must be one that the local government has the authority to undertake. The sources of this authority are both the state constitution and

4. *See* Hawkins v. Town of Dallas, 229 N.C. 561, 50 S.E.2d 561 (1948).

5. Data General Corp. v. County of Durham, 143 N.C. App. 97, 545 S.E.2d 243 (2001); Whitfield v. Gilchrist, 348 N.C. 39, 497 S.E.2d 412 (1998).

6. *See* State v. Smith, 289 N.C. 303, 222 S.E.2d 412 (1976); *and* Houpe v. City of Statesville, 128 N.C. App. 334, 343, 497 S.E.2d 82, 89, *disc. rev. denied*, 348 N.C. 72, 505 S.E.2d 871 (1998) (applying the rule in State v. Smith applies to municipalities).

state statutes. Under the constitution, local governments are authorized to levy taxes only for a public purpose. North Carolina courts have held that this same limitation applies when local governments spend money, even money from sources other than taxes.[7] Thus, when a local government enters into a contract, the expenditure must be for a public purpose. It is sometimes difficult to determine what constitutes a public purpose; and the courts have noted that the concept is one that changes with time, reflecting changing attitudes about what governments should do.[8]

In addition to the constitutional public purpose limitation, North Carolina local government contracts must be authorized by statute. North Carolina local governments do not have inherent powers; they only have those powers that have been conferred expressly upon them by the state legislature or that are necessarily implied in express powers. Local government authority in North Carolina is more restricted than that of local governments in "home rule" states. In home rule states, local governments have broad authority to act unless a state law specifically restricts that authority. Thus, the fact that a local government in another state can enter into a particular contract does not necessarily mean a similar contract will be legal in North Carolina. It is also important to note that the constitutional limitation takes priority over statutory authority, so that even if a statute authorizes a particular contract, a court could find both the statute and the contract to be invalid if they violate the public purpose limitation.

If a statute does not authorize a particular contract, the contract is considered *ultra vires*—beyond the power of the local government—and it is invalid. An *ultra vires* contract cannot be enforced, even under the court's equitable powers (see Question 4), and cannot be validated by ratification (see Question 10); a court will not allow a remedy under any theory if the result is beyond the local government's authority.[9] Examples of expenditures that have been judged invalid due to lack of authority include an unrestricted donation to a chamber of commerce,[10] compensation to a landowner where the local government had no legal liability,[11] and compensation to employees beyond the amount provided by statute.[12]

---

7. Hughey v. Cloninger, 297 N.C. 86, 253 S.E.2d 898 (1979); City of Greensboro v. Smith *ex rel.* City of Greensboro, 241 N.C. 363 , 85 S.E.2d 292 (1955); Dennis v. City of Raleigh, 253 N.C. 400, 116 S.E.2d 923 (1960).

8. Maready v. City of Winston-Salem, 342 N.C. 708, 720, 467 S.E.2d 615, 623 (1996) (upholding expenditures for industrial recruiting).

9. Bowers v. City of High Point, 339 N.C. 413, 424, 451 S.E.2d 284, 292 (1994); Rockingham Square Shopping Ctr., Inc. v. Town of Madison, 45 N.C. App. 249, 262 S.E. 2d 705 (1980). *But see* Lewis v. City of Washington, 309 N.C. 818, 310 S.E.2d 610 (1983).

10. Horner *ex. rel* City of Burlington v. Chamber of Commerce of Burlington, 231 N.C. 440, 57 S.E.2d 789 (1950); *Dennis*, 253 N.C. 400, 116 S.E.2d 923.

11. Jenkins v. Henderson, 214 N.C. 244, 199 S.E. 37 (1938).

12. *Bowers,* 339 N.C. 413, 451 S.E.2d 284.

6. Can a local governing board enter into a contract that binds its discretion or the discretion of future governing boards?[13]

The general rule is that contracts entered into by a local government continue to be binding on that entity throughout the term of the contract, even if the governing board or individual who created the obligation leaves office. North Carolina courts have held, however, that a local government cannot enter into a contract that prevents the governing board (whether the current board or future boards) from exercising certain essential discretionary powers.[14] Examples of contracts involving these types of powers include contracts that promise to rezone property (legislative power), to levy or not levy a tax, to lay out or close a particular street, or to charge or freeze a particular rate or special assessment.

Since the limitation on binding discretion is based on public policy rather than on constitutional principles, the state legislature can enact laws that authorize local governments to enter into specific types of contracts that bind governing board discretion. It has done so in a few limited circumstances. For example, local governments have specific statutory authority to agree to levy taxes or maintain a certain fee rate as part of a bond transaction[15] and cities have authority to enter into annexation agreements.[16]

Most of the contracts local governments enter into are common commercial transactions necessary to carry out the regular business of the entity. They rarely involve issues requiring the governing board's unrestricted exercise of discretion. Thus, in most cases, a contract entered into by one board or individual, assuming it is otherwise valid, must be honored by successors in office and by the unit as a whole throughout the term of the contract.

Individual Authority to Contract

7. Who has authority to contract on behalf of a local government?

Both the common law and state statutes require that a contract must be entered into by a person or board with the authority to contract on behalf of the entity that will be bound by the contract. A local government is not bound by a contract entered into by an individual who does not have authority to contract on its behalf.[17] North Carolina law provides that the governing board of a city, county, or local school unit is the body that has authority to act for the local

---

13. *See generally,* David M. Lawrence, "Contracts That Bind the Discretion of Governing Boards," *Popular Government* 56 (Summer 1990), 38–42.

14. Plant Food Co. v. City of Charlotte, 214 N.C. 518, 199 S.E. 712 (1938).

15. G.S. 159-46, -93.

16. G.S. 160A-58.21 through -58.28.

17. L & S Leasing, Inc. v. City of Winston-Salem, 122 N.C. App. 619, 471 S.E.2d 118 (1996); Community Projects for Students v. Wilder, 60 N.C. App. 182, 298 S.E.2d 434 (1982).

government and this includes the authority to contract.[18] The governing board can delegate its authority to others within the organization unless a statute specifically requires action to be taken by the governing board. The formal bidding statute, for example, requires that contracts in the formal range be awarded by the governing body.[19] That statute also authorizes governing boards to delegate the authority to award contracts for the purchase of apparatus, supplies, materials, and equipment.[20] (See Question 113.) Other contracts subject to the formal bidding statute must be awarded by the governing board.

A delegation of authority to contract may be either *explicit* or *implicit.* An example of explicit delegation might be found in a city charter or in a county or school policy adopted by the governing board delegating to the manager or other official the authority to enter into contracts on behalf of the local government. A governing board might also adopt a resolution explicitly delegating authority for awarding purchase contracts as permitted under the formal bidding statute or in other circumstances, including informal contracts where the statutes do not require the governing board to award contracts. In addition, a job description or personnel policy could constitute an explicit delegation of contracting authority if it has been approved by the governing board. Thus a purchasing agent or department head may have authority to contract if it is part of his or her job responsibilities as defined by the board.

In many cases, however, the board does not explicitly identify the individuals within the unit that have authority to contract. If the local government regularly pays and performs contracts entered into by many different individuals within the unit, a court might find that these individuals have implicit authority to contract or that the contracts have been ratified. (See Question 10.) Implicit authority is inferred from the actions of the board in approving and authorizing payment of contracts. For example, if the unit issues procurement cards, petty cash, or blanket purchase orders to employees, it would be hard to argue later that these employees did not have authority to contract on behalf of the unit.

It is better for the board to be explicit about who has authority to contract than risk a court ruling based on pattern and practice. If procedures for contracting are not clearly defined, a court might reasonably conclude that everyone in the organization has implicit authority to contract on behalf of the unit.

8. Is the authority to execute a contract the same as the authority to approve a contract?

No. It is very important to distinguish between the authority to *enter into* a contract, and the authority to *execute* (sign) a contract. As discussed in Question 16, execution of the contract is a formality that is used to prove assent. Contracts are sometimes, but not always, executed at the same time that they are approved. In some cases, for example, the board may approve a contract which is later executed by the manager. Even if a contract is properly executed,

18. G.S. 160A-12; 153A-12, 115C-36.
19. G.S. 143-129(b).
20. G.S. 143-129(a).

it is not enforceable against the entity if it was not approved or authorized by someone with authority to contract on behalf of the entity. The fact that someone has authority to execute a contract does not necessarily mean he or she also has authority to approve a contract, although it may constitute evidence of implicit authority if there is no explicit delegation.

9. Can a local government be liable on contracts under the doctrine of apparent authority?

Courts developed the concept of *apparent authority* to apply in situations where a person did not have actual authority but acted in a way that led someone reasonably to believe that he or she did have authority. This doctrine protects innocent parties who are misled by the actions of an agent who seems to be acting on behalf of a principal but is without actual authority to do so. In the case of contracts with governmental agencies, however, courts have held that the doctrine of apparent authority does not apply.[21]

For example, a local government has a policy requiring all contracts costing over $100,000 to be approved by the governing board. A department head orders $175,000 worth of equipment. The vendor erroneously assumes that the department head has the authority to make the purchase. The vendor will not be able to enforce the contract because the department head had no authority to make the purchase; and the department head's actions will not substitute for actual authority since the doctrine of apparent authority *does not apply* to contracts with governmental entities.

Since most governmental entities operate under contracting laws and requirements that are publicly available, courts have ruled that people who contract with governments are charged with the knowledge of those procedures and cannot argue that they were misled.[22] Even though this may not always actually be true, courts have been strict in enforcing the rule that a local government will not be legally responsible for a contract entered into by someone who had no authority, apparent or actual, to act on its behalf.

10. Can an individual's lack of authority be cured by ratification?

Yes. Ratification is an action by the person or entity with legal authority, usually the governing board of the local government in this context, after initial action has been taken by someone who does not have proper authority. Ratification should be accomplished by express action of the board. In some cases, however, a court might interpret other acts, such as authorizing payment of a contract entered into without proper authority, as ratification.[23] A contract cannot be ratified, however, if it is invalid because the local government does

---

21. Nello L. Teer Co. v. North Carolina State Highway Comm'n., 265 N.C. 1, 10, 143 S.E.2d 247, 254 (1965); L & S Leasing, Inc. v. City of Winston-Salem, 122 N.C. App. 619, 471 S.E.2d 118 (1996).

22. *L & S Leasing, Inc.*, 122 N.C. App. at 622, 471 S.E.2d at 120.

23. Bell Atlantic v. DRR, Inc., 114 N.C. App. 771, 774, 443 S.E.2d 374, 376 (1994); 10 McQuillin Mun. Corps. (hereinafter McQuillin) § 29.17 (3d ed. 1990).

not have authority rather than because a particular individual lacked authority. In order to ratify a contract, the governing board must have the legal authority to enter into it.[24]

Budgetary Authority

11. What does it mean to have proper budgetary authority for a contract?

One of the most important functions of the governing board is to decide how the local government's money will be spent. Boards do this by adopting an annual budget ordinance that, in varying degrees of detail, makes appropriations that give direction to the employees in the unit and establish the legal limitations on how funds will be spent during the ensuing fiscal year. Under the Local Government Budget and Fiscal Control Act,[25] all contractual obligations must be supported by an appropriation that authorizes the expenditure. In addition, at the time the obligation is incurred, there must be an unencumbered balance remaining in the appropriation sufficient to pay the obligation owed in the current fiscal year.[26]

State law requires the finance officer or a deputy finance officer[27] to certify that these two requirements have been met and requires that a preaudit certificate signed by the finance officer be contained in every written contract before it is issued.[28] This certificate is commonly preprinted on purchase orders. A similar certificate must appear on disbursements.[29] Preaudit compliance is commonly incorporated into computerized finance and accounting systems which automatically check for availability of funds at the point that a requisition or purchase order is created.

North Carolina law enforces the board's budgeting decisions by providing that any obligation that is not supported by an appropriation and any contract on which the preaudit certificate has not been completed is void and unenforceable.[30] In addition, an individual who incurs an obligation or pays any

---

24. Insurance Co. v. Guilford County, 226 N.C. 441, 449, 38 S.E. 2d 519, 525 (1946); McQuillin, §29.108.

25. G.S. 159-7–41. Parallel provisions exist under the School Budget and Fiscal Control Act. *See* G.S. 115C-441.

26. G.S. 159-28(a); G.S. 115C-441(a). In the case of "special funds of individual schools," under G.S. 115C-448, it appears that since these are not budgeted funds, the preaudit requirement does not apply to contracts obligating only these funds.

27. 25. G.S. 159-25 authorizes the delegation of finance officer duties to any other employee to whom the duties of budget officer may be assigned. *See* G.S. 159-9.

28. The statute requires that the preaudit certificate read substantially as follows: "This instrument has been preaudited in the manner required by the Local Government Budget and Fiscal Control Act." This statement is followed by the signature of the finance officer. G.S. 159-28(a). *See* G.S. 115C-441(a) (local school units).

29. G.S. 159-28(d); G.S. 115C-441(d).

30. G.S. 159-28(a); G.S. 115C-441(a); L & S Leasing, Inc. v. City of Winston-Salem, 122 N.C. App. 619, 471 S.E.2d 118 (1996); Watauga County Bd. of Election v. Town of Boone, 106 N.C. App. 270, 416 S.E.2d 411 (1992).

funds in violation of the statute is personally liable for any funds committed or disbursed.[31]

A North Carolina Court of Appeals case suggests that there may be a very narrow set of circumstances under which the failure to include the preaudit certificate may not render a contract void.[32] That case involved a contract promising severance pay, a contingent liability, no part of which became due during the year in which the certification would have been made. Though the court in this case held that the contract was enforceable against the town, this holding would not appear to apply to most commercial contracts entered into by local governments under which payments are due during the year the contract and preaudit certificate are executed.

12. Can local governments enter into contracts that extend beyond the current fiscal year?

Yes. Identical statutes in Chapters 160A and 153A of the North Carolina General Statutes (hereinafter G.S.) specifically authorize cities and counties respectively to enter into "continuing contracts, some portion or all of which are to be performed in ensuing fiscal years."[33] The statutes require, however, that when a continuing contract is entered into, the governing board must appropriate funds in each subsequent year sufficient to pay the amount due under the contract in that year.[34] Similar provisions in the statutes governing budgeting by local school units provide authority for schools to enter into continuing contracts.[35]

Since a continuing contract binds the governing board's budgeting authority in future years, it is advisable to obtain the board's approval before entering into continuing contracts even though the statutes do not specifically require it.

13. Are there special procedures for lease-purchase or installment-purchase contracts?[36]

Lease-purchase and installment-purchase contracts are used to finance purchases or construction projects and, in some cases, they do require special procedures. There are actually two different arrangements local governments can use to pay for purchases or to finance improvements over time. Although they are often both referred to as lease-purchase contracts, the more commonly used arrangement is more properly identified as an installment-purchase contract.

---

31. 29. G.S. 159-28(e) ; G.S. 115C-441(e).

32. *See* Myers v. Town of Plymouth, 135 N.C. App. 707, 714, 522 S.E.2d 122, 126 (1999).

33. G.S. 160A-17; 153A-13.

34. *See* G.S. 159-13(15); 160A-17; 153A-13.

35. *See* G.S. 115C-432(b)(4).

36. *See generally*, David M. Lawrence, *Financing Capital Projects*, 2d ed. (Chapel Hill, N.C.: Institute of Government, The University of North Carolina at Chapel Hill, 1994) §§ 105, 406.

Under a lease-purchase contract, a local government leases equipment with either an option or an obligation to purchase it at the end of the contract term. Generally, under this arrangement the unit does not take title to the property until the purchase obligation occurs or the option to purchase is exercised. Under this arrangement, no security interest (mortgage) in the property is given by the unit; it is not necessary because the seller still has title to the property and can simply take the property back if the unit doesn't make its lease payments or defaults in some other way. For cities and counties there are no special requirements for entering into this type of lease-purchase contract, except that these contracts are subject to the competitive bidding statutes (see Chapter II) and should be approved by the governing board as continuing contracts (see Question 12). The authority to enter into these types of contracts is G.S. 160A-19 (for cities) and G.S.153A-165 (for counties). Local school units have limited authority to use this method of contracting under G.S. 115C-528(b) only for the purchase of "school buses; mobile classroom units; photocopiers; and computers, computer hardware, computer software, and related support services."[37] Additional procedural requirements apply to school contracts under this statute as described below.

Under an installment-purchase contract, a local government takes title to the property at the beginning of the contract and gives the seller or a financial institution a security interest in the property, allowing that party to take the property back if the local government defaults. The courts have held that local governments must have specific statutory authority to mortgage public property.[38] Installment-purchase contracts are specifically authorized for cities, counties, and several other local government entities in G.S. 160A-20. Local school units are authorized to enter into installment-purchase contracts under G.S. 115C-528(c) only for the purchase of "school buses; mobile classroom units; photocopiers; and computers, computer hardware, computer software, and related support services."[39] As noted above, installment-purchase contracts are not legal if they are entered into by units of government that are not covered by any of the statutes listed above or if they are for transactions that are not covered by those statutes.

Local governments, including local school units, are authorized to use both installment-purchase and lease-purchase contracts for guaranteed energy savings contracts[40] as provided in G.S. 143-64.17C. In addition, G.S. 153-158.1 authorizes counties to acquire property for use by local school units. Under

---

37. G.S. 115C-528(a). The term of a contract entered into under this section shall not exceed the useful life of the property purchased. An option to upgrade property is included in the useful life and may be exercised without additional bidding. G.S. 115C-528(d).

38. Vaughn v. Commissioners of Forsyth County, 118 N.C. 636, 24 S.E. 425 (1896).

39. G.S. 115C-528(a). The term of a contract entered into under this section shall not exceed the useful life of the property purchased. An option to upgrade property is included in the useful life and may be exercised without additional bidding. G.S. 115C-528(d).

40. A guaranteed energy savings contract, as authorized under Chapter 143, Article 3B, Part 2, G.S. 143-64.17, et seq., is a contract that provides for energy saving improvements to facilities the cost of which are guaranteed to equal the energy savings over the term of the contract.

this authority, counties may use their broader authority under G.S. 160A-19 and -20 to finance purchases for the local school units.

Some installment-purchase and lease-purchase contracts are subject to specific procedural requirements. These contracts should be approved by the governing board as continuing contracts (see Question 12), even though the statutes may not specifically require it. Under G.S. 160A-20, a public hearing preceded by at least ten days public notice is required for installment-purchase contracts involving real property, including construction or repair contracts.[41]

Installment-purchase contracts in certain circumstances must also be approved by the Local Government Commission (LGC), a branch of the State Treasurer's Office responsible for overseeing local government finances and debt. For cities, counties, and other local governments subject to G.S. 160A-20, LGC approval is required for contracts involving improvements to real property, including construction or repair contracts, and for other contracts that meet all three of the following requirements: (1) the contract period, including optional renewals or extensions, extends for five years or more; (2) the contract requires the unit to make payments to a third party who may or may not be a party to the contract; and (3) the total contract amount, including optional renewals or extensions, is at least $500,000 or a sum equal to "one tenth of one percent" of the unit's total tax base, whichever is less. Contracts for the purchase of motor vehicles or voting machines are exempt from LGC approval, as are contracts entered into under grants from the state or federal government and loan agreements under the North Carolina Solid Waste Management Loan Program.[42]

For local school units, G.S. 115C-528 establishes separate approval requirements for lease-purchase and installment-purchase contracts. As noted earlier, the statute allows the use of these contracting methods only for specified types of contracts. In addition, the statute requires that these contracts be approved by the LGC and the county commissioners.[43] County commissioner approval is not required, however, as long as the term of each contract is less than three years and the total amount financed during a three-year period does not exceed either $250,000 or an amount equal to three times the local unit's annual state allocation for classroom materials, equipment, and instructional supplies, whichever is less. Contracts that exceed this dollar limit or extend beyond three years must be approved by the county commissioners under G.S. 115C-441(c1) and are treated as continuing contracts for capital outlay under that statute. A contract entered into under G.S. 115C-528 must be approved by the LGC if it has a term of five or more years and obligates the unit to pay a total of $500,000 or more.[44]

---

41. G.S. 160A-20(g).

42. G.S. 160A-20(e); 159-148(b). A different test for Local Government Commission approval of hospital authority installment-purchase contracts is set forth in G.S. 131E-32.

43. G.S. 115C-528(e), (f).

44. G.S. 115C-528(f). This statute provides that contracts under G.S. 115C-528 are considered financing agreements subject to Article 8 of Chapter 159 of the General Statutes, with certain exceptions.

14. What is a nonappropriation clause, and does its presence mean that the contract is not a continuing contract?

A nonappropriation clause in a lease-purchase or installment-purchase contract allows the local government to terminate its obligation to make payments under the contract without being forced to raise taxes to meet that obligation. The North Carolina Supreme Court relied on the presence of a nonappropriation clause, among other things, to conclude that an installment-purchase contract does not constitute a pledge of the tax power, which would require approval by taxpayers.[45] Although this clause may give the board some discretion that, if exercised, relieves it of the obligation to budget funds for continuing contracts (see Question 12), this discretion is rarely exercised. The market for installment-purchase agreements, by not exacting a high price for contracts containing nonappropriation clauses, reflects the assumption that such clauses will rarely be exercised.[46] In addition, some contracts may provide that exercise of the nonappropriation clause is a breach of contract for which the local government may be required to pay damages.

There are no North Carolina cases addressing the question of whether the presence of a nonappropriation clause means that the contract is not a continuing contract within the meaning of state budgeting laws. (See Question 12.) The governing board's legal obligation under continuing contracts is to appropriate funds that are due under the contract in each fiscal year. A nonappropriation clause gives the governing board the legal ability to avoid that obligation since, if the board decides to exercise its nonappropriation right under the contract, nothing is due under the contract after the decision becomes effective. From a practical standpoint, however, the right to nonappropriate rarely is exercised, so contracts containing these clauses should be treated as continuing contracts for purposes of board approval and budget planning.

15. What is a nonsubstitution clause, and what is a deficiency judgment?

These are two provisions addressed in G.S. 160A-20 and G.S. 115C-528, the statutes that authorize installment-purchase contracts. (See Question 13.) A nonsubstitution clause is a limitation that is placed in a contract by the seller. It prevents the local government from exercising its authority not to appropriate funds to make payments on the contract and then substituting different equipment to carry on the same function or activity. The statutes prohibit nonsubstitution clauses that would prevent the unit from replacing the property that was the subject of the contract or would prevent the unit from continuing to provide the service or activity for which the property was used.[47] Local government officials should review contracts carefully, since standard contracts from vendors often contain nonsubstitution clauses. If a local govern-

45. Wayne County Citizens Ass'n v. Wayne County Bd. of Comm'rs, 328 N.C. 24, 399 S.E.2d 311 (1991).

46. *See* David M. Lawrence *Financing Capital Projects,* 2d ed. (Chapel Hill, N.C.: Institute of Government, The University of North Carolina at Chapel Hill, 1994), 25–27.

47. G.S. 160A-20(d); G.S. 115C-528(h).

ment enters into an installment-purchase contract that contains such a clause, a court would not allow the vendor to enforce it. It is unclear whether a court would deem the entire contract to be invalid or just the illegal provision, although the latter result is probably the most likely.

The statutes also provide that a seller cannot obtain a deficiency judgment against a local government that breaches an installment-purchase agreement.[48] This prevents a seller from obtaining money damages from the local government if the security interest in the property is not sufficient to pay the outstanding amount due at the time a contract is breached. In other words, the seller's remedy is limited to the value of the property being purchased, even if that value ends up being less than the amount due under the contract at the time of breach.

Given the limitations on the seller's remedies, the market would not work as well as it does if local governments did not exercise good faith and follow through with their obligations to make payments under installment-purchase contracts except in cases of serious fiscal crisis.

Contract Formalities

16. Do all contracts have to be in writing?

No. There is no general legal requirement that a contact must be in writing, though some contracts must be in writing because a statute requires it. A writing is almost always necessary, however, to enforce a contract, primarily to prove that the party against whom enforcement is sought did in fact agree to the contract and to prove what the terms of the agreement are.

A statute that requires a contract to be in writing is called a "statute of frauds," a term developed under the English legal system from which our legal system evolved. A statute of frauds is really a statute to *prevent* fraud; it requires a writing signed by the party against whom enforcement is sought to prevent a fraudulent claim that the person made a promise he or she did not fulfill. Several North Carolina statutes require written contracts; some are particular to local governments, and some are not.

All contracts made by or on behalf of cities must be in writing.[49] A city contract that is not in writing is void, but the governing board can cure this defect by expressly ratifying the contract. (See Question 10 for further discussion of ratification.) There is no parallel statute that requires county contracts to be in writing. The formal bidding statute, G.S. 143-129, however, requires all local government contracts that are within its scope to be in writing. (See the "Dollar Thresholds" chart in Appendix 1 and Questions 31 through 54 for information on which contracts are subject to formal bidding.)

Another important writing requirement is contained in the Uniform Commercial Code (UCC). The UCC was developed to modernize and standardize the law governing commercial transactions, eliminating variations from state to

48. G.S. 160A-20(f); G.S. 115C-528(i).
49. G.S. 160A-16.

state and removing many of the technicalities in the common law of contracts. In North Carolina, the UCC has been adopted as Chapter 25 of the General Statutes. The provisions governing contracts for the sale of goods are contained in Article 2, beginning at G.S. 25-2-101. Article 2 requires that all contracts (not just local government contracts) for the sale of goods exceeding $500 must be in writing.[50] A contract that does not satisfy this requirement is still enforceable in certain situations specified in the statute if both parties are "merchants" within the definition of the statute.[51] In most cases local governments meet this definition. In addition, while the common law requires that contracts specify all of the essential terms of the agreement, the UCC modifies common law contract requirements relating to the contents of a writing[52] and the formalities for a valid signature.[53]

Other writing requirements are found in Chapter 22 of the North Carolina General Statutes. Of most significance to local governments is the requirement of a writing for any contract or deed evidencing the sale of land or any interest in land, including an easement; any sale or lease of mining rights; and any other lease of more than three years in length.[54]

As a general rule, when a writing is required by statute, the writing must contain all of the material terms of the agreement and must be signed (or contain some other proof of assent or indication of an intent to be bound) by the parties or their authorized representatives in order to satisfy the requirement. As noted above, these rules are modified under the UCC for contracts involving the sale of goods.

Even when not required by statute, a writing serves some important purposes, the most significant being the clear expression of the agreement between the parties. In addition, for local governments the written document—usually a purchase order—incorporates the fiscal and departmental approvals required by statute and by local policy and provides documentation for the annual audit. Computers have eliminated much of the paper involved in the contracting process, but the information that was contained on paper contracts can still be created and preserved in electronic transactions and files.

17. Does the written record of a resolution or ordinance adopted by a local government satisfy a writing requirement?

No. The North Carolina Supreme Court has held that the board's actions as recorded in the minutes do not satisfy a statutory requirement that a contract be in writing.[55] The board's assent to a proposed agreement as reflected in meeting minutes or in a resolution or ordinance adopted by the board could

---

50. G.S. 25-2-201(1).
51. G.S. 25-2-104.
52. G.S. 25-2-201(1) (quantity is the only contract term that must be contained in the writing).
53. G.S. 25-1-201(39) (a signature can be "any symbol executed or adopted by a party with present intention to authenticate a writing.").
54. G.S. 22-2.
55. Wade v. City of New Bern, 77 N.C. 460 (1877).

create a binding contract when no statute requires a written contract. Where a written contract is required, however, only a separate document will satisfy this requirement.

18. Can a faxed or other electronic document satisfy a writing requirement?

Yes. While there are no North Carolina cases directly addressing this question, legislation at the federal and state level has provided significant legal authority for the use of electronic contracts. The federal Electronic Signatures in Global and National Commerce Act (E-SIGN) and the state Uniform Electronic Transactions Act (UETA) both contain provisions stating that a contract may not be denied legal effect or enforceability solely because an electronic record was used in its formation.[56] The Electronic Commerce in Government Act[57] provides an additional source of authority for electronic transactions by public agencies. This act establishes a mechanism for certification of electronic signatures for use in transactions with public agencies. None of these statutes requires the use of electronic transactions. Instead, they provide for legal enforceability of such transactions where the parties agree to use them.

If a local government uses or accepts electronic documents in its contracting process, some additional considerations are warranted. First, it is important to bear in mind that electronic contracts must meet all other legal requirements in order to be valid—not just the writing requirements that may apply. Thus, for example, while it may be legally permissible to accept a bid bond or performance bond electronically (see Questions 87 through 92 for a discussion of bid bonds and Question 129 for a discussion of performance and payment bonds), these are guarantees provided by third parties and the local government may want to require additional documentation to avoid fraudulent submissions. In addition, statutes specifically governing use of electronic means in the bidding process must be complied with in order for the resulting contract to be valid. (See Questions 81 and 82.) Finally, care should be taken in the competitive bidding context to ensure that procedures that allow both written and electronic submission do not create advantages or disadvantages based on the method chosen.

19. Who has the authority to sign contracts on behalf of a local government?

The statutes don't expressly assign responsibility for signing contracts, leaving it to the governing board to assign this responsibility to one or more individuals. It is common for the mayor, chair, or other presiding officer of the governing board to sign all official documents, including contracts, although this is a matter of common practice, not statutory directive. Governing boards also typically authorize the manager to sign contracts, sometimes setting a

---

56. *See* G.S. 66-317(b) (UETA), *and* 15 U.S.C. § 7001(a) (E-SIGN).
57. Chapter 66, Article 11A of the North Carolina General Statutes, G.S. 66-58.1 through 66-58.12.

dollar limit on this authority. Others commonly assigned this responsibility include the finance officer and purchasing agent.

It is important to distinguish, as discussed in Question 8, between executing (signing) a contract and authorizing or approving the underlying obligation it represents. Courts have emphasized, for example, that a governing board chair or mayor cannot individually authorize a contractual obligation, even though he or she may have individual authority to execute contracts.[58] The board can, of course, delegate to the same individual the authority to both approve and sign contracts, except where a statute requires that contracts be approved by the board. (See Question 113.)

20. Is a witness or a corporate seal required when contracts are executed?

Only conveyances of real property require a seal, and writing "[seal]" next to the signature is sufficient to satisfy that requirement.[59] In addition, placing a seal on a contract lengthens the period of time within which legal challenges involving the contract must be brought.[60] Although attesting, witnessing, or notarizing a signature provides proof of its authenticity, there is no general statutory requirement that these formalities accompany local government contracts.

---

58. Abbott Realty Co. v. City of Charlotte, 198 N.C. 564, 152 S.E. 686 (1930).

59. *See* William A. Campbell, *North Carolina Guidebook for Registers of Deeds*, 7th ed. (Chapel Hill, N.C.: Institute of Government, The University of North Carolina at Chapel Hill, 1994), 40, n.26.

60. G.S. 1-47(2).

Chapter II
Competitive Bidding Requirements

Underlying Purposes of Competitive Bidding

21. Why are there competitive bidding requirements for public contracts?

Most public agencies, whether local, state, or federal, must comply with some kind of competitive procedure when awarding contracts involving significant expenditures of public funds. North Carolina statutes establish competitive bidding procedures for certain types of contracts awarded by the state and local government units. The North Carolina Supreme Court has stated that the purpose of the competitive bidding law

> is to prevent favoritism, corruption, fraud, and imposition in the awarding of public contracts by giving notice to prospective bidders and thus assuring competition which in turn guarantees fair play and reasonable prices in contracts involving the expenditure of a substantial amount of public money.[1]

22. Is the main purpose of competitive bidding to get the lowest price?

Even though many people assume that government competitive bidding primarily aims at getting the "low bid," there are really two distinct and sometimes competing purposes: fairness and value. Both of these requirements stem from the fact that public funds are being used.

23. What does fairness require in the context of public contracting?

Fairness is an essential component of any competitive bidding process. As the North Carolina Supreme Court opinion cited in Question 21 illustrates, fairness is not just a way to ensure low prices. It is a separate end, designed to prevent favoritism and ensure an open, objective process that is applied consistently to all participants. *State and Local Government Purchasing*, a publication of the National Association of State Purchasing Officials, notes that "[a] unique characteristic of competitive public procurement is its underlying principle that the prices themselves are not as critical as the fairness and impartiality of the process used to obtain them."[2] Indeed, maintaining the integrity of

---

1. Mullen v. Town of Louisburg, 225 N.C. 53, 58–59, 33 S.E.2d 484, 487 (1941).
2. The Council of State Governments, *State and Local Government Purchasing*, 4th ed. (Lexington, Ky.: CSG, 1994), 15.

the process may at times result in higher prices. For example, a bid which materially deviates from specifications or fails to comply with the mandated procedure *must* be rejected, even if the result is a higher cost to the contracting agency and, therefore, to the public. Indeed, the rules governing the evaluation of responsiveness in bidding (see Question 101 and Appendix 4) are designed to ensure fairness between competitors. When evaluating bids and when implementing all the mandated competitive procedures, public agencies must ensure that the process is fair to all those participating.

24. Can a local government consider best value rather than just lowest price when bidding and awarding contracts?

Value connotes more than just low price. The concern in public purchasing for prices stems, of course, from the fact that public funds are being used and must be conserved. As noted in Question 21, competition is designed to ensure reasonable prices. However, it is widely accepted that conservation of funds does not always mean choosing the lowest bid. An item of poor quality purchased at a low price does not represent the best investment of public funds if it requires frequent repair, does not function properly, or does not last long. Indeed, the North Carolina bidding statute specifically requires consideration of quality and performance when awarding contracts. (The amount of discretion afforded to the awarding authority under this statute is discussed in Questions 117 through 120.)

25. Do the goals of fairness and value ever conflict?

There can be a tension between obtaining value and ensuring fairness. Quality is a subjective term and is certainly open to different interpretations in a given purchase. Furthermore, if the unit takes steps to define the level of quality it seeks, it may narrow the field of competitors by eliminating some products that do not meet the identified standards. A balance must be struck so that competition is not *unreasonably* restricted yet the level of quality is sufficient to ensure value, not just low price. This means that restrictions on competition must be justified. (Preparation of specifications is discussed in more detail in Questions 55 through 65.) In these cases, competition may be lessened in favor of higher value. By the same token, sometimes value is sacrificed in favor of fair competition. For example, strict application of bidding procedures required by statute may at times require rejection of the best bid because it does not meet specifications.

The dual purposes underlying the competitive bidding laws and the need to balance them should be considered when interpreting and applying the specific provisions described below. These purposes should also be considered when deciding how to proceed in the numerous situations that arise in the competitive bidding arena that are not directly addressed by a statute or case.

Sources of Legal Requirements

26. Where can I find the competitive bidding requirements in the North Carolina General Statutes?

Chapter 143, Article 8 of the North Carolina General Statutes (hereinafter G.S.) contains most of the provisions governing competitive bidding of public contracts. Most of the requirements for competitive bidding are contained in G.S. 143-129. Appendix 2 to this *Legal Guide to Purchasing and Contracting* contains the key statutes affecting local government purchasing.

Entities Covered by Competitive Bidding Statutes

27. Which local governments are required to comply with competitive bidding requirements?

The formal bidding statute, G.S. 143-129, applies to the following agencies: the state,[3] any institution of the state, and any political subdivision of the state, including counties, local school units, and municipalities. The statute also states that contracts must be awarded pursuant to its procedures when they involve an expenditure of "public money" in the amounts specified in the statute. Generally, the term public money describes funds held by public agencies, so the statute should be interpreted to apply to any covered public agency that enters into the types of contracts at the dollar levels covered by the statute.

28. Are there any governmental units that are exempt from the competitive bidding requirements?

Separate statutory provisions exempt public housing authorities, hospital authorities, soil and water conservation districts, and joint municipal power agencies from the competitive bidding requirements.[4] The exemption for housing authorities also probably applies to housing authority purchases made by a city that has constituted itself a housing authority under G.S. 157-4.1.

---

3. The state and its agencies are governed by this statute only for construction and repair contracts. Contracts for purchase of equipment, materials and supplies by the state and its agencies are governed by Article 3 of Chapter 143 of the North Carolina General Statutes (hereinafter G.S.). Community colleges are also governed by Article 3 procedures for purchase contracts by virtue of G.S. 115D-58.5(b).

4. Public housing authorities, G.S. 157-9; hospital authorities, G.S. 131E-23(d); soil and water conservation districts, G.S. 139-8(11); and joint municipal power agencies, 159B-11(10).

29. Do nonprofit organizations or other quasi-public organizations that receive public funds have to comply with the bidding laws?

The general rule is that contracts made by a private entity are not subject to the competitive bidding requirements. The formal bidding statute, G.S. 142-129, requires bidding where there is an expenditure of public money. (See Question 27.) Even if a private entity receives funds from a local government, the funds are considered private once they are received by the private entity. In other words, the characterization of the contracting entity as either public or private determines the characterization of the funds held by that entity and determines whether bidding is required.

In some cases, however, courts have looked beyond the legal character of a particular organization to determine whether the laws governing public entities apply. The North Carolina Court of Appeals has held that the public records law applies to a private nonprofit hospital.[5] The court reached this result because it found extensive involvement by a public entity (a county) in the oversight and control of the private entity's (the hospital's) operations. Evidence of this involvement included the amount of funding or other direct support provided by the county as a percentage of the hospital's total budget, the county's power to appoint members of the hospital board, the county's present and future ownership of the hospital property, and the fact that the hospital represented itself to the public as a public agency by using the name of the public entity with which it was connected. Several cases involving private organizations with significant ties to local governments have reached similar results.[6]

The court decisions in these cases make sense. It would seem inappropriate for a public agency to be able to avoid laws—such as the public records, open meetings, and bidding laws—that apply to public agencies simply by setting up private nonprofit agencies and transferring to them the duties previously carried out by the local government. On the other hand, it is quite common and clearly legal for public agencies to contract with private entities to carry out public functions the local government has authority to conduct.[7] It is only when a private entity has significant connections to a public entity that it could be considered public for purposes of particular laws that govern public entities. A single contract between a private entity and a public entity—for example, a contract with a private company to collect garbage—is unlikely, by itself, to constitute sufficient involvement to require the private company to comply with competitive bidding requirements. On the other hand, an entity such as an economic development commission—consisting of members ap-

---

5. *See* News & Observer Publ'g Co. v. Wake County Hosp. Sys., Inc., 55 N.C. App. 1, 284 S.E.2d 542 (1981), *petition for disc. review denied,* 305 N.C. 302, 291 S.E.2d 151 (1982), *appeal dismissed,* 459 U.S. 803 (1982). *See generally* Joseph S. Ferrell, "Organization and Powers of County and City Hospitals," in *Hospital Law In North Carolina,* Anne M. Dellinger, ed. (Chapel Hill, N.C.: Institute of Government, The University of North Carolina at Chapel Hill, 1985), 14–18.

6. *See* Frayda S. Bluestein, "Privatization: Legal Issues for North Carolina Local Governments," *Popular Government* 62 (Winter 1997) (Chapel Hill, N.C.: Institute of Government, The University of North Carolina at Chapel Hill), 33–39.

7. *See* G.S. 160A-20.1; 153A-449.

pointed by local governments within a region, supported with significant contributions from those local governments, and endeavoring to accomplish economic development initiatives on behalf of the local government—might be considered a public agency for purposes of the competitive bidding laws.

30. Are volunteer fire departments required to comply with the competitive bidding laws?

The answer to this question depends upon the specific legal status of the volunteer fire department. If the fire department is a department of a county or city, the bidding laws apply. However, many volunteer fire departments are organized as private, nonprofit corporations. In these cases, the county levies a tax (using either a special tax district or general countywide taxes) and contracts with the volunteer fire department to provide fire protection services in designated areas. In most cases, these tax dollars are the primary source of funding for the fire department. As noted in Question 29, if the fire department is a private entity, the money is no longer considered public money once it is paid under the contract. If the fire department decides to buy a fire truck or build a fire station, the contract it enters into does not involve the expenditure of public funds. (The contract between the *county* and the fire department does involve the expenditure of public funds. However, as discussed in Question 34, the contract for fire protection is a service contract and is not covered by the bidding laws.)

Under the analysis that was used in the hospital case discussed in Question 29, the volunteer fire department's heavy reliance on tax dollars might cause it to be considered an agency of the county for purposes of the bidding laws even though it is organized as a private, nonprofit corporation. Unlike most private entities with which a local government might contract for services, volunteer fire departments rely heavily on their contracts with local governments and most would not survive without the tax-generated payment for their services. Indeed, in some cases, the tax rate is set in accordance with the specific budgetary request of the private volunteer fire department. It is not clear, however, whether the court would extend the analysis of the hospital case to this situation. Volunteer fire departments operate more independently and with less county control and supervision than the nonprofit hospital analyzed in that case.

Given the uncertainty about the application of the bidding laws in this situation, the county may choose to include in its contract with the volunteer fire department a requirement that the department use competitive bidding when contracting for construction or purchasing equipment. This might be desirable for reasons separate from the legal issues. First, the public agency may want to ensure that the money it gives the fire department is spent wisely and fairly. Second, the public may have a perception that these funds are public, even though the strict legal definition does not apply. This may be particularly true where money is generated from a special tax district designated for fire protection. If the public entity (whether a county or a city) that funds the fire department does not require the volunteer fire department to abide by bidding procedures, there is no other legal requirement that clearly requires it.

Contracts Covered by Competitive Bidding Statutes

31. Do the competitive bidding procedures apply when the unit is spending money under federal or state grants or money from other outside sources?

Cities, counties, and local school units have specific authority to accept grants and loans from the federal and state governments and to comply with requirements that are attached to those grants or loans.[8] Outside funding sources may, for example, impose competitive bidding requirements that differ from those otherwise required under state bidding laws; and local governments are authorized to comply with those requirements. However, if federal or state grants or loans do not include separate competitive bidding requirements, then the state law requirements apply. In fact, unless there is a specific statute that exempts a particular contract from competitive bidding, the local government should assume that the bidding procedures apply to any contract that is within the scope of the statute regardless of the source of funds that will be used to pay it.

32. What if funds are donated to the unit on condition that they must be used to purchase a particular item or to construct a facility using a specified contractor?

The statutes governing the general powers of cities, counties, and local school units provide authority to receive donated property. These powers also provide the authority to receive donated funds.[9] In general, this authority should also include the ability to receive donated funds subject to conditions that are otherwise lawful. However, there is no exception in the competitive bidding statutes for contracts made using donated funds; and the power to receive donations may not be so broad as to authorize a donation containing a restriction that, if accepted, would violate the law. A donation specifying a particular purchase or contractor may require the unit (depending upon the type of contract and amount of money involved) to violate the competitive bidding laws. It could be argued that the condition does not violate public policy since, but for the donation, there would be no public funds to spend. It is not clear whether a court would accept this argument or whether it would defer to the legislature to create an explicit exception. In light of this uncertainty, local governments should consider suggesting that the donor purchase and donate the item rather than donating funds or that the limitation on the donation be eliminated or restructured to allow for compliance with applicable bidding requirements. Note also that a donation that requires the purchase of a particular item may still be subjected to competition if the item may be supplied by more than one vendor.

---

8. G.S. 160A-17.1, made applicable to counties by G.S. 153A-14; G.S. 115C-47(7) (schools).

9. G.S. 153A-11 (counties); 160A-11 (cities); G.S. 115C-410.

33. What types of contracts are covered by the bidding laws?

The competitive bidding statutes apply to two categories of contracts: contracts for the purchase or lease-purchase of "apparatus, supplies, materials, and equipment" (referred to in this *Legal Guide to Purchasing and Contracting* as "purchase" contracts) and contracts for construction or repair work.[10] Within each of these categories, the statutes establish dollar limitations (see the "Dollar Thresholds" chart in Appendix 1), which determine the level of competition required. There are many local government contracts that do not fall within either of these two categories and are, therefore, not subject to any mandatory competitive requirements. In addition, several statutory exceptions remove contracts from bidding requirements that would otherwise apply, or provide alternative procedures that may be used at the local government's option. These statutory exemptions and alternatives are discussed in Questions 40 through 47.

Although not defined in the statutes, the terms apparatus, supplies, materials, and equipment have been held to denote "particular types of tangible *personal property*."[11] Similar terms can be found in Article 2 of the Uniform Commercial Code (UCC), which applies to sales of "goods,"[12] and the North Carolina sales tax law, which applies to "personal property that may be seen, weighed, measured, felt or touched, or is in any other manner perceptible to the senses."[13] Cases interpreting these other laws are sometimes helpful in analyzing whether particular contracts are covered by the bidding statutes.

34. Are contracts for services subject to the competitive bidding laws?

Service contracts other than those for construction or repair work are not covered by the competitive bidding laws. It's not that the statute exempts service contracts. They're simply not covered by the two categories of contracts that are listed in the bidding statute. A particular group of services—architectural, engineering, surveying, and construction management at risk—are subject to separate procedural requirements.[14]

The statute does not define what is meant by "repair," and that word could be interpreted to include repair of equipment. However, in the context of the phrase "construction or repair work" it is probably more reasonable to interpret repair as being limited to repair to public facilities, including buildings, utilities, and roads, and to treat repair of equipment as a service and thus not subject to competitive bidding requirements.

---

10. This *Legal Guide to Purchasing and Contracting* deals with purchase contracts. For a thorough discussion of requirements for public construction and repair contracts, *see* A. Fleming Bell, II, *Construction Contracts with North Carolina Local Governments,* 3d ed. (Chapel Hill, N.C.: Institute of Government, The University of North Carolina at Chapel Hill, 1996).

11. Mullen v. Town of Louisburg, 225 N.C. 53, 58, 33 S.E.2d 484, 487 (1934) (emphasis added).

12. *See* G.S. 25-2-102; 25-2-105.

13. G.S. 105-164.3(46).

14. G.S. 143-64.31. *See,* A. Fleming Bell, II, *Construction Contracts with North Carolina Local Governments,* 3d ed. (Chapel Hill, N.C.: Institute of Government, The University of North Carolina at Chapel Hill, 1996): 37–39.

35. What is the definition of a service contract, and what are some examples?

Although they are not defined in the statutes, service contracts are generally distinguished from purchase contracts in that they call for personal performance of work rather than delivery of a tangible item. Common examples of service contracts include contracts for the purchase of legal, banking, and accounting services; janitorial, recycling, and solid waste collection or disposal services; and insurance.

36. Do the competitive bidding requirements apply to contracts that are a mixture of goods and services?

Some contracts involve both a service and the purchase of tangible property. For example, a contract for aerial mapping may involve aerial photography —a service—but also has a tangible product—the resulting map. A carpeting contract involves purchase of the carpet but may also include the service of installation. The bidding laws do not specifically address this situation.

Based on cases from other jurisdictions and analogies to the tax laws and the Uniform Commercial Code (UCC), discussed in Question 33, the best approach is to try to determine which is the predominant aspect of the contract. This inquiry may be stated in several ways: Is the service component of the contract incidental (in terms of relative cost or importance to the contracting unit) to the purchase of supplies or equipment? Is the tangible item the end product of a service? If the service aspect predominates, the contract is properly characterized as a service and need not be bid. However, if the tangible property aspect predominates, the entire contract should be bid.

The North Carolina Supreme Court used the predominance approach to conclude that a contract for removal of sludge from a waste treatment system was a service contract rather than a sale of city property.[15] (One of the issues in the case was whether the competitive rules for disposing of public property applied to the contract.) Under the UCC, the courts have used the same reasoning to conclude that a physician who prescribes medication is not a merchant who deals in the sale of goods as defined in the UCC since the essence of the transaction is the professional service provided, not the sale of goods.[16]

Another approach is to separate the tangible and service components. This leaves the unit free to negotiate the service contract while complying with the bidding requirements for the tangible component. This should only be done where it is practical and will result in overall cost savings to the unit and should not be done solely to avoid competitive bidding requirements.[17]

---

15. Plant Food Co. v. Charlotte, 214 N.C. 518, 522, 199 S.E. 712, 715 (1938).

16. Batiste v. American Home Prod. Corp., 32 N.C. App. 1, 6, 231 S.E.2d 269, 272, *disc. review denied*, 292 N.C. 466, 233 S.E.2d 921 (1977).

17. G.S. 143-133 prohibits dividing contracts to evade the competitive bidding requirements.

37. How does the "predominant aspect" rule of interpretation apply to specific contracts, such as contracts for goods that include installation?

Applying this rule of interpretation to the examples discussed in Question 36, the aerial photography is the predominant aspect of the aerial mapping contract and the map is the result of that work. As such, the contract should be characterized as a service and is not subject to competitive bidding. (Note, however, that aerial mapping is a form of surveying and is subject to the special rules that govern selection of surveyors.)[18] On the other hand, purchase of the carpet is the predominant aspect of a contract for carpeting, even if the contract includes installation. This will usually be the case with purchase contracts that involve installation, unless the installation is particularly complicated. In some cases, installation work may constitute construction and thus require bidding and licensing under laws governing construction or repair work. For example, a contract to install a new air conditioning unit involves the purchase of equipment plus installation, but the installation may require electrical or other licenses, in which case it could properly be treated as a construction contract. Many similar borderline cases arise, and there are no cases to provide guidance. The predominant aspect rule provides a basis for making case-by-case judgments about how to treat such contracts for bidding purposes.

38. Are local governments required to bid computer software contracts?

Almost all units of government have occasion to purchase and upgrade computer systems consisting of both computer hardware and software. Clearly, computer hardware falls within the definition of "apparatus, supplies, materials, or equipment" and is subject to bidding procedures depending upon the estimated cost. Most computer software probably falls within the definition as well, especially if it already exists in a tangible form at the time of the purchase. However, some computer software is designed by a professional specifically to meet the user's needs. Applying the predominant aspect rule of interpretation described in Question 36, a contract of the latter kind may be considered a service contract since the skill and expertise of the computer consultant predominate and the software program is the end-product of that work.

The North Carolina sales tax law contains a definition that supports the above interpretation. The sales tax law, which applies to tangible personal property, applies to computer software but "custom computer software" is excluded. Custom software is defined as software "written in accordance with the specifications of a specific customer." Custom software does not include "prewritten software that can be installed and executed with no changes to the software's source code other than changes made to configure hardware or software."[19]

Thus, local governments should assume that contracts for computer hardware or software are subject to competitive bidding unless they primarily

18. G.S. 143-64.31.
19. G.S. 105-164.3(46); 105-164.13 (43).

consist of custom design or other services. There are, however, unique aspects of computer hardware and software purchases that may justify consideration of several alternative approaches.

Since many computer contracts involve a mixture of hardware, software, and services, the legislature has established a more flexible procedure, which may be used as an alternative to a traditional competitive bidding process at the option of the local government. Under G.S. 143-129.8 (discussed more fully in Question 45), local governments may use a "request for proposals" and engage in limited negotiations with the selected vendor, subject to the limitations contained in the statute. In some cases, a local government's software needs can be satisfied by a unique software system available from only one source. The sole-source exception in G.S. 143-129(f) provides authority to purchase without bidding in these situations. (See Question 43). It is important to distinguish, however, between the software and the hardware, which are often offered in a single contract. The software may be a sole-source item, but the hardware is usually widely available. If it is impractical to separate the purchases to isolate the sole-source component, the "request for proposals" procedure under G.S. 143-129.8 may be the most appropriate method of procurement.

Another common question about computer purchases is whether an upgrade to a computer system must be bid. If an upgrade involves purchase of supplies and equipment costing more than the formal bid threshold amount, the purchase is generally subject to bidding. In some cases, however, a computer upgrade may amount to a sole-source purchase if the software and equipment must be compatible with existing equipment and can only be supplied by one company. In those cases, the unit may purchase under the sole-source exception. (See Question 41.f.)

Finally, some computer systems may be leased rather than purchased. As noted in Question 42, a lease is not subject to bidding. It is important, however, to make sure that the contract is properly characterized as a lease. If a contract is called a lease, but is in fact a contract for a term that equals or exceeds the useful life of the equipment or software, it should properly be characterized as a sale. In the case of computer software, the vendor may have no practical intention of repossessing the property. In these cases, it would be inaccurate to characterize the contract as a lease.

39. Are contracts for demolition work covered by the competitive bidding statutes?

Since bidding is required for "construction or repair" work and demolition is neither, competitive bidding is not required for demolition work. This work ranges from highly specialized services, such as imploding a building, to more commonplace requirements such as removing structures or debris in order to clear a site for new construction. In the latter case, the work may be a part of the grading or clearing contract that forms a part of a construction project and should be bid as construction.

40. Are there special rules for the purchase of food or food services?

The statutes contain several provisions that establish separate rules for food and food service contracts. These apply only to local school units. First, G.S. 115C-264 creates an exception from the bidding requirements for the purchase of supplies and food for food services programs operated by the schools. (See Question 41.q.)

Another statute, G.S. 143-64, requires local school units, community colleges, and universities to competitively bid contracts that "involve the sale of juice or bottled water." This requirement appears to require bidding for any type of contract that involves these products, including contracts for vending machines and concessions, as well as direct purchases of the product. The statute authorizes the unit to establish quality standards for these beverages and to use those standards in accepting or rejecting bids.

Local school food services are required to give preference in food purchases to high-calcium foods and beverages. Under G.S. 115C-264.1, these are defined as "foods and beverages that contain a higher level of calcium and that are equal to or lower in price than other products of the same type or quality." This preference does not apply to purchases for individuals if the high-calcium product would interfere with their proper treatment or care.

41. Which contracts are exempt from the competitive bidding requirements?

There are several statutory exemptions from the competitive bidding requirements. Recognizing the strong policy of public protection that underlies the competitive bidding laws, the courts have strictly construed bidding exceptions and are likely to limit their application where there is any doubt. Accordingly, local government officials should conclude that bidding is not required only if the situation is clearly covered by an explicit exception.

The following sections describe exceptions from the requirements of Article 8 of Chapter 143. This means that they are exceptions to both the formal bidding requirements of G.S. 143-129, as well as the informal bidding requirements of G.S. 143-131, since both of these statutes are within Article 8. Some of these exceptions apply only to purchase contracts, while others apply to both purchase and construction contracts, as noted in the descriptions that follow.

a. Purchases from other units of government [143-129(e)(1)]

Local governments are not required to comply with the competitive bidding statutes when they contract for the purchase of apparatus, supplies, materials, or equipment from any federal agency or any other governmental unit within the United States. A parallel exception in G.S. 160A-274 specifically authorizes the sale, lease, and exchange of property between state and local government units without complying with the property disposal procedures.[20] This

20. The coverage of the two provisions may not be exactly parallel. The exception to the bidding law authorizes purchases from the federal government and the property

exception to the competitive bidding law also specifically allows local governments to bid at any surplus sales of any government within the United States. This exception applies only to purchase contracts.

b. Emergencies [143-129(e)(2)]

Bidding is not required "in cases of special emergency involving the health and safety of the people or their property." This exception applies to both purchase and construction or repair contracts. The North Carolina Supreme Court has interpreted this exception very narrowly, so the exception will be available legitimately only in rare circumstances.

That narrow interpretation came in *Raynor v. Commissioners of Louisburg.*[21] The town contracted without receiving bids for installation and repair of equipment in its power plant. A major part of the contract also included the purchase of several new diesel engines. The contract was clearly within the scope of the bidding statute. When challenged, the town relied on the emergency exception to justify its failure to bid the contract. The court summarized the town's explanation this way:

> The town was operating its water, sewage and power system with four engines, some of which were old and needed replacement. . . . Some of this machinery was said to have passed the age at which replacements are ordinarily made. . . . [T]he town was growing. . . . demands upon the power plant would increase. . . . [I]f there should be a breakdown of one or more engines in the plant, sufficient protection would not be afforded the citizens in the furnishing of water for consumption and sewage and against fires. . . . [B]ecause of the national emergency existing with respect to the public defense, not only were these conditions accentuated, but it was becoming, and would become more difficult to secure proper machinery or material for repair and replacement.[22]

The court held that these facts did not constitute an emergency sufficient to justify the failure to comply with the bidding procedures.

This case establishes several essential elements for an emergency to be exempt under the statute. The emergency must be present, immediate, and existing. It may not be a condition that is merely anticipated and may never actually occur. If the condition can be foreseen in time to take action to prevent harm to the public (or if the required bidding procedure can be completed before any harm would occur), the emergency exception cannot be invoked. The court noted that advertisement for bids would have required only one week and the contractor could have been required to "proceed with dispatch in making the desired replacements." This suggests that if harm to the public can be averted through temporary measures while proper bidding is being conducted, the emergency exception cannot be used to avoid bidding.

---

sale provision applies to a broad listing of local units, the state, "or any other public district, authority, department, agency, board, commission or institution." It is not clear whether the property sale provision applies to such agencies out of the state or to the federal government.

21. 220 N.C. 348, 17 S.E.2d 495 (1941).

22. *Raynor,* 220 N.C. at 353, 17 S.E.2d at 499.

The court also emphasized that the failure to take proper precautions to prevent the need for an expedited contract will not be accepted as a justification for exemption from the bidding requirements. The court's hostility to such a situation is demonstrated in the following quotation from the *Louisburg* case:

> It is not to be supposed that [the legislature] intended to make it possible for municipal officers to avoid advertising for bids for public work by merely delaying to take action to meet conditions which they can foresee until danger to public health and safety has become so great that the slight further delay caused by advertising will entail public calamity.[23]

Under this interpretation, the emergency exception is most likely to apply only in situations of natural disaster or other sudden and unforeseeable damage to property.

Where an emergency does exist, the governing board should adopt a resolution setting out the facts constituting the emergency (either before or as soon as possible after the purchase). As the court made clear in the Louisburg case, however, the board's resolution is not binding on a court. The court can review all of the information available about the situation (not just the facts in the board's resolution) and determine if, in the view of the court, the emergency exception legitimately justifies the failure to comply with the bidding requirements.

Two additional issues should be considered regarding emergency situations. First, as noted in Question 42, a lease of equipment, which may be the most practical solution to an emergency need, is not subject to bidding. Second, if the local government expects to seek reimbursement from federal or state aid sources, emergency contracts for goods or services should be structured to comply with the requirements of those agencies. It is often the case that these agencies will require competition for emergency contracts that are not otherwise subject to bidding under state law.

c. Group purchasing programs [143-129(e)(3)]

This exception allows local governments to purchase from suppliers who are selected through a group purchasing program that is a "formally organized program that offers competitively obtained purchasing services at discount prices to two or more public agencies." These programs are often established for particular types of operations, such as for hospitals or utilities, and may include participating units from across the country. There are very few limitations on its application other than that the group purchasing program must use a competitive process to select the vendors. The statute does not require that the process mirror the requirements under the North Carolina statutes. The exception is only valid for purchases that are a part of the program, so local government purchasers should make sure to verify that vendors can document their status under the program and that purchases under this exception are restricted to those items and prices that were established

---

23. Raynor v. Commissioners of Louisburg, 220 N.C. 353, 354, 17 S.E.2d 495, 499 [quoting Safford v. City of Lowell, 151 N.E. 111 (Mass. 1926)].

under the group purchasing program contracts. This exception applies only to purchase contracts.

d. Change order work [143-129(e)(4)]

Competitive bidding is not required for construction or repair work undertaken "during the progress" of a project that was initially bid. This exception applies only to construction or repair contracts and is generally understood to be the authorization to contract for change order work during an ongoing construction or repair contract without soliciting bids. There is no numerical percentage, dollar limit, or other direction in the statute about how much work may be done under this exception. However, a reasonable rule of interpretation would be that the work must be within the scope of the original project and not so substantial in amount or kind so as to invalidate the original bid procedure.[24]

e. Gas, fuel, and oil [143-129(e)(5)]

Purchases of gasoline, diesel fuel, alcohol fuel, motor oil, fuel oil, or natural gas are not subject to the formal bidding requirements. These purchases are subject to the informal procedures of G.S. 143-131. (See Questions 130 through 136.)

f. Sole-source purchases [143-129(e)(6)]

The bidding laws contain a fairly broad exception for sole-source purchases. The sole-source exception provides that the formal bidding requirements do not apply when

(1) performance or price competition for a product are not available;
(2) a needed product is available from only one source of supply; or
(3) standardization or compatibility is the overriding consideration.

Purchases made under this exception must be approved by the governing board; and, notwithstanding other authority to delegate the responsibility for awarding contracts, authority to award sole-source contracts cannot be delegated.

Although there is no case to date interpreting this exception, it is important to note that it should be applied with attention to the presumption in favor of competitive bidding noted earlier in Question 41. For example, a local government may conclude that it is most efficient and desirable to standardize on a particular make of vehicle in order to minimize fleet maintenance and repair costs. While the broad language of the exception may suggest that standardiza-

---

24. *See* A. Fleming Bell, II, *Construction Contracts with North Carolina Local Governments,* 3d ed. (Chapel Hill, N.C.: Institute of Government, The University of North Carolina at Chapel Hill, 1996), p. 55–58 (discussing change orders and additional work).

tion is a basis for purchasing without bidding, the unit should solicit competition where it is available consistent with the standardization policy. If there are multiple vendors of the preferred vehicle type, the unit should solicit bids in accordance with the statutory requirements.

A question often arises about whether the requirement of board approval under the sole-source exception applies to contracts in the informal range. The exception applies to all contracts that are subject to bidding, whether formal or informal. Thus, a contract in the informal range that is made under this exception would have to be approved by the governing board. This may seem unwieldy, however, to some units that do not generally bring informal range contracts before the board, and it may be impractical due to the scheduling of board meetings. An alternative approach is to proceed under the informal bidding procedures without invoking the sole-source exception. This would involve soliciting bids from any possible sources and proceeding with the bid from the only available source. As noted in Question 135, the informal procedure does not require receipt of a minimum number of bids—a single bid is legally sufficient. This approach would, therefore, comply with the informal bidding requirements and could also identify any available competition that might exist.

In addition to the sole-source exception discussed above, public hospitals are exempt from bidding in any of the following special circumstances listed in the sole-source exception:

(1) a particular medical item or prosthetic appliance is needed;
(2) a particular product is ordered by an attending physician for his or her patients;
(3) particular products are purchased for over-the-counter resale;
(4) particular products are desired for experimental, developmental, or research work; or
(5) equipment is already installed, connected, and in service and the governing body determines that it should be purchased.

The governing body of the hospital is required to keep a record of all purchases made under this exception, and that record is subject to public inspection.

g. Information technology goods and services [143-129(e)(7); 143-129.8]

Local governments may purchase "information technology"[25] through contracts awarded by the state Office of Information Technology Services, which specializes in these types of contracts and has several flexible procurement methods from which to choose in conducting its work. This exception overlaps

25. Information technology is defined in G.S. 147-33.81(2) as "electronic data processing goods and services, telecommunications goods and services, security goods and services, microprocessors, software, information processing, office systems, any services related to the foregoing, and consulting or other services for design or redesign of information technology supporting business processes."

with the exception in G.S. 143-129(e)(9), discussed in Question 41.i., which more broadly authorizes local governments to purchase from contracts awarded by any state agency. Another alternative method for purchasing information technology goods and services is set forth in G.S. 143-129.8, discussed more fully in Question 45.

h. Guaranteed energy savings contracts [143-129(e)(8)]

Local governments have authority under Chapter 143, Article 3B, Part 2 of the General Statutes to enter into "guaranteed energy savings contracts." Under these contracts, the vendor makes improvements to a public facility that will generate savings in energy costs sufficient, over the term of the contract, to pay for the cost of the improvements.[26] Separate procedures apply to these contracts as set forth in the statutes;[27] therefore, they are exempted from the otherwise applicable bidding requirements.

i. State contract purchases [143-129(e)(9)]

The central agency that is responsible for purchasing on behalf of state agencies and community colleges is the Division of Purchase and Contract (the Division) within the Department of Administration. The Division establishes term contracts for a wide variety of commodities and has historically allowed local governments to participate in those contracts at their option. An exemption in the bidding statute allows local governments to purchase from these contracts if the contractor is willing to extend to the local government the same or more favorable prices, terms, and conditions as those established under the state contract. The statute does not require the local unit to advertise nor does it require local board approval for a purchase under this exception. There is also no requirement that the option for local governments to use the contract be a part of the original contract with the vendor. This exception applies to contracts awarded by any North Carolina state agency. As noted above, this exception overlaps with the exception for purchases from contracts awarded by the Office of Information Technology Services, which is a state agency.

There is also some overlap between the "piggybacking" exception (see Question 41.l. below and Appendix 3) and the state contract exception, but there are important differences. While the piggybacking exception allows the purchase of goods that were the subject of a contract awarded by any other public agency anywhere in the country, the state contract exception only applies to items available under contracts awarded by a North Carolina state agency. Another difference is that the time limitation and board approval requirements in the "piggybacking" exception do not apply to the state contract exception. For purchases from North Carolina state contract vendors, the state contract would be simpler to use than the "piggybacking" exception.

---

26. G.S. 143-64.17(3).
27. *See* G.S. 143-64.17A, -64.18B.

Finally, it is important to note that, like the "piggybacking" exception, the state contract exception does not create any obligation on the part of the state contract vendor to honor the state contract prices in a sale to a local government. The state does, however, make it possible for local governments to become a party to some state contracts. If a local government takes advantage of this opportunity and becomes a party to the contract, the successful vendor for the contract is obligated to sell to the local government at the contracted price and the local government is bound to purchase any items it desires under that contract as if the local government had awarded the contract to the vendor itself.

j. Purchase of used goods [143-129(e)(10)]

Local governments may purchase used apparatus, supplies, materials, or equipment without complying with the competitive bidding requirements. This exception recognizes the situation that usually exists with used equipment, which is that each item is unique in terms of age and condition, making bidding impractical. The exception does not apply, however, to remanufactured, refabricated, or "demo" items. For purposes of the exception, the statute defines a "demo" item as one that is used for demonstration and is sold by the manufacturer or retailer at a discount.

k. Construction management at risk [143-129(e)(11)]

Local governments are authorized to use the construction management at risk method for building construction contracts under G.S. 143-128.1. Selection of a construction manager at risk is subject to the provisions of G.S. 143-64.31, and other procedures for these contracts are set forth in G.S. 143-128.1; therefore, they are exempted from the otherwise applicable bidding requirements in G.S. 143-129.[28]

l. Previously bid or "piggybacking" contracts [143-129(g)]

The so-called "piggybacking" exception authorizes local governments to purchase without bidding from a person or entity that has, within the past twelve months, contracted to furnish an item to any other public agency. Specifically, the previous contract must have been awarded by the federal government, any federal agency, any state government or state agency anywhere in the country, or any local government anywhere in the country. Despite the common name for these contracts, the exception does not actually involve

28. For information on the legislation creating the authority to use construction management at risk and other contruction methods, see Frayda Bluestein, *Purchasing and Contracting,* in *North Carolina Legislation 2001* (Chapel Hill, N.C.: Institute of Government, The University of North Carolina at Chapel Hill, 2002), 235–253.

"piggybacking" on another government's contract. Purchases under this exception are made directly from the vendor under a new contract, not as part of the prior contract, and no approval or action by the other government is required. The vendor must be willing to supply the item to the local government for the same or more favorable prices and other terms. In addition, the prior contract must be one that was entered into following a public bid process substantially similar to the one contained in G.S. 143-129.

Contracts made under this exception must be approved by the local governing board at a regularly scheduled meeting; and notice of the intent to award the contract without bidding must be published no less than ten days prior to the meeting. As in the case of sole-source contracts, and notwithstanding other authority to delegate the responsibility for awarding contracts, the authority to award contracts under this exception cannot be delegated. A more detailed set of questions and answers regarding this exception, including suggested language to meet the advertisement requirement, can be found in Appendix 3 of this *Legal Guide to Purchasing and Contracting.*

This exception provides that purchases may be made under this exception when the responsible officials determine it to be in the best interest of the unit. This suggests that some effort should be made to determine that the price and terms offered by the supplier are as good or better than those that could be obtained through bidding. If a supplier makes or proposes to make a competitive offer in response to the notice of intent to waive bidding, the unit should conduct a competitive bidding process even though the statute does not explicitly require it.

Finally, it is important to note that the item purchased by the local government must be *the same* as the item sold under the previously awarded contract. Although there is great temptation to modify the contract by selecting alternate options or making other modifications to suit the particular needs of the local government, this should be kept to an absolute minimum. The likely basis for this very broad exception is that, since another agency has recently conducted a bidding process, the local government is allowed to "piggyback" on that process without having to repeat it. If, however, the local government, in effect, modifies the specifications for the item to be purchased such that the outcome of the original bid might have been different, the basis for the exception is destroyed. In this situation, the exception is no longer valid for the purchase and a contract awarded would be void for failure to comply with the bidding requirements. (See Question 143.)

m. Transportation authority purchases [143-129(h)]

Regional public transportation authorities[29] and regional transportation authorities[30] are authorized to use a "request for proposal" method of purchasing apparatus, supplies, materials, or equipment as an alternative to the other-

---

29. Created pursuant to Article 26 of Chapter 160A of the North Carolina General Statutes.

30. Created pursuant to Article 27 of Chapter 160A of the North Carolina General Statutes.

wise applicable bidding requirements under G.S. 143-129. The statute, G.S. 143-129(h) specifies the procedures these agencies must use when purchasing under this alternative method.

n. Solid waste management facilities [143-129.2]

A unique statutory procedure allows local governments to contract for the design, construction, operation, management, and maintenance of highly complex and innovative solid waste management facilities, including facilities involving energy recovery. The statute creates an exemption from the competitive bidding laws for these facilities, but it also establishes a request-for-proposals procedure that must be followed. However, the statute *does not exempt* construction work for any "facility or structure which is ancillary to the solid waste management facility and which does not involve storage and processing of solid waste or [energy or materials recovery]."[31] Examples of ancillary facilities listed in the statute are roads, water and sewer lines to the facility, transfer stations, scale houses, administration buildings, and residue and bypass disposal sites.

Questions arise about what kinds of solid waste facilities may be constructed under this exception. For example, is a lined landfill a solid waste management facility for purposes of this exception? The statute does not define "solid waste management facility" but does incorporate by reference definitions in G.S. 130A-290, which defines the term quite broadly as "land, personnel and equipment used in the management of solid waste."[32] However, the procedure established in the statute suggests that it should only be used for complex systems involving innovative technology and the need for unification of design, construction, operation, management, and maintenance in one contract. Lined landfills and other more conventional solid waste management approaches do not appear to be within the scope of this exception.

o. Use of unit's own forces (force account work) [143-135]

Local governments are not required to comply with competitive bidding requirements for construction or repair work undertaken using the permanent work force of the unit if the project is within the dollar thresholds set forth in the statute. (See the "Dollar Thresholds" chart in Appendix 1.) However, the unit must still comply with the competitive bidding laws for any equipment, supplies, or materials that it purchases to use on the project. The language of the statute suggests that in order for the project to lawfully be conducted with the unit's own forces, the *entire* project, including the cost of labor and materials, must be within the statutory dollar limit, and must be conducted entirely with the unit's own forces. The statute also prohibits local governments from dividing projects in order to evade the limitations under this section.

---

31. G.S. 143-129.2(f).
32. G.S. 130A-290(39).

p. Purchases of goods and services from nonprofit work centers for the blind and severely disabled [143-129.5]

Local governments may purchase goods and services directly from a nonprofit work center for the blind and severely disabled, as defined in G.S. 143-48, without complying with the otherwise applicable bidding requirements in G.S. 143-129.

q. Supplies and food for school food services [G.S. 115C-264]

Local school units are exempt from the competitive bidding requirements for the purchase of supplies and food for food services programs operated by the schools. Some of these programs are federally funded and carry their own separate competitive bidding requirements. This exception applies only to local school units. (See Question 40.)

42. Do lease contracts have to be bid?

No. The competitive bidding requirements apply to purchases, as well as lease-purchase or installment-purchase contracts, which are contracts in which either the seller or a third party allows the unit to pay for an item over time.[33] The competitive bidding requirements *do not apply* to lease (also called rental) contracts, under which the unit does not intend to and does not have the option to purchase the goods. Competitive bidding does apply when there is an option to purchase, no matter how it may be described or where in the term of the contract it may fall and regardless of whether the unit intends to exercise it. Specific limitations on and procedures for installment-purchase (often called lease-purchase) contracts are contained in G.S. 160A-20 (cities, counties, and other local governments) and G.S. 115C-528 (local school units).[34] (See Question 13.)

It is also important to make sure that lease contracts are not leases in name only but are, in fact, consistent with the definition of a lease. Though there are no cases on this issue in the bidding context, other sources of law provide guidance. A contract that is called a lease but is in fact for a term that equals or exceeds the useful life of the equipment would likely, if challenged, be characterized as a sale and would be subject to the bidding requirements.[35] As stated in a treatise on North Carolina contract law, "The existence of residual value in the goods that reverts to the lessor indicates that a lease is present."[36]

---

33. G.S. 143-129(a); 160A-19; 153A-165, and 115C-528.

34. *See* David M. Lawrence, *Financing Capital Projects*, 2d ed. (Chapel Hill, N.C.: Institute of Government, The University of North Carolina at Chapel Hill, 1994), § 205 ("Installment Purchase Contracts and Certificates of Participation").

35. While there is a distinction between operating and capital leases under generally accepted accounting principles, this standard should probably not be used in this context to determine whether a contract is a true lease. The accounting standard is developed based on a different set of concerns and does not parallel the analysis that has been used in contract law.

36. *See* John N. Hutson Jr. and Scott A. Miskimon, NORTH CAROLINA CONTRACT LAW (Mathew Bender & Co., Inc., LEXIS Publishing, 2001), 460 [analyzing § 1-203(37) of

If the leased property has nominal or no residual value, or the vendor has no practical ability or intent to repossess the property (as may be the case for some "leased" computer software), it is not appropriate to characterize the contract as a lease, especially if this characterization is primarily intended as a justification for avoiding the application of the bidding requirements.

43. Do sole-source items have to be bid?

A specific exception in the statute, G.S. 143-129(e)(6), authorizes sole-source purchases without bidding, subject to certain procedural requirements. (See Question 41.f.)

44. Is bidding required when a local government purchases items from a state contract vendor?

A specific exception in the statute, G.S. 143-129(e)(9), authorizes local governments to purchase from a state contract vendor without bidding. (See Question 41.i.)

45. What is the "request for proposals" procedure that is authorized for information technology goods and services?

Chapter 143 contains a provision, G.S. 143-129.8, which gives local governments more flexibility in purchasing information technology goods and services. As stated in the statute, this provision recognizes "the complex and innovative nature of information technology goods and services, and . . . the desirability of a single point of responsibility for contracts that include combinations of purchase of goods, design, installation, training, operation, maintenance, and related services. . . ."[37] The statute authorizes local governments to use a request-for-proposals procedure rather than an invitation for bids (see Question 66 for a discussion of the difference between these procedures). This provision is available as an alternative to the traditional bidding methods, which may be used at the option of the local government.

For purposes of this statute, information technology is defined as "electronic data processing goods and services, telecommunications goods and services, security goods and services, microprocessors, software, information processing, office systems, any services related to the foregoing, and consulting or other services for design or redesign of information technology supporting business processes."[38] Note that this definition includes some types of contracts, such as services, that are not subject to competitive bidding. (See Question 34.) Local governments are not obligated to use either the competitive bidding or the request for proposals procedures for contracts that consist only of services. The definition also includes some contracts, such as computer hardware and other "goods," that could easily be purchased as commodities

---

the Uniform Commercial Code, which distinguishes a lease from a sale with a security interest].

37. G.S. 143-129.8(a).

38. G.S. 143-129.8(a) (citing G.S. 147-33.81(2)).

under the traditional competitive bidding requirements. As noted earlier, however, both computer software contracts and other contracts that involve a combination of goods and services can be complicated and are not necessarily well-suited to the traditional bidding process called for under G.S. 143-129. For these reasons, local governments should consider using the more flexible procedures under G.S. 143-129.8 for information technology contracts.

Solicitations under this statute must be advertised in the same manner as is required for contracts that are subject to bidding under G.S. 143-129(a). (See Questions 71 through 74.) The statute provides for a range of procurement methods and a flexible standard for awarding contracts which allows the unit to choose the contract that best meets its needs, even if it is not the lowest cost proposal. Factors to be used in evaluating proposals must be included in the request for proposals.[39] Another important aspect of this statute is the provision that allows the local government to negotiate with any proposer in order to obtain a final contract that best meets the needs of the unit. In order to preserve the fairness of the competitive process, the statute limits the scope of these negotiations. Negotiations "shall not alter the contract beyond the scope of the original request for proposals in a manner that: (i) deprives the proposers or potential proposers of a fair opportunity to compete for the contract; and (ii) would have resulted in the award of the contract to a different person or entity if the alterations had been included in the request for proposals."[40] This limitation prevents the owner from substantially changing the terms of the solicitation after proposals have been received in a way that would be unfair to actual or potential participants in the process, while still providing the flexibility that is important given the potential range of differences among proposals that might be received in the information technology field.

In order to preserve the confidentiality of proposals during the evaluation and negotiation process, the statute provides that proposals are not subject to public inspection until a contract is awarded.[41] Note that proprietary information that meets the statutory definition of a trade secret is exempt from disclosure under a separate exception in the public records law.[42]

The statute does not specifically require that contracts under this alternative procedure must be awarded by the governing board. Therefore it appears that the award may be made by the board or by staff under a delegation of authority from the board. (See Question 7.)

46. What procedures apply to purchases from North Carolina Correction Enterprises?

The state prison system produces a number of items that local governments may buy without complying with any competitive bidding procedures. Since Correction Enterprises is part of a state agency, the exception discussed in Question 41.a. for purchases from other units of government applies. G.S. 148-70

39. G.S. 143-129.8(b)(2).
40. G.S. 143-129.8(c).
41. G.S. 143-129.8(d).
42. *See* G.S. 132-1.2

actually creates a preference for Corrections Enterprises products, but this only applies to state agencies. Another provision in the statute prohibits requiring competition when purchasing from Correction Enterprises, and this provision does apply to local governments.

47. Can a local government piggyback on another governmental unit's contract without going out for bids if a vendor who has a contract with the other unit is willing to provide the goods at the same price?

Yes. An exception to the bidding requirements, G.S. 143-129(g), specifically authorizes this, subject to certain procedural requirements. (See Question 41.l. and Appendix 3.) Local governments having similar needs for particular items can also pool their requirements to obtain volume discounts by cooperatively bidding those items. A broad statute, G.S. 160A-461, authorizes local governments to undertake cooperatively any function they have the authority to carry out, including purchasing. Cooperative bidding procedures are discussed in more detail in Question 156.

Application of Dollar Thresholds

48. What are the dollar thresholds for formal and informal procedures?

The dollar thresholds are set out in the "Dollar Thresholds" chart in Appendix 1. Some local governments operate under local acts that vary the thresholds established by general law.

49. Do the dollar thresholds apply to the cost of each item or to the total contract amount?

The dollar thresholds apply to the total amount of the contract that will be awarded to any one contractor. G.S. 143-133 specifically prohibits dividing contracts to avoid competitive bidding.

50. Are local governments required to identify and consolidate all of their needs for particular items before going out for bids in order to avoid the statute's prohibition on dividing contracts?

No. There are many legitimate reasons for spreading out purchases over time, including limited storage facilities, fluctuating prices, insufficient or staggered revenue sources, or noncentralized purchasing. Successive purchases of identical items over a short period of time, however, are likely to draw the attention of the unit's auditor or other observers of the purchasing process, particularly if multiple contracts are awarded to the same vendor.[43]

---

43. *See* Fuqua v. Rockingham County Bd. of Soc. Servs., 125 N.C. App. 66, 479 S.E.2d 273 (1997) (splitting invoices to avoid bidding violated state law and was upheld as basis for dismissing employee).

51. How does a local government generate the estimated cost in order to determine the level of competition required?

The formal bidding statute does not contain any specific requirements for establishing estimates of contract costs. Purchasing officials must make a good faith estimate based on historical or comparative pricing information. In the case of construction or repair work, they may rely on a design professional's estimate.

52. What if a good faith estimate suggests that the informal bidding procedure should be used but one or more of the bids actually exceeds the informal bidding limit?

The formal bidding statute applies to contracts *estimated* to cost at or above the formal threshold. The informal bidding statute is worded differently. It applies to contracts *costing* (not estimated to cost) the statutory amount. If all of the bids received after informal competition exceed the informal bid threshold amount, the contract must be readvertised using the formal procedures. However, if one or more bids are within the informal range and are otherwise acceptable, a contract may be awarded even though some of the bids are in the formal range.

53. Are taxes and delivery costs included in the estimate when determining what level of bidding is required?

Yes. Even though local governments are entitled to reimbursement of sales tax, the total amount of the contract, including taxes, delivery, and any other charges to be paid by the local government under the contract, should be included when determining which procedures are required. Specifications often require that taxes be set out separately or that taxes not be included in the bid. This makes sense for several reasons. First, it avoids any ambiguity about whether taxes are included in the bid that may cause confusion or allow for manipulation by bidders after bids are opened. In addition, many local governments do not include taxes on their purchase orders and, instead, pay taxes out of a separate account set up to accommodate reimbursement. Despite these acceptable practices, there is no indication in the bidding laws that taxes may be excluded in determining the total cost of the contract.

54. What if a change order or other modification made to an informally bid contract after it has been awarded and executed brings it above the formal limit?

Contracts sometimes require modification due to changes in circumstances or unforeseen conditions that increase the amount of the expenditure above the original contract amount. Subject to some restrictions (see Question 41.d.), these types of changes are certainly legal. Although the statutes do not specifically say so, it seems clear that, if reasonable increases bring an informally bid contract into the formal range, the law does not require that the contract be relet under formal procedures.

In determining what constitutes a reasonable change, local government officials should take great care to ensure that the changes made after a contract is awarded are not so significant in quantity or kind that they could be viewed as an abuse or avoidance of the competitive bidding laws. If changes arise after bids are opened and analyzed but before a contract is awarded, officials should avoid the temptation to award the contracts as bid and then make the changes by change order after the contract is executed. In one case, a court held officials personally liable for funds paid to a contractor under a contract that was significantly increased after it was awarded. The court found that the officials and the contractor knew that more work was required and conspired to avoid proper procedures.[44] When the need to make significant changes in a contract becomes evident before the contract is awarded, the appropriate action is to reject all of the bids and readvertise the contract as revised using the procedures that apply based on the estimated cost with the changes.

Specifications

55. What are specifications, and what purposes do they serve?

Specifications form the basis of the competitive bidding process and of the resulting contract. The specifications describe for the bidders what is being sought, provide the basis for comparing bids, and are generally incorporated by reference into a contract (usually a purchase order) to become the successful bidder's legal obligations under the contract.

56. Do the statutes contain specific requirements for how specifications should be prepared?

The competitive bidding statutes are virtually silent about the requirements for preparing specifications for purchasing apparatus, supplies, materials, or equipment. For construction or repair contracts, several state statutes dictate that materials specified must provide for broad competition[45] and restrict manufacturers or those with financial interests in a product from preparing specifications for governmental entities.[46] Despite the lack of statutory guidance, specifications play an important legal and practical role in the purchasing process. Legal issues involving specifications are discussed in Questions 58 through 60.

57. Where can local government officials find the information they need to prepare good specifications?

Purchasing officials must often rely on the technical expertise of those requesting the materials to develop a written description of items to be purchased.

---

44. Moore v. Lambeth, 207 N.C. 23, 175 S.E. 714 (1934).
45. G.S. 133-3.
46. G.S. 133-1; 133-2.

In addition, trade associations and vendors can supply technical specifications that are very useful. Local government officials writing specifications must be careful to inspect vendor specifications before incorporating them into a solicitation since they may restrict competition.

Perhaps the greatest resource for specifications is other units of government. National and state organizations of purchasing professionals provide opportunities to exchange specifications and other valuable information. In addition, the North Carolina Division of Purchase and Contract maintains standard specifications and makes them available to local governments upon request. Even for the most complex purchase, a survey of other units by phone, e-mail, or fax is likely to turn up someone who has purchased similar items before.

Local governments should take several precautions when using specifications from other units. First, it is essential to make sure that all aspects of the specifications are modified to conform to local policies, terms and conditions, and other information in effect in the unit issuing the bid so that the borrowed specifications do not conflict with other general information accompanying the solicitation. It may also be useful to find out how the specifications worked for the unit that originally issued them and what problems, if any, arose during the bid process or after the contract was awarded. This information may provide an opportunity to improve upon the specifications before using them again.

58. Are there any legal limitations on how specifications are prepared?

The requirement of fairness that underlies the bidding laws (see Questions 21 and 23) dictates that specifications must be prepared in a way that provides ample opportunity for competition.[47] Thus any narrowing of competition in the specifications must be justifiable. Of course, the bidding statute itself provides that quality is a factor in awarding contracts; therefore, quality can also be considered when preparing specifications. Local governments are not required to prepare specifications that are as broad as possible. Rather, specifications may delineate the quality that is being sought and may eliminate possible competitors if the product they offer does not meet the unit's needs. Creating a balance between demanding quality and maintaining reasonable opportunity for competition is easier to describe than it is to achieve. Substantial background research may be required in some cases to develop specifications that reflect the features and quality levels desired, but this work is necessary in order for the unit to obtain value for the tax dollars spent.

59. Is it legal to specify brand names?

There is no statute or case that specifically addresses this question. The answer really derives from the analysis in the answer to Question 58: Brand

---

47. *See* Sperry Corp. v. Patterson, 73 N.C. App. 123, 124, 135 S.E.2d 642, 644 (1985); Raynor v. Commissioners of Louisburg, 220 N.C. 348, 350, 17 S.E.2d 495, 497 (1941).

names may be specified if there is no other product that meets the needs of the unit, although this is rarely the case. On the other hand, brand names are often useful as a shorthand way to communicate to vendors the specific qualities, functions, or characteristics that are being sought. In order to take advantage of this shorthand while still not limiting competition, specifications often call for a particular brand "or equal." This allows sellers of other brands the opportunity to demonstrate that their product meets the needs of the unit. It is, of course, still up to the unit to decide whether competing products *do* meet the unit's requirements; and this determination must be made within the legal limitations described in the previous answer. That is, products may not be unreasonably excluded, and the unit must be able to justify any determination that a product is not an equal to what is specified.

It is important to distinguish between a brand name specification and a sole source. (See Question 41.f.) Even if bids are limited to a specific brand, there is usually more than one supplier of that brand, so competition is still possible and should be sought.

60. Does the desire to standardize equipment justify specifying a particular brand?

In some cases, a local government may increase efficiency and save money by limiting purchases to a particular brand. For example, if the unit services its own fleet of vehicles, it may save money by limiting its stock of supplies and its personnel training program to one make of vehicle. Another example might involve standardization of computer or copying equipment in order to avoid having more than one service contract. If the unit can document that such cost savings actually exist, standardization is legally justifiable. Units should continue to compare costs of different manufacturers each time they purchase new equipment, however, since performance and repair costs change over time and may eventually justify expanding to other manufacturers. Standardization of materials to be used in construction or repair projects is subject to additional limitations under G.S. 133-3.

61. What is an "approved products" or "qualified products" list?

A local government can survey the available products on the market and determine which among them meet the quality and other characteristics the unit requires. In some cases, this process may involve testing or other evaluation of products against predetermined criteria. Once evaluation is complete, the specifications can list the specific brands or products that will be accepted. This method is preferable to the use of "or equal" in specifications because it gives suppliers an opportunity to demonstrate their goods before the specifications are promulgated and provides clearer guidance to bidders about what will be accepted. If the specifications list a brand "or equal," bidders must go through the expense of submitting a bid and awaiting a determination by the unit after the bids are received. Of course, the principles of fairness and competition apply to an approved products list in the same manner as described in Question 58, and products may not be unjustifiably excluded from such a list.

62. Are there state rules requiring purchase of products with recycled content or purchase of remanufactured or reused materials?

A state law that applies to state agencies, community colleges, and local school units requires these entities to encourage and promote the purchase of products with recycled content.[48] The statute prohibits the use of specifications that explicitly discriminate against materials with recycled content except where necessary to protect the health, safety, and welfare of the citizens.[49] State law also requires these entities to report on the amount of products purchased, and another statute establishes an annual goal of 50 percent for the purchase of paper and paper products with recycled content equal to 50 percent.[50]

Another provision requires local governments and state agencies, or any person contracting with these entities, to use products made from recycled steel.[51]

Finally, state law limits a local government's ability to use a provision in any agreement or contract that prohibits reusing, remanufacturing, or refilling a toner or inkjet cartridge. G.S. 75-36 makes any such provision void as a matter of public policy. This provision does not prevent a vendor from requiring the use of new or specified toners or inkjet cartridges as a condition of the warranty under a maintenance contract. As noted in Question 41.j., purchase of remanufactured or refabricated items does not fall within the scope of the used goods exception to the bidding requirements.

63. What is a performance specification, and when should one be used?

A performance specification describes what the desired product or service must do, rather than describing the product or service itself. This type of approach is particularly useful for purchasing computer systems, for example, where there are many different products on the market and the products vary in design. Even when a commodity, such as a utility vehicle, is being purchased, elements can be included in the specifications to solicit information from the bidders about the performance of the vehicle (mileage, load capacity, repair record, and so forth), and to inform bidders about the anticipated use of the vehicle so they can bid a product that is capable of meeting the articulated need. Advantages of performance specifications include potential for increased competition (because particular products or brands are not specified) and increased flexibility in bidder response. One disadvantage is that bids may be more difficult to compare, since bidders may be offering very different products in response to the same specifications. In evaluating bids submitted under a performance specification, attention must be focused on how well the proposal will meet the performance requirements as well as on the cost of obtaining different levels of performance.

---

48. G.S. 143-58.2(a).
49. G.S. 143-58.2(b).
50. G.S. 143-58.2(f); 143-58.3.
51. G.S. 130A-309.14. This requirement only applies if the product can be acquired competitively within a reasonable time, at a reasonable price, and meets applicable performance requirements.

64. What is the purpose of a pre-solicitation or pre-bid conference?

An effective way to improve specifications is to ask all interested or potential bidders to attend a meeting with representatives of the unit either before specifications have been developed (pre-solicitation) or after specifications are promulgated but before the bid opening (pre-bid). The purpose of a pre-solicitation meeting is to communicate to suppliers the unit's needs and to get information from the suppliers about their products. This information can then be compiled and used to develop specifications. If a particular site is involved or other special conditions exist, meeting at the location where the product will be installed and used can avoid errors in bids.

A pre-bid conference gives potential bidders who have obtained specifications an opportunity to ask questions and clarify particular aspects of the specifications and also to identify problems or errors in the specifications. In these meetings, representatives of the unit can ensure that all bidders get the same information. In addition, if the conference discloses a need for corrections or additions to the specifications, these can be recorded and sent out as written addenda. (See Question 74.) Pre-bid conferences should be publicized to all potential bidders and should be scheduled at a location and time that is convenient for bidders. Some local governments provide a written record of all questions and answers: this avoids later misunderstandings about what was said and can also be provided to bidders who were unable to attend.

65. Can the local government make attendance at a pre-bid conference or site visit mandatory and reject the bids of contractors who do not attend?

Although there is no specific authority to require attendance at a pre-bid conference, the authority for a mandatory pre-bid conference or site visit is probably implicit in the unit's authority to structure its bid process in a manner that ensures the receipt of accurate and acceptable bids. Local governments do have specific authority to prequalify contractors on construction contracts,[52] and it could be argued that attendance at a pre-bid conference is part of a prequalification process. Although the published advertisement required for formal bids represents a strong policy in the statutes in favor of allowing wide participation in bidding, requiring interested bidders to attend a mandatory pre-bid conference seems justifiable in cases where there are unusual site conditions or where the solicitation is particularly complicated. It is advisable to include notice of a pre-bid conference in the advertisement if attendance will be mandatory.

The difficult question that sometimes arises with mandatory pre-bid conference or site visit requirements is what to do about a bidder who does not attend the mandatory pre-bid conference or site visit and who submits an otherwise acceptable and low bid. It would be unfair to other bidders who have made the effort to attend, sometimes at great expense, if someone who did not attend is allowed to bid. Such a bid should be considered nonresponsive. (See

52. G.S. 143-135.8.

Question 101.) Another option in this situation is to extend the bid opening date, if time permits, and provide an additional pre-bid conference opportunity. Bidders who attended the first meeting would not be required to attend the second one, and information provided at both meetings would be provided to all bidders.

Given these potential complications, and the possibility of a challenge to the authority of the unit to require attendance at a pre-bid conference, local governments should always consider the need for a mandatory pre-bid conference carefully to make sure that the potential benefits will outweigh the risks.

Types of Contracts and Solicitations

66. What are the differences between an IFB or RFB, an RFP, and an IFQ or RFQ, and which of these are North Carolina local governments allowed to use?

These terms are commonly used in the contracting process. Except for the statute authorizing the use of a request for proposals for information technology goods and services (see Question 45), these terms are not used in North Carolina's bidding statutes and have no legal significance under those laws. They do have commonly understood meanings and differences.

An IFB or RFB (invitation or request for bids) usually indicates that a sealed bid procedure is being used. The essence of such a procedure is that detailed specifications are made available in advance, bids usually consist of a lump sum cost for specified items, bids are received and evaluated for compliance with specifications, and a contract is awarded to the lowest responsible bidder. Based on this common understanding of IFBs or RFBs, this is the most accurate way to describe solicitations promulgated under North Carolina's formal bidding statute.

An RFP (request for proposals) is typically used for service or other contracts where development of detailed specifications is not practical. An RFP is usually written as a performance specification, delineating the result desired and asking the responders to propose a method of reaching that result. This is the method that is authorized under G.S. 143-129.8 for information technology goods and services. (See Question 45.) Since responses to an RFP may vary widely, a sealed bid process is generally not used with an RFP. Often the proposals are followed by negotiations or by a separate sealed bid procedure based on new specifications developed after reviewing initial proposals. In some cases, proposals may be divided into technical and cost components, with the cost portion opened only if the technical proposal is satisfactory. This protects an unsuccessful respondent from unnecessary price exposure.

RFPs can legally be used under G.S. 143-129.8 subject to the procedures required under that statute. (See Question 45.) They can also be used for contracts that are subject to the competitive bidding statutes, though this method of solicitation does not fit easily with the requirements of those statutes. Indeed, it may be misleading to contractors to call a solicitation under the bidding laws an RFP, given the commonly understood meaning of that term. If an

RFP approach is used for a contract that is subject to the bidding requirements, *it is essential that the statutory procedures are incorporated into the RFP process.* From a legal standpoint, it doesn't matter what you call the process as long as it meets the statutory requirements. This means that for contracts that are subject to competitive bidding, the RFP must be advertised, proposals must be sealed, and no negotiations may be conducted after proposals are opened.

RFPs can also be used for contracts that are not subject to the competitive bidding requirements, particularly service contracts. For these contracts, the RFP procedure can be structured in whatever manner the local government deems appropriate and may include negotiations following receipt of the proposals. The procedure to be used, as well as the standard by which contracts will be awarded, should be clearly described in the RFP.

An IFQ or RFQ[53] (invitation or request for quotes) usually indicates an informal procedure and accurately describes the requirement under North Carolina's informal procedure for contracts involving small dollar amounts. (See the "Dollar Thresholds" chart in Appendix 1 and Questions 130 through 136.) Quotes generally do not have to be sealed and often are given over the telephone or electronically (by fax or e-mail). A quote is generally as legally binding as a bid, except that oral quotes may not be binding if a written contract is required. (See Question 16.)

67. Can a local government trade in surplus property as part of a competitive bidding process for the purchase of new equipment?

Yes. Generally, local governments must dispose of surplus property under the procedures established in Article 12 of Chapter 160A.[54] Under G.S. 143-129.7, however, local governments may simultaneously purchase and trade in apparatus, supplies, materials, and equipment, without separately having to comply with the property disposal procedures. The statute provides that the amount offered for the surplus property to be traded in can be considered in determining the lowest responsible bidder. This is typically accomplished by providing a place on the bid form for the bidder to list the trade-in allowance or the amount the bidder is willing to offer to purchase the surplus property. The award is then made to the lowest responsible bidder, considering the purchase price as reduced by the trade-in amount offered.

To avoid confusion in evaluating bids, the bid form and specifications should clearly instruct bidders as to whether the trade-in offer is mandatory or whether a bid will be accepted without it. The local government may want to make the trade-in optional in order to reserve the right to dispose of the property by separate sale if this approach might bring a higher sale price.

---

53. "RFQ" can also refer to a request for qualifications, used in a qualification-based solicitation, such as the one used to select design professionals under G.S. 143-64.31 or in a prequalification of bidders.

54. These provisions apply to cities and are made applicable to counties under G.S. 153A-176 and to local school units under G.S. 115C-518(a). For more information on local government property disposal, see David M. Lawrence, *Local Government Property Transactions in North Carolina*, 2d ed. (Chapel Hill, N.C.: Institute of Government, The University of North Carolina at Chapel Hill, 2000).

It is also important to recognize that a purchase that includes the trade in option under G.S. 143-129.7 is essentially an exception to compliance with the otherwise applicable property disposal procedures. This exception only applies when the purchase is made under the bidding statutes. Thus, for example, if a local government wishes to contract for a *lease* of equipment without bidding (see Question 42) and include a trade-in, the exception does not apply and the property disposal procedures must be used. Note, however, that under those procedures, property with a low dollar value may be sold under a delegation from the governing board using informal procedures.[55]

68. Can a local government solicit bids to lock in a price without committing to a particular quantity of items to be purchased, and, if so, how does the unit determine what level of bidding is required?

Yes. This type of contract is variously called a fixed-price, an indefinite-quantity, a requirements, or a term contract. Bids are solicited to lock in prices for a specified term. Under a requirements contract, the local government's obligation is to purchase all of its needs for the specified item from the successful bidder, and the bidder's obligation is to supply all of the unit's needs during the term of the contract. In other cases the unit might set a maximum and minimum quantity to give the bidder some security.

When the quantities to be purchased under these contracts are uncertain, it is difficult to know the amount of the contract for purposes of determining what bidding procedures apply. The best approach is to estimate the quantities, based on historical or anticipated usage, and if the prices based on the estimated quantities are likely to exceed the formal threshold, the formal procedures should be used for the initial bid.

Execution of contract documents is somewhat confusing under an indefinite quantity or term contract. The initial bid documents, specifications, and contract award documents should set out the terms of the agreement during the course of the contract. Thereafter, individual purchase orders are typically used to order quantities as needed. The initial contract is a binding agreement, but the amount of money obligated is not determined. Therefore, the individual purchase orders establish the periodic financial obligation and are the instruments that should be preaudited. (See Question 11.)

69. Can a local government include in a contract an option to renew the contract for additional terms or to purchase additional quantities at the unit's discretion?

Yes, as long as the option is contained in the original specifications so that all of the bidders are informed of the option and can account for it in their bids. The contract terms should specify the conditions (if any) on renewal or increase in quantities and the method and procedures the unit will use to notify the contractor that the unit is exercising its option. A statement reserving

55. *See* G.S. 160A-266(c).

to the unit the option to purchase additional quantities is very useful since it is common to discover additional needs after a contract is awarded. Including such a statement avoids having to rebid the contract to purchase additional items.

70. Can a renewal or additional-quantities provision in a contract allow for a price adjustment?

If the original contract is one that was formally bid, a later price adjustment should be linked to a fixed index (such as the Consumer Price Index or other commodity index) or other identified standard so that it does not amount to a renegotiation of the price.

Formal Bidding Procedures (Requirements Found in G.S. 143-129)

Advertisement

71. Where must bid opportunities be advertised?

Bids for contracts in the formal range must be solicited by advertisement "in a newspaper having general circulation" in the contracting unit's area or by electronic means or both.[56] Where bids are advertised in the newspaper, a separate statute, G.S. 1-597, defines the characteristics a newspaper must have in order for the advertisement to be valid. Specifically, the paper must be one that has a general circulation (that is, a circulation open to anyone who wishes to subscribe) to actual paid subscribers, that has been given second-class mail status, and that has been regularly and continuously issued in the area at least one day per calendar week for approximately six months prior to the advertisement. The statute has several exceptions and conditions, including special rules for municipalities located in more than one county. In addition, G.S. 1-598 provides that a sworn affidavit by an official of the newspaper stating that the paper meets the definition in the statute can be used as evidence that the requirements of the statute have been met. This type of affidavit is commonly requested when advertisements for bids are placed and is retained by the unit as proof of both the qualification of the newspaper and of the fact and date of advertisement for compliance with the bidding statute.

Advertisements for bid opportunities are commonly placed in the legal notices section of the newspaper. This is a good practice since it is the place where those interested in these types of advertisements are likely to look. Nothing in the statute, however, specifies where in the newspaper the advertisement must appear, and the advertisement requirement is satisfied no matter where in a qualifying publication the advertisement appears.

A decision by the local government to advertise bid opportunities electronically *instead* of in the newspaper, must be approved by the local governing

---

56. G.S. 143-129(b).

board. This approval may take the form of a resolution authorizing electronic advertisement for particular contracts or a blanket resolution authorizing electronic advertisement generally for all contracts. Another option is a resolution authorizing electronic advertisement and delegating to the manager, superintendent, or other official (or both) the authority to determine or establish a policy on what type or combination of types of advertisement will be used for particular contracts. It is important to note that local governments are free to use electronic advertisement *in addition* to newspaper advertisement without approval from the governing board.

The statute does not define what it means to advertise electronically, leaving it open to the local governments to determine the particular methods to use. Examples of electronic advertisement include posting opportunities on the local government's Web site, the state's Web site, or other Web sites that post this sort of information. A direct e-mail to one or more contractors probably would not satisfy the requirement for electronic advertisement. Instead, it would seem more consistent with the concept of an advertisement for the information to be posted and more broadly available.

There is no established or statutorily defined way to document the electronic advertisement of bidding opportunities. For bids posted on the local government's Web site or self-posted on another Web site, the unit might wish to develop a system of internal documentation that reflects the date on which the information was made accessible to the public. For notices placed on third-party Web sites, the local government could obtain an affidavit or certification similar to those used for newspaper advertisement that documents the date and location of the posting.

Electronic advertisement is a cost effective and increasingly common way to distribute information (including specifications which can be downloaded by interested bidders) about upcoming bids. In deciding how and where to publicize bidding opportunities, local government officials should consider that the advertisement serves at least two purposes. One is, of course, to provide information to potential bidders about the opportunity to submit bids, although the widespread practice of providing individual notice to bidders (either by mail or electronically) in addition to the advertisement is the way this is usually accomplished. (See Question 75.) The other purpose is to provide notice to the public that the local government is undertaking a purchase or construction contract. In consideration of both of these purposes, local government officials should strive to use electronic venues for publicizing bidding opportunities that are reasonably accessible to both potential bidders and citizens.

72. When and for how long must the advertisement for a bid opportunity appear?

The statute requires that the advertisement must appear "at a time where at least seven full days shall lapse between the date on which the notice appears and the date of the opening of bids."[57] Even though the statutory advertising

57. G.S. 143-129(b).

period is relatively short, local governments should, whenever possible, set the bid-opening date based on the length of time bidders will need to adequately prepare complete and accurate proposals.[58] Failure to do so may result in incomplete or erroneous bids, rejection of bids, and readvertisement or in a reduction in competition. In some cases, however, time becomes a factor; and officials want to open bids as soon as legally possible after the advertisement appears.

73. What information must be in the advertisement of a bid opportunity?

The statute identifies three things that must be contained in the advertisement: the time and place where plans and specifications of proposed work (for construction or repair) or a complete description (for purchases) may be obtained, the time and place of the bid opening, and a statement reserving to the governing body of the unit the right to reject any and all bids.[59]

For construction projects the advertisement will often contain a description of the contractor licensing required for the job. Although this is not required by the bidding statutes, the licensing laws require that contractors must have appropriate licensing before bidding on a job and require those preparing specifications to notify potential bidders of the licensing requirements.[60]

Although it is common for local governments to include additional information in the advertisement, units should be cautious not to make the advertisement unnecessarily lengthy. A lengthy advertisement is, of course, more costly. Perhaps more importantly, the unit should avoid lulling potential bidders into thinking that they can submit a bid without obtaining more detailed information from the unit at the specified time and place. A concise description of the project or purchase should be sufficient to allow the reader to determine if he or she is interested in obtaining more information about the solicitation.

74. Can a local government change the date of a bid opening after the advertisement for the bid opportunity has appeared?

Sometimes a local government must make changes in specifications after they have been distributed to potential bidders. Such a change is called an "addendum," and is typically distributed to all of the potential bidders who have obtained specifications. Sometimes these changes or other events may extend the time needed to respond to the bid invitation, and the bid opening date must be changed. Bidders can be notified individually of the new bid opening date by addendum.

---

58. For construction and repair contracts, recommendations of those in the construction industry suggest bid preparation times based on the size of the project. Professional organizations of architects and general contractors in North Carolina have formed a "Joint Cooperative Committee" to develop recommended practices for construction projects. Joint Recommendation No. 1 contains recommended minimum time periods ranging from twenty-one to thirty-five days, depending upon the type and estimated cost of the project. Copies of the Joint Recommendations can be obtained by contacting the Carolinas Associated General Contractors in Raleigh, North Carolina.

59. G.S. 143-129(b).

60. G.S. 87-13, 87-15.

It could be argued that the unit must publish a new advertisement reflecting the new bid opening date. The advertisement is an essential part of the statutorily mandated procedure. Thus, if it becomes necessary to change any of the information that must be contained in the advertisement by statute, including the date, time, or location of the bid opening, the unit may have to readvertise and hold the bid opening no earlier than one week from the date the new advertisement appears. On the other hand, since the addendum is sent to all interested bidders who have obtained specifications, failure to readvertise may not result in actual harm. There is no case in North Carolina that gives guidance on this issue. The safest course is to readvertise whenever possible if the bid opening date is changed.

It is not necessary to readvertise if a change is made that affects information contained in the first advertisement that *is not* mandated by the statute, such as the description of the scope of the project or characteristics of the product to be purchased. Failure to readvertise where significant changes are made, however, could be detrimental to the process. A major purpose of the advertisement is to give notice to those who might be interested in bidding. Any change that could influence whether someone reading the advertisement would consider submitting a bid should be readvertised.

75. Are local governments required to maintain bidders lists and to send individual notice of bidding opportunities to bidders?

The advertisement is the only notice of public contracting opportunities that is required by law. However, it has become a true formality. Most local governments obtain competition by maintaining lists of individuals and businesses interested in doing business with the unit and by sending or e-mailing individual notice of specific contracting opportunities to these and other potential bidders. A bidders list typically contains complete information about suppliers known to the unit, including the commodities they supply; their status as minority businesses, if applicable; and their response rates or bidding histories with the unit. Computer programs have been developed to facilitate cross-referencing this information, making it easily accessible for specific solicitations.

Nothing in the statutes requires units to have or maintain bidders lists or to provide individual notice of bidding opportunities, but these are essential steps in obtaining competition. Bidders lists are developed using numerous sources, including vendor application forms, which can be developed by the unit; vendor sales visits or exhibits at conferences; and contacts with other units of government. Some government agencies use electronic databases or services to identify bidders and make bidding opportunities known. Use of these resources is perfectly legal, but it does not substitute for the statutorily mandated advertisement.

76. If a local government maintains a bidders list, is it required to list all suppliers who wish to be listed? Can the local government remove bidders from the list?

Bidders are not legally entitled to receive individual notice of contracting opportunities. As long as the required advertisement has been published or posted electronically, the unit has complied with all of its legally mandated notice obligations. Nonetheless, where the unit does send individual notice to bidders, it should do so equitably and should place limitations on the notice, if necessary, in a manner that is reasonable and supportable. (Even when practices or procedures are optional, they should be carried out in a nondiscriminatory and nonarbitrary manner.) For example, it is reasonable and perfectly legal to exclude or remove from the list bidders who have failed to respond to previous notices or to limit the number of notices to keep costs down. Limitations based solely on the volume and cost of mailings should, where possible, be made using objective criteria for bidders based on location, responsiveness to past solicitations, or similar information.

77. If a bidder is removed from the bidders list, does that mean that the bidder is disqualified from bidding?

No. Excluding someone from the bidders list is different from disqualifying a bidder or refusing to accept his or her bid. Since there is no requirement that bidders be notified individually, it would be difficult for a bidder to argue that he or she has a right to receive notice. The requirement to advertise for bids, however, implies that people generally do have a right to submit a bid. Merely removing someone from the bidders list or failing to send individual notice of a bid does not amount to a disqualification or refusal to accept a bid.

78. Can a local government disqualify bidders based on prior poor performance or other factors?

Local governments do not have specific statutory authority to disqualify bidders, that is, to identify bidders from whom the unit will refuse to accept a bid. It can be argued, however, that such authority is implicit in the unit's authority to award bids to the lowest responsible bidder and that the decision to disqualify a bidder amounts to a determination in advance that the bidder is not responsible. In addition, local governments have specific authority to prequalify bidders on all construction projects.[61] Disqualification could be viewed as an exercise of the authority to prequalify.

Since the competitive bidding statutes reflect a strong policy of keeping bidding opportunities open, bidder disqualification procedures should be very carefully developed and implemented. Units must document the bases upon which a bidder can be disqualified, and the bases should relate to the bidder's ability to successfully perform the contract and the criteria comprising

---

61. G.S. 143-135.8.

responsibility as identified by the courts. (See Question 117.) This information is best if it is based on the unit's own experience with the bidder, but the unit can also rely on the documented experience of others or on the potential bidder's lack of experience. Although it is not clear whether a hearing must be provided to the bidder prior to disqualification (see Question 145 for a discussion on violation of constitutional rights), the unit should give the bidder an opportunity to respond to ensure that the unit acts with complete information. Finally, disqualification procedures must be time-sensitive, so that the information relied upon is recent enough to be valid and so that the disqualification is not permanent. A bidder should be provided an opportunity to appeal to be reinstated upon a showing that the basis for disqualification has been cured or that recent contracts have been successfully performed. In light of the uncertainty about a unit's statutory authority for disqualification and the significant impact it has on the bidder, local governments should exercise caution and seek guidance from their attorneys before undertaking this action.

Bid Opening

79. Are sealed bids always required in the formal bidding process, and why are they used?

The formal bidding statute requires that bids must be sealed.[62] Two other methods of receiving bids are also authorized: reverse auctions and electronic bids. These are discussed in more detail in Questions 81 and 82. The use of sealed bids is closely linked to the underlying purposes of the bidding statutes: economy and fairness. Sealed bids provide confidentiality, ensuring that prices and terms will not be disclosed and that bidders will remain on an equal footing prior to the bid opening. In addition, setting a fixed time and place for receiving bids (assuming there is no collusion) gives bidders an incentive to provide their best prices without knowing what others will propose. A sealed bid procedure is less flexible than other procedures that allow for negotiation, but the underlying assumption is that bidders who do not have an opportunity to negotiate will provide their best price the first time.

80. What should be done if a bid is erroneously opened by an employee of the unit prior to the bid opening?

Under the bidding statute, it is a misdemeanor to open or disclose the contents of an envelope or package prior to the time set for a bid opening with knowledge that it contains a bid and without the permission of the bidder.[63] The criminal sanction for opening a sealed bid reflects the importance of maintaining security in the competitive bidding process to avoid collusion, fraud, disclosure, or any other impropriety. Nonetheless, it does happen, usually

62. G.S. 143-129(b).
63. G.S. 143-129(b).

where bids are not properly marked, that an employee of the unit erroneously opens a sealed bid before the official time for bids to be opened. A person is not subject to criminal sanction for opening a bid if it is not properly marked or if for any other reason the person does not know that the envelope or package contains a bid. If a bid is erroneously opened, the responsible official should reseal the bid as soon as possible to avoid exposing the bid contents, notify the bidder of the error, and disclose the fact of the error at the bid opening in order to avoid potential questions about the resealed envelope. Special care should be taken to ensure that the contents of the bid are not disclosed and that the chain of custody of the documents is not broken.

The concern for security that is reflected in the sealed bid requirement also suggests that units should take special care to organize filing and handling systems for bids that minimize the number of employees involved and maximize the security and reliability of the chain of custody of these documents. A common practice designed to minimize problems with erroneous bid-opening is to provide bidders with return envelopes clearly marked with the bid number or other information so that they are easily identified when received by the unit. In addition, the use of a time and date stamp when bids are received can help document the chain of custody.

81. Are local governments authorized to receive bids electronically?

A separate statute, G.S. 143-129.9, authorizes local governments to receive bids electronically as an alternative to otherwise applicable requirements. As a practical matter, this option applies only to the formal, sealed bid requirement in G.S. 143-129, since the informal statute, G.S. 143-131, does not specify the form in which bids may be received. This statute applies only to contracts for the purchase of apparatus, supplies, materials, or equipment. The exclusion of construction or repair contracts from the statute suggests that electronic bids are not permitted for these contracts in the formal range. As noted earlier, however, the informal bidding requirements in G.S. 143-131 appear to allow for the receipt of electronic bids for both purchase and construction contracts in the informal range.

The statute provides that a local government that receives bids electronically for contracts in the formal range must establish procedures "designed to ensure the security, authenticity, and confidentiality of the bids to at least the same extent as is provided for with sealed paper bids."[64] In addition, the local government must apply the requirements for advertisement, timeliness of the receipt of bids, the standard of award, and all other aspects of the formal bidding requirements that are not inconsistent with the electronic bidding method.[65] An increasing number of software applications and service providers are becoming available to local governments that wish to receive bids electronically. It is likely that systems developed specifically for use by public agencies will comply with the general requirements of the statute.

---

64. G.S. 143-129.9(a)(2).
65. G.S. 143-129.9(b).

82. Describe the "reverse auction" alternative to the formal bidding procedure that local governments are authorized to use.

Another alternative method authorized under G.S. 143-129.9 is the "reverse auction." The statute defines a reverse auction as "a real-time purchasing process in which bidders compete to provide goods at the lowest selling price in an open and interactive environment."[66] Under this method, the bidders' prices are revealed during the process and bidders may continue to submit bids until the end of the auction period. The statute authorizes local governments to conduct reverse auctions themselves or to use a third party provider, including the state, to conduct the reverse auction on their behalf. As with electronic bids, the local government must apply the requirements for advertisement, timeliness of the receipt of bids, the standard of award, and all other aspects of the formal bidding requirements that are not inconsistent with the reverse auction bidding method. If the local government uses a reverse auction system developed by the state electronic procurement system, the state's process satisfies the local government's obligations under this statute.

Reverse auctions are authorized for purchase contracts only (not for construction or repair contracts). A separate provision in the statute provides that reverse auctions shall not be used for the purchase of "construction aggregates, including but not limited to, crushed stone, sand, and gravel."[67] As noted in the previous question, since the informal bidding statute, G.S. 143-131, does not specify the method by which bids must be received, it is possible that local governments can use a reverse auction for construction or repair contracts in the informal range, though this might conflict with the limitation in the statute that the record of informal bids received is not subject to public inspection until the contract has been awarded.[68]

83. Do bid openings have to be public meetings of the governing board?

Although the formal bid statute requires that bids be opened in public, it does not specifically require that bids be opened at a board meeting. Indeed bid openings are typically held as separate events, with the results reported to the board or other authorized official for award.

Where the board delegates to the manager or purchasing official the authority to award contracts under G.S. 143-129(a), the matter does not have to come before the governing board at all.

84. Who can or must attend a bid opening, and how is a bid opening conducted?

The statute requires that bids must be opened in public,[69] so anyone can attend a bid opening. Bid openings are typically conducted at the offices of the

66. G.S. 143-129.9(a)(1).
67. G.S. 143-129.9(c).
68. G.S. 143-131(a).
69. G.S. 143-129(b).

local government awarding the contract, the time and place having been specified in the advertisement and bid documents. Bid openings are usually conducted by an employee authorized to handle the bids. It is advisable to have at least two representatives of the local government at a bid opening, especially if no one else is present, in case questions arise about events or actions that took place. The person handling the bids typically announces when the time for receiving bids is ended and then reads out the names of the bidders and the amounts of their bids. In some cases, a determination can be made at that time that certain bids are not acceptable, for example, if a required bid bond or other component of the bid is not attached. Otherwise, evaluation of the bids is conducted at a later time, and no statement about the apparent successful bidder should be made. Conduct at bid openings is largely a matter of common practice rather than something that is dictated by statute.

85. Can members of the public, including the bidders present at the bid opening, look at the bids after they are opened but before the evaluation or award has been made?

By operation of the public records law,[70] formal bids are subject to public inspection once they are opened. (As noted in Question 134, informal bids are not subject to public inspection until after the contract is awarded.) This means that they must be made available for inspection, subject to reasonable limitations necessary to maintain their integrity and to properly conduct the bidding procedure. Most officials conducting a bid opening allow those present to inspect the documents but not to take custody of them, even for the purpose of copying them. It is essential that the unit maintain custody of the bids to avoid any possibility that bids might be changed or that portions might be misplaced, removed, or altered. After the initial opening, responses to requests for copies of bids should be made in accordance with the unit's policies for other public records. In addition, it is a common practice for the unit to prepare and distribute to all bidders and other interested parties a bid tabulation listing the names of the bidders and the bid amounts, although this is not legally required.

There is only one exception to the rule that formal bids are public records once they are opened. The public records law provides an exception for information contained in a bid that meets the definition of a trade secret under state law and that is so designated at the time the bid is submitted.[71] The local government must make a determination under this exception that information claimed to be confidential by bidders actually satisfies the terms of the statutory exception for trade secrets before the documents legally can be withheld from public inspection.[72]

---

70. G.S. 132-1.

71. G.S. 132-1.2.

72. For more information about this exception, see David M. Lawrence, *Public Records Law for North Carolina Local Governments* (Chapel Hill, N.C.: Institute of Government, The University of North Carolina at Chapel Hill, 1997), 131–140, 187–190.

86. Can a late bid be accepted if the bidder can show it was the fault of a delivery company or some other agent and not directly the fault of the bidder?

The formal bidding statute does not provide any explicit basis for accepting a late bid. This leaves the question open to interpretation and could be viewed as leaving it to local governments to establish circumstances under which late bids will be accepted. Courts have ruled, however, that failure to comply with the bidding procedures renders the resulting contract void. (See Question 143.) In addition, a late bid is nonresponsive, and it could be argued that it is unfair to the other bidders to accept late bids. (See Question 101.) Even if the other bidders do not object to considering a late bid, or waive this objection, compliance with the bidding requirements is essential to the validity of the contract and cannot be waived by the bidders. Most local governments take the view that it is the bidder's responsibility to get the bid to the appropriate place at the appropriate time and that the bidder is responsible for the acts of any agents or carriers hired to deliver the bid. In the rare circumstance in which a bid is merely seconds late so that the competitive advantage is nominal, and where no exposure of bids has yet occurred, it might be legal to accept a bid after the bidding period has been declared closed. It is difficult to determine, however, the amount of time after the close of bids that may be considered nominal. This suggests that a rigid rule of not accepting bids after the time for bid opening has passed may be the best policy.

If a bid is received before the bid opening but is not opened at the bid opening due to the fault of the local government, on the other hand, the bid should be considered. On rare occasions a bid is misplaced by employees of the local government and is discovered after the bid opening. This usually happens because the bid is not clearly marked. As long as the unit can document that the bid was actually received before the bid opening, it is appropriate to open and consider the bid under these circumstances. The use of a date and time stamp for all incoming mail to the purchasing department is extremely useful in documenting receipt of bids in these situations. It may be necessary, in this situation, to provide additional notice and open the bid in public, in order to comply with the statutory requirement of a public bid opening and to avoid allegations of fraud or favoritism.

Bid Bond or Bid Deposit

87. What is a bid bond or bid deposit, and when is one required?

Bids on contracts for construction or repair work in the formal bidding range must be accompanied by a bid bond or deposit in the amount of not less than 5 percent of the bid. This security is held by the local government to guarantee that the successful bidder will execute the contract and provide performance and payment bonds if required. (For a discussion of when these bonds are required, see Question 129.) If a bidder backs out of his or her bid or refuses to enter into a contract, the unit may retain the bid deposit or seek payment under the bid bond. In effect, the bid bond provides compensation—perhaps a form of liquidated damages—for the cost of accepting a higher bid or repeating the bidding process when these actions are necessitated by a bidder's failure to execute a contract. If the bidder has made a clerical error, a bid can be withdrawn without forfeiting the bid bond. (See Question 105.) This is different, however, from the performance bond, which guarantees that the bidder will *perform* the contract once it has been executed. (See Question 129 for a discussion of performance and payment bonds.)

Although bid bonds are not required for purchase contracts, local governments may require them in circumstances they deem appropriate. It is important to bear in mind that if a local government requires a bid bond this may increase the cost of the contract, since the bidders must incur costs to obtain a bid bond. In addition, if a bidder fails to provide a bid bond when the specifications call for one, the local government will be required to reject the bid as nonresponsive, since the failure to obtain the bid bond would give the bidder a competitive advantage. (See Question 101.) For these reasons, local governments should require bid bonds only when it is determined that the benefits will outweigh the cost and risk of error.

In some cases, particularly with purchase contracts, the distinction between bid bonds and performance bonds is blurred. For many purchases, there is no formal contract that is executed by both parties. Instead, the unit issues a purchase order to the successful bidder with the expectation that the items will be delivered according to the terms of the bid. The unit often retains the bid bond until the goods are delivered, using it to secure performance rather than to secure execution of a contract. Under the legal contract formation principles of offer and acceptance, the bid is an offer and the award and issuance of a purchase order constitutes acceptance. (See Question 4.) Under the Uniform Commercial Code, which applies to the sale of goods,[73] the issuance of the purchase order is sufficient to create a legally binding contract, at which point the bid bond technically is extinguished. It does not appear that the bid bond can legally serve as security for performance—or liquidated damages for breach of contract—after this point in the transaction, although it is commonly used for this purpose.

88. Can a bid bond or bid deposit be accepted if it is submitted in a form other than the ones listed in the statute?

For construction or repair contracts in the formal range the bidding statute allows the bid deposit to be made in the following forms: cash, a cashier's check, a certified check on a bank or trust company insured by the Federal Deposit Insurance Corporation, or a bid bond executed by a corporate surety licensed under the laws of North Carolina.[74] Bidders sometimes submit bid deposits in the form of a personal or corporate check or a letter of credit or similar form of security. Although these instruments may be as secure as those listed in the statute, the specificity of the statute suggests that only those listed may be accepted. Since the specified forms of security are part of the mandatory bidding statute, local governments probably do not have authority to

73. G.S. 25-2-201.
74. G.S. 143-129(b).

establish local policies providing that different forms will be accepted. Bid security is not required for purchase contracts, so local governments that opt to require it may designate the type that will be allowed.

89. If a bid is not accompanied by a proper bid deposit, can the bid be accepted if the bidder can provide the proper bid deposit before the contract is awarded or soon after the bid opening?

The competitive bidding statute provides that "[n]o proposal shall be considered or accepted . . . unless *at the time of its filing* the same shall be accompanied by a [bid deposit or bond]."[75] This language suggests that a bid deposit or bond in the right amount and the right form must accompany the bid no later than the time of the bid opening.

90. How is the amount of the bid deposit calculated for contracts where the amount of work or quantity to be purchased is not specified?

In some cases a request for bids is based on unit prices and estimated quantities, so the total amount of the contract is not known. (See Question 68.) For construction projects, sometimes the unit will ask for prices on alternates, leaving to the unit the choice of whether to include that work, depending upon the prices offered. In these situations, it is difficult to calculate 5 percent of the bid amount in order to comply with the statutory bid deposit requirement.

For purchase contracts with open-ended quantities, the unit can estimate a quantity for the sole purpose of the bid-deposit calculation, making clear in the specifications that it reserves the right to purchase more or less than the estimated quantity at the price offered, depending upon needs. For construction contracts with alternates, the bid deposit should cover the maximum amount for which a contract *could* be awarded, that is, the total amount of the bid including all alternates, since the unit has the option of awarding a contract up to that amount.

It is unclear, however, if the unit is required to reject a bid accompanied by a bid bond or deposit that doesn't cover all alternates or the total estimated quantities. The local government may legally be able to accept a bid as long as the bid bond or deposit amounts to 5 percent of the amount of the contract *actually awarded*, even though this may not be determined until the bids are evaluated.

91. If a bid is received without the proper bid deposit, can it be counted for purposes of the three-bid requirement?

The statute does not specifically address this question, and there has been no clarifying case to date. Since the statute says that a bid *shall not be considered* unless it is accompanied at the time of its filing by the proper bid deposit, it would not seem appropriate to count it when determining how many

75. G.S. 143-129(b) (emphasis added).

bids have been received. As noted in Question 93, three bids are required only for construction or repair contracts in the formal range.

92. Can a local government accept a faxed bid bond?

The answer to this question is not entirely clear. The bid bond must be submitted in a form that is legally enforceable. As noted earlier, state law recognizes the validity of electronic contracts where the parties agree to use them. (See Question 18.) Under this authority, it would appear that the local government could agree to accept a faxed bid bond as long as the parties (including the surety company) agree to use this form of contract.[76] If faxed documents are to be accepted, it is important for the specifications to indicate this so that all bidders will be aware of this option.

Number and Form of Bids

93. How many bids must be received under the formal bidding procedure before a contract can be awarded?

Three bids are required *only for construction or repair contracts* in the formal bidding range.[77] *There is no minimum number of bids that must be received for a purchase contract to be awarded, regardless of the cost of the contract.* Therefore, as long as the advertisement for the opportunity to bid is properly placed and the specifications are properly drawn (that is, are not unjustifiably narrow—see Question 58), a purchase contract can legally be awarded even if only one bid is received. Some local governments have established local policies requiring three bids for purchase contracts or for contracts in the informal range. These policies are binding on the units that have adopted them, but are not mandated by state law.

94. Can a local government accept a faxed bid in a formal bidding procedure?

As noted earlier (see Question 81), local governments have authority to accept formal bids electronically only for purchase contracts under G.S. 143-129.9. A faxed bid could be accepted as part of an alternative process under that statute. A faxed bid would not comply, however, with the sealed bid procedure in G.S. 143-129. A faxed bid is not sealed and could not be accepted unless it is first placed in a sealed envelope. Although it is possible for an employee of the unit receiving bids to place the bid in a sealed envelope, this would seem to undermine the purpose of receiving sealed bids and could expose the unit to question or criticism if the bidder were to allege that a portion

---

76. Note that while the agreement of the bidder to use a faxed document may be implicit by his or her submission of the document with the bid, the surety is a third party whose agreement may not be evident from the actions of the bidder.

77. G.S. 143-132.

of the document was missing or altered. Another option would be for the bidder to place a representative at the location of the incoming fax and have that person place the bid in a sealed envelope for submission. This would satisfy the sealed bid requirement and keep government employees out of the chain of custody and free from possible criticism.

Local governments that choose to allow faxed bids should clearly indicate this in the specifications and should delineate the procedures and requirements for submitting them.

95. If a bid is submitted but is determined to be unacceptable (nonresponsive) after it has been received and evaluated, does it count as a bid for purposes of the three-bid requirement?

The statutes contain no guidance on this question, but a good rule of interpretation is that as long as a bid constitutes a serious effort to make an offer it should be counted as a bid, even if it is later rejected as being incomplete or inaccurate. Thus an envelope containing a "no bid" statement or letter should not be counted as a bid. On the other hand, a bid that upon evaluation is determined to be incomplete or nonresponsive should be counted.

There is one possible exception to this rule. If the basis for rejecting the bid is the bidder's failure to submit the proper bid deposit or bond on a construction or repair project, there is a strong argument that the bid should not be counted. Since the statute states that a bid *cannot be considered* unless accompanied by the bid deposit or bond, it seems that it should not be considered for any purpose, including the three-bid requirement. (See Question 91.) As noted in Questions 87 and 93, this concern only applies to construction or repair contracts since state law does not require three bids or bid bonds for purchase contracts.

96. What should be done if a bid solicitation for a construction or repair contract in the formal range generates fewer than three bids?

The statute that requires three bids for construction or repair contracts, G.S. 143-132, provides that if fewer than three bids are received, the unit must readvertise the project. The second advertisement must appear for at least the minimum time required by the statute (see Question 72) before the second bid opening. All of the same rules and procedures apply to the second bid opening as to the first, except that after the second advertisement, a contract can be awarded even if fewer than three bids are received.

97. Can the unit make any changes in the specifications in the second round of bidding?

The statute does not address this question. To remain consistent with the purpose of the statute, however, it would be proper to refrain from making any significant changes in the specifications, since the intent of the requirement to repeat the process is to try twice to get three bids on a particular set of specifications. If significant changes are made, the unit would have to receive three bids the second time or repeat the advertisement based on the new specifications if fewer than three are received (resulting in a total of three advertisements). This may be worth doing if the unit feels that significant changes in the specifications are desirable for the project or wants to obtain better competition.

Since there are no cases or guidelines in the statute about what constitutes a significant change, local governments can consider the purpose of the advertisement requirement in making judgments. If the proposed changes in the specifications would affect the range of bidders that would be interested in bidding or would significantly change the amount or form of the bids received after the first advertisement, the first advertisement should not be counted toward the three-bid requirement.

98. What should be done with bids already received if readvertisement of a bid opportunity is necessary?

The statute is silent about this question. There is no prohibition on opening the bids;[78] but the common practice is to leave the bids sealed and either return them to the bidders or keep them to be opened at the next bid opening, if the bidder indicates that this is his or her preference. Once the bids are opened, they are available for public inspection under the public records law. (See Question 85.) Since the statute does not specifically require that the bids be opened in the case of a rebid, bidders usually prefer that they remain unopened to avoid exposing prices.

In some cases, the local government might determine that opening the bids is in the best interest of the unit. For example, if only one bid is received and there is unlikely to be additional competition after a second advertisement, the local government may choose to open the bid to prevent the bidder from increasing the price in the second bid.

The decision about how to handle bids between the first and second advertisement should be made by the local government, balancing the desire to be fair to the bidders with the overall best interest of the unit, which includes the desire to minimize the expenditure of tax dollars.

99. What if a contract for construction or repair work was estimated to cost more than the formal threshold amount but the estimate was very close to the threshold and fewer than three bids were received?

In this case, it may be in the best interest of the unit to open the bids. If even one bid is below the formal bid threshold and is otherwise acceptable, the contract can be awarded to that bidder. (See Questions 52 and 131.) If the contract amount is within the informal range, a contract can be awarded even if fewer than three bids are received. Because the wording of the informal bidding statute[79] refers to the actual amount of the contract, not the estimated

---

78. The only explicit prohibition on opening bids contained in the bidding statutes is in G.S. 143-132(b), which provides that when bidding on construction projects under the dual bidding method, if at least three single-prime bids are received but no complete set of separate-prime bids is received, the separate-prime bids cannot be opened.

79. G.S. 143-131.

amount, even one bid within that range is sufficient to award a contract. If one or more bidders is present at the bid opening, the government representative handling the opening might even consider asking the bidders if their bids are within the informal range. If the unit wishes to avoid unnecessarily exposing the bids, however, the safest approach is to refrain from opening the bids and to readvertise the project according to the formal bidding requirements.

Evaluating Bids

100. Who is responsible for evaluating the bids and determining which bidder should receive the award of the contract?

Either the governing board or the individual to whom the board delegates responsibility under G.S. 143-129(a) (see Question 113) is responsible for making the award to the lowest responsible bidder. The process of evaluating bids is usually carried out by the unit's staff or by an architect or engineer under contract with the unit in the case of major construction or repair projects. After evaluating the bids, the staff member or agent makes a recommendation of award to the governing board or to the person to whom the board has delegated the authority to make awards. The recommendation should include a summary of the bids and an explanation supporting the recommended award, especially if the recommended award is not the low bid. (See Question 115.)

101. What is the legal standard for evaluating bids, and under what circumstances may or must a bid be rejected?

Bids must be evaluated to determine if they comply with the specifications issued for the contract. The legal standard and commonly used term for this process is the evaluation of "responsiveness." As articulated by the North Carolina courts and other courts considering this issue, a public body must determine whether the bid "conforms substantially" with the specifications or whether it contains a "material variance" from specifications.[80] This standard is embodied in many standard specifications which contain language to the effect that the unit "reserves the right to waive minor irregularities." It recognizes that there are variations among products and proposals and that minor deviations do not disqualify bidders.

Under the legal standard for responsiveness, however, a bid that contains a *material* variance from specifications cannot be accepted. To do so would be unfair to the other bidders. Thus the court defines a material variance as one that gives a bidder "an advantage or benefit not enjoyed by the other bidders."[81] A comprehensive discussion of the responsiveness standard and the types of advantages that have been ruled by courts around the country to constitute material variances is set forth in Appendix 4. Whether a deviation from

---

80. Professional Food Serv. Management v. North Carolina Dep't of Admin., 109 N.C. App. 265, 269, 426 S.E.2d 447, 450 (1993).

81. *Professional Food Serv. Management*, 109 N.C. App. at 269, 426 S.E.2d at 450.

specifications or an omission in a bid is material must be determined on a case-by-case basis. The local government may deem an omission to be material based on how important the omitted feature is to the unit. In other cases, the local government must consider whether the aspect that varies from the specifications is one which represents a cost to other bidders who complied with it or whether the variation is one which the average bidder would have considered to be within the scope of the specifications as written.

102. What if there is an ambiguity or omission in a bid that makes it difficult to determine what is being bid? Can the local government contact the bidder to resolve the question?

Inquiries of bidders during the bid evaluation period should be kept to a minimum and should be handled very carefully. Once the bids are opened, the bidders have the opportunity to know the prices offered by other bidders and see the bids. An inquiry about an ambiguity in a particular bid might give that bidder an opportunity to improve his or her position or correct a mistake that might otherwise be a basis for rejecting the bid. Inquiries should only be made if the unit is confident that the inquiry would not place the bidder in a position of unfair advantage with respect to the other bidders.

103. What if there is a discrepancy in a bid between the unit price and the extension?

The standard rule of interpretation in bidding is that where there is a discrepancy between the unit price and the extension (the unit price multiplied by the number of units estimated or required in the bid), the unit price governs. Even though this rule is universally accepted, it is still unclear whether the local government has the authority to fix a discrepancy that is apparent in a bid or whether, instead, the bid must be either rejected as nonresponsive or accepted based on the lowest price evident from the bid. One way to avoid this problem is to clearly state in the specifications that the local government will apply the rule that the unit price governs in resolving unit price/extension discrepancies. For additional discussion of price ambiguities in bids, see Appendix 4.

104. Is the local government required to reject a bid if it is not made on the proper bid form or if the form is not properly completed?

In many cases, bid specifications explicitly require that bids be submitted on the form provided. This is an effective way of ensuring that bidders complete all aspects of the bid, thus reducing the variation among proposals and avoiding problems in evaluating bids. The bid form may contain detailed questionnaires that are essential for evaluating the bids. Failure to use the proper bid form or to complete it properly, however, is not always fatal to a bid. As long as the necessary information is contained in the bid and the unit can evaluate the bid without inappropriate consultations with the bidder (see Question 102), the failure to use or complete the proper bid form can be considered a minor variation and can be waived. For further discussion of this issue, see Appendix 4.

Errors in Bids and Bid Withdrawal

105. What if a bidder discovers a mistake in his or her bid and wishes to withdraw the bid?

The competitive bidding statutes include a provision for withdrawal of a bid.[82] Under G.S. 143-129.1, a bidder must notify the agency in writing of his or her request to withdraw within seventy-two hours after the bid opening, or a longer time as specified in the bid specifications. The time period for notice of withdrawal is short in order to avoid manipulation of the bidding process, and to provide time for hearing the request without delaying the contract award. The opportunity to extend the time beyond seventy-two hours is primarily to allow for circumstances in which the seventy-two hours would expire on a weekend or holiday. A suggested approach is for local governments to include language in their specifications and policies that requires written notice of a request to withdraw a bid to be submitted within seventy-two hours, not including Saturdays, Sundays, or other days (such as holidays) on which the local government offices are closed.

In order to justify withdrawal, the bidder must demonstrate that a substantial error exists and that the bid was submitted in good faith. The mistake must be "clerical in nature as opposed to a judgment error."[83] Furthermore, the statute specifies that the error must be due to "an unintentional and substantial arithmetic error or an unintentional omission of a substantial quantity of work, labor, material or services made directly in the compilation of the bid" that can be shown by objective evidence drawn from work papers, documents, or materials used to prepare the bid. The request for withdrawal must be heard promptly by the agency. Since the statute does not specifically require action by the governing board, it appears that the hearing could be held by staff upon delegation of the board. If the board finds that the mistake is the kind for which withdrawal is permissible, the withdrawal may be allowed without forfeiture of the bid deposit. (See Question 87.) If, however, the mistake is based on poor judgment rather than clerical error, the request must be denied and the bid deposit is forfeited. A bidder who has requested withdrawal does not have the option of going forward with the contract and living with or correcting the mistake. Indeed the statute prohibits a bidder who has requested withdrawal from receiving any part of the contract, even if it is rebid.

106. If a bid is withdrawn for a mistake, does it count for purposes of the three-bid requirement for construction or repair contracts?

Yes. The bid-withdrawal statute specifically provides that it does.

---

82. G.S. 143-129.1.
83. G.S. 143-129.1.

107. What if a bidder who has made an error that affects the price can show that, even with an adjustment to correct the error, he or she is still the lowest responsible bidder? Can the appropriate adjustment legally be made?

No. There is no authority in the bidding statutes for allowing a bidder to adjust his or her bid. Furthermore, it would be completely inconsistent with the fairness principles of the competitive bidding statutes to allow such an adjustment. It would also provide opportunities for fraud and collusion as bidders could intentionally create mistakes and then ask for corrections—or not ask for corrections—after seeing the other bid prices. As a rule, bidders should not be allowed to adjust or modify their bids in a formal bidding process.

108. What if the local government, rather than the bidder, discovers an error in a bid? Is the bidder required to withdraw?

Sometimes the bid evaluation process discloses an error or omission in a bid. As noted in Question 101, with some errors the unit is *required* to reject the bid as nonresponsive.[84] In some cases, however, a bid appears complete on its face but the price is noticeably out of line with the other bids, suggesting a possible error. In this case, both the local government and the bidder have choices to make. If the pricing error is due to a clerical error and meets the requirements for withdrawal, the bidder may choose to, although he or she is not required to, withdraw. If the error is one of judgment, the bidder does not have the option of withdrawing. The options for the local government in this situation are somewhat unclear. It could be argued that the unit has an obligation to the taxpayers to force the bidder to perform the contract, even if it means the bidder suffers a loss. On the other hand, many purchasing professionals recognize that the bidder's performance under such a contract—especially if it involves ongoing performance such as construction or repair work—is likely to be unsatisfactory and that the overall cost to the unit may be more than it would have been if the bid had simply been rejected and the unit had gone with the next lowest responsible bidder. It is unclear, however, if there is legal authority to reject a bid under these circumstances.

Negotiating with Bidders

109. Can the local government ever negotiate with a bidder after the bids are opened but before the contract is awarded?

The formal bidding statute allows the unit to negotiate with bidders only in one situation: when all of the bids exceed the "funds available for the project or purchase."[85] In this case the statute authorizes (but does not require) the

---

84. The article in Appendix 4 discusses in more detail the relationship between the responsiveness requirement and mistakes that might justify withdrawal.

85. G.S. 143-129(b).

local government to negotiate with the lowest responsible bidder and make "reasonable changes in the plans and specifications" as necessary to bring the contract price within the funds available. It is not clear what constitutes "reasonable" changes, but the major concern in making such changes should be fairness to the other bidders and to the integrity of the bidding process. The assumption underlying this limited authority to negotiate seems to be that minor changes are unlikely to make a difference in the positions of the bidders, so readvertisement with revised specifications is not necessary. Therefore, changes that could affect the positions of the bidders might exceed the authority provided in the statute. Significant changes could include changes in quantity (a major increase or decrease in materials or in the amount of work in proportion to the total contract) or changes in kind (a significant change in the type of materials to be used or purchased, or in the overall design, approach, or method as compared with the original specifications).

110. If the local government is not successful in negotiating with the lowest responsible bidder, can it pursue negotiations with the next lowest responsible bidder?

The statute does not appear to allow this. It says that if negotiations are not successful, the local government is authorized to readvertise the project, incorporating into new specifications the changes necessary to bring the project within budget. Readvertisement may be repeated as many times as necessary to secure an acceptable contract within the funds available for the project.

111. What does "available funds" mean for purposes of this provision? Is the unit limited to the actual budgeted amount?

The statute does not define "available funds," but there is no reason to interpret it narrowly to mean those funds originally budgeted for the item or project. It should be interpreted to mean the funds legally available from any source, including funds that can be used from other accounts or other sources or by virtue of a reallocation or budget amendment.

112. Can the local government negotiate with the lowest responsible bidder on price only, without making changes in specifications?

If all the bids exceed the funds available and the contract can't be changed without substantially reducing its usefulness, the local government may have no choice but to abandon the project or purchase unless the price can be adjusted. The lowest responsible bidder might be willing to reduce his or her price rather than lose the contract completely. There is nothing in the statutes that specifically addresses this situation. As long as there is no evidence of fraud, collusion, or undue pressure by the local government upon the contractor, however, it does not appear that there would be any legal basis for challenging this type of negotiation.

Awarding Contracts

113. Who is legally authorized to award contracts on behalf of a local government under the formal bidding statute?

The governing body is responsible for awarding formally bid contracts. G.S. 143-129(a) authorizes the governing body to delegate to the manager or chief purchasing official the authority to award contracts for the purchase of apparatus, supplies, materials, and equipment. The board can make the delegation subject to any restriction as to dollar amount or other conditions the governing board deems appropriate. In addition, the person to whom authority is delegated must comply with all of the requirements in the competitive statutes. As noted earlier, contracts made under the sole-source and "piggybacking" exceptions must be approved by the governing board even if authority has been delegated for other purchase contracts. (See Questions 41.f. and 41.l.) The statute does not authorize the governing board to delegate the authority to award contracts for construction or repair work in the formal range.

114. Must contract awards be made at a meeting, or any particular kind of meeting, of the board; and what is the procedure for award when authority is delegated?

The only way the governing board can take action is at an official meeting, so awards made by the governing board must be made at an official meeting of the board. However, except in the case of contracts awarded under the piggybacking exception (see Question 41.l.), nothing in the statute requires that contract awards be made at regular meetings or at any particular kind of meeting. As long as the required notice of the meeting has been made properly and provided that a quorum is present, a contract may be awarded at a regular, special, or emergency meeting of the governing board.

If the authority to award contracts has been delegated to the manager or chief purchasing official, the award will be made administratively. The statute does not specify any requirements for notice or additional procedures to be followed when awarding contracts under delegated authority.

115. Are there any particular findings that must be made before a contract can be awarded?

Formal bids are often awarded based on a recommendation from a staff member or the independent contractor (architect, engineer, or consultant) who handled the bid advertisement and evaluation. The board or official awarding the contract should make sure that the statutory requirements have been fulfilled before the contract is awarded. This can be done by establishing policies and procedures for staff to follow.

The decision to award a contract is not of a judicial nature so no specific findings are required. Nonetheless, in cases where a bid other than the low-dollar bid is chosen or where bids have been rejected or withdrawn, the basis for the decision should be reflected in the record of the decision, whether it is an administrative record or the official minutes of the board. Where the awarding authority accepts the recommendation of staff, the documentation of the award may be accomplished by simply incorporating the memorandum containing the recommendation into the minutes or administrative record.

116. Can a local government award a contract in one budget year for an item to be paid for out of the next year's budget?

Yes. Toward the end of the budget year, local governments may find it useful to take bids and award contracts for items that have been budgeted for the following year. This is legal, and constitutes a continuing contract. (See Question 12.) It is important to make sure that the payment terms agreed to, or documentation associated with the contract, make clear to the vendor when payment will be made. There is some question about the appropriate handling of the preaudit requirement (see Question 11) on this type of contract since no funds will be due in the year that the contract is made. The best approach is to complete the preaudit certificate in the year that the contract is made, and make sure that internal systems are in place to encumber the funds in the following year. Some jurisdictions actually issue a new purchase order in the following year, usually because the purchase order system is used to encumber the funds, but the law probably does not require the creation of a new document as long as the obligation to budget the funds that become due under the contract is satisfied.

Lowest Responsible Bidder Standard for Award

117. Does a local government have the authority to award a contract to someone other than the lowest bidder?

The formal bidding statute requires that contracts be awarded to the "lowest responsible bidder or bidders, taking into consideration quality, performance and the time specified in the proposals for the performance of the contract."[86] The only North Carolina case interpreting this standard to date held that "the term responsibility implies skill, judgment and integrity necessary to the faithful performance of the contract, as well as sufficient financial resources and ability."[87] In that case, the governing board had requested that the two lowest bidders provide information regarding their experience, finances, and personnel so the consulting architect could evaluate the relative responsibility of the bidders. The low bidder refused to provide the information, asserting that as the low bidder meeting specifications and licensing requirements, his

86. G.S. 143-129(b). The plural "bidders" is probably included because, where a construction or repair project is bid on a separate-prime basis, the award would be made to multiple bidders.

87. Kinsey Contracting Co. v. City of Fayetteville, 106 N.C. App. 383, 385, 416 S.E.2d 607, 609, *disc. review denied,* 332 N.C. 345, 421 S.E.2d 149 (1992).

company was entitled to the award. The court rejected this assertion. Therefore, under the ruling in this case, it is clear that the board has the authority to consider a number of factors in determining whether the low-dollar bid has been submitted by the lowest *responsible bidder,* and that the board is not required automatically to award to the lowest *responsive bidder.* (See Question 101 for discussion of responsiveness.)

118. Is the local government required to prove that the lowest bidder is not responsible in order to award to another bidder?

The answer to this question is not clear. One interpretation of the statutory language is that as long as the lowest bidder is responsible, the award must go to that bidder. Under this reading, the "quality, performance, and time" considerations would be used to determine the threshold question of responsibility. The statute could, on the other hand, be interpreted to allow the local government to award to a higher bidder who is determined to be *more* responsible, without demonstrating that the lowest bidder is not responsible. Under this reading, the quality, performance, and time would be considered in addition to responsibility in determining the best value to the unit.

Local governments are understandably reluctant to engage in a process designed to prove that a contractor is not responsible. The governmental entity, its officials, and others who might have information about the past performance of contractors may be reluctant to go on record with negative comments about contractors. Unsubstantiated information could result in liability for defamation or other injury to the business or personal reputation of the parties involved. In some cases, however, the lowest bidder may simply not have sufficient experience, skill, or financial or other resources for the project at hand, even if he or she is otherwise a capable and responsible contractor. It is appropriate and within the scope of the local government's authority to award to a better qualified bidder in this situation.

In effect, the awarding authority may make a determination that the lowest bidder is not responsible *for a particular project,* but a local government should avoid making judgments or conclusions about the responsibility of a bidder that are any more broad than necessary to award a particular contract. It is necessary, for the protection and proper expenditure of public funds, to make a determination that the contractor who receives a contract can successfully complete the work within the time and budget provided. With this in mind, local governments should not hesitate to obtain information about contractors and should not shy away from awarding to a higher bidder who is qualified to complete the project satisfactorily. The North Carolina Court of Appeals has held that it will not second-guess the judgment of the local government in a contract-award case and that the burden is on the challenger of such a decision to show that there has been fraud, abuse of discretion, or other illegal action on the part of the awarding authority.[88]

---

88. Kinsey Contracting Co. v. City of Fayetteville, 106 N.C. App. 383, 384, 416 S.E.2d 607, 608, *disc. review denied,* 332 N.C. 345, 421 S.E.2d 149 (1992).

119. How much discretion does the local government have to award a purchase contract to a higher bidder? Can the award go to a higher bidder who offers a higher quality of equipment?

The discussion of the lowest responsible bidder standard for awarding contracts in cases from North Carolina and other states usually focuses on construction or repair contracts. Indeed, the only case interpreting the standard in North Carolina to date involved construction. (See Question 117.) However, the standard of award also applies to purchases of apparatus, supplies, materials, and equipment. For these contracts, the differences between bidders are more likely to result from differences in the equipment they are offering, rather than from the performance, experience, skill, or financial resources of the bidder.

If specifications are drawn broadly to promote competition among manufacturers and suppliers, there may be variations in quality and suitability of products offered. A narrow reading of the statute would require a local government to accept the lowest bid that meets the minimum requirements in the specifications. This interpretation, however, conflicts with the purpose of conserving public funds and does not necessarily promote fairness. Since the legislature has specifically directed the board to consider quality, performance, and time when awarding contracts, it seems reasonable to conclude that the board has the discretion to purchase more expensive equipment if it is of higher quality or better suited to the needs of the local government, since this will constitute the best investment of public funds. This issue has not been addressed by the courts and therefore must be left to the judgment of the local government on advice of counsel.

120. How much and what kind of documentation is required if the local government awards a contract to someone other than the low bidder?

There is no clear answer in either the statutes or cases to this very important question. Local governments should try to obtain the best and most reliable information available and should include in the record of the contract award decision (either the minutes of the board meeting at which the contract is awarded or the administrative record maintained by an official with delegated authority to award contracts) any information upon which they have relied. The unit's own experience with a contractor or item of equipment is the best evidence it can use. Experience by others is also useful, as are reported studies of equipment performance, such as those contained in *Consumer Reports* and trade publications.

Although there are no cases on the subject, it does not appear that the awarding authority has to establish beyond a reasonable doubt or to an absolute certainty the superiority of a contractor or product that is not the lowest bid. The terms responsibility, quality, and performance are subjective and require the exercise of judgment and discretion in awarding contracts. The courts will not set aside the exercise of this discretion unless the challenger demonstrates that there has been abuse of discretion, fraud, collusion, or some other illegal activity. (See Question 118.) Failure to articulate the basis for a decision, however, may be used as evidence of arbitrariness or may leave the awarding authority open to allegations of fraud or abuse of discretion.

An important way to obtain the necessary information to evaluate bidders is to require the bidders themselves to demonstrate their qualifications as part of the bidding process. Appropriate questions can be included in the specifications so that bidders will have the responsibility to provide documentation of their qualifications, or of the adequate performance of their products. This provides a good starting point for the analysis and evaluation of bids for award. As noted earlier, the *Kinsey* case makes clear that failure to provide this information when it is requested as part of the bidding process is grounds for rejection of the bid. (See Question 117.)

Preferences

121. Can a local government establish a preference for local bidders?

Local governments have no statutory authority to establish preferences of any kind and are bound by the "lowest respnsible bidder" standard when awarding contracts that are subject to the bidding requirements. (See Question 117.) The fact that a bidder is local cannot, by itself, be a basis for awarding a contract to a higher bidder. Some argue that doing business with local companies will help build and maintain the local government's tax base. (This of course depends on how "local" is defined and whether such a policy stirs other jurisdictions to adopt similar policies, which might ultimately cause losses for local companies.) Local governments do have authority to engage in local economic development,[89] but this authorization does not include the use of the contracting function to provide what amounts to a subsidy to a local company that is not otherwise the lowest responsible bid.

In some cases, local companies may provide better, more cost-effective, or more timely service. These factors can legally be considered under the lowest responsible bidder standard, which explicitly allows consideration of quality, performance, and time. Local governments are not, however, entitled to *assume* that a local company will be superior in these areas and should be careful to document the basis for a decision based on these factors. (See Question 120.)

Local governments can promote local businesses by making sure they are given notice of opportunities to bid and can use local businesses for convenience when purchasing small items or obtaining quotes for informal bids. The governing board could legally adopt a policy of sending individual notice of bidding opportunities only to local bidders, since the statute does not require such notice in the first place and local governments may have authority to establish a local preference for contracts that are not subject to the competitive bidding requirements. (See Question 33.) Boards considering this option should evaluate whether the loss of competition and potential cost savings is outweighed by the benefit to be gained from promoting local businesses in this way.

---

89. G.S. 158-7.1.

122. Doesn't state law establish a preference for minority-owned and women-owned businesses?

No. State law requires local governments to establish goals for participation by minority-owned and women-owned businesses in major building construction projects and requires local governments to identify good faith efforts that must be taken to attain these goals.[90] The statute specifically states, however, that contracts must be awarded to the lowest responsible bidder and without regard to race, religion, color, creed, national origin, sex, age, or handicapping condition.[91] Local governments also have the authority to comply with minority business participation requirements imposed as a condition of receiving grants or loans from the federal or state governments and can incorporate those requirements into the basis for awarding contracts.[92]

Local school units are required to report annually on the percentage of goods and services purchased and bids received from minority-owned, female-owned, disabled-owned, disabled business enterprises, and nonprofit work centers for the blind and severely disabled.[93] This is a reporting requirement only and does not require particular efforts in contracting with the listed groups, although the statute does contain general language encouraging and promoting the use of "small, minority, physically handicapped and women contractors in state purchasing of goods and services."[94]

Post-Award Procedures

123. Must a local government contract be approved by any entity other than the local governing board?

Certain contracts that involve long-term financing commitments, particularly those in which the item being purchased is pledged as security for the financing, must be approved by the Local Government Commission, a division of the State Treasurer's Office organized to oversee local government borrowing activity. In addition, some financed purchases by local school units must be approved by the board of county commissioners. For a more complete discussion of these contracts and approval requirements, see Question 13.

124. Is a binding contract created as of the moment the board or designated official awards the contract?

The answer to this question is somewhat unclear. Under traditional contract law principles, a bid constitutes an offer which may either be accepted or

---

90. G.S. 143-128.2.
91. G.S. 143-128.2(h).
92. G.S. 160A-17.1(3a) (G.S. 160A-17.1 is made applicable to counties by G.S. 153A-14); G.S. 115C-47(7) (schools).
93. G.S. 143-48(b).
94. G.S. 143-48(a).

rejected by the local government.[95] (See Question 4.) The bidder's offer is, in some cases, secured by the bid deposit or bond. Under the competitive bidding statute, once the board awards a contract, the successful bidder must execute a contract and provide adequate performance and payment bonds if required. (For a discussion of when these bonds are required, see Question 129.) Failure to do these things allows the local government to retain the bid deposit or bond, unless the bid has been withdrawn because of a mistake as provided in the statutes. (See Question 105.)

It is relatively easy to describe the bidder's obligation. Under this statutory scheme the *bidder* is bound by the offer from the time it is submitted and until it is either rejected, legally withdrawn, or accepted. It is less easy to determine the point at which the *local government* is bound and to answer the related question of whether the board's action in awarding a contract creates a binding obligation on the part of the local government. There is no North Carolina case directly answering this question. Among cases from other jurisdictions, some hold that the contract is created by the award, while others rule that a binding contract does not come into being until all of the statutory procedures have been completed. If applied to North Carolina, the latter view would mean that a binding contract is not created until the bidder has submitted the required performance and payment bonds and both the bidder and the local government have executed a written contract. (See Question 16.)

125. Can a local government rescind its award of a contract under the competitive bidding statutes?[96]

If the local government is not bound by a contract until it has executed the contract (as discussed in Question 124) there is still a question about how much authority the local government has to rescind its decision to award to a particular bidder between the time of award and the execution of the contract. There is no North Carolina case addressing this question. Some cases from other jurisdictions suggest that the act of executing a contract following award is a ministerial one and that the time for exercising discretion to choose bidders is before award, not after. There is nothing in the statute, however, to suggest that the board could not, if faced with new information or for other good cause, reconsider and rescind its award prior to executing a contract.

A local government might improve its legal authority to do this by including in the specifications and the award decision a standard provision stating that the award represents a preliminary determination as to the qualification of the bidder and that no legally binding acceptance of the offer occurs until the

---

95. For a discussion of this issue and analysis of cases from other states, see Frayda S. Bluestein and Jaye Sitton, "Can a Local Government Rescind Its Award of a Contract Under North Carolina's Formal Bidding Statute?" *Local Government Law Bulletin* 52 (December 1993) (Chapel Hill, N.C.: Institute of Government, The University of North Carolina at Chapel Hill).

96. *See* Frayda S. Bluestein and Jaye Sitton, "Can a Local Government Rescind Its Award of a Contract Under North Carolina's Formal Bidding Statute?" *Local Government Law Bulletin* 52 (December 1993) (Chapel Hill, N.C.: Institute of Government, The University of North Carolina at Chapel Hill).

awarding authority has executed a contract. Local governments should be careful to rescind the award of a contract only when absolutely necessary. Bidders commonly rely on the "notice of award" as the authority to begin mobilizing resources and acquiring materials for a project or purchase. Bidders might seek to recover these out-of-pocket costs in a lawsuit if the awarding authority's failure to go forward with the contract appears to be in bad faith or otherwise without justification.

126. Can a local government award a contract contingent upon obtaining necessary funding or some other condition?

North Carolina law suggests that a conditional award of a contract does not constitute valid acceptance sufficient to form a contract.[97] These cases rely on traditional contract principles that require a meeting of the minds and an unequivocal and unqualified acceptance in order to create a contract. It is not clear from these cases, however, what must be done following award to create the contract. One possibility is that the awarding authority must ratify or re-award the contract once the contingency is removed, for example, once anticipated funding is secured. Another possibility is that the award is deemed insufficient until such time as the contingency is removed.[98]

During the time in which funding, regulatory approval, or other contingencies are pending, the bidder is not entitled to withdraw and is bound to go forward with the contract once it is awarded, so long as the period of delay is not unreasonably long or does not exceed the terms specified in the bid documents. (See Question 124.) In addition, there is nothing that prevents a local government from soliciting bids prior to obtaining funding or subject to other contingencies that may be resolved prior to the award of the contract.

127. Is the bidder relieved of his or her obligation if the local government takes too long to award or execute a contract?

There are several legal provisions on which bidders might rely to argue that they are not bound by their bids after passage of significant periods of time. First, many specifications contain provisions setting a minimum period of time during which bids must remain valid, commonly sixty to ninety days. The bid specifications may also contain a statement that the award will be made within or no later than a certain number of days after bids are received and that the local government will issue a notice to proceed within a certain time after award. In addition, the competitive bidding statute provides that the bidder must forfeit his or her bid bond if the bidder fails to execute the contract within ten days or fails to provide satisfactory performance and payment bonds.[99]

---

97. Henderson & Corbin, Inc. v. West Carteret Water, Corp., 107 N.C. App. 740, 421 S.E.2d 792 (1992); William Muirhead Constr. Co. v. Housing Auth., 1 N.C. App. 181, 160 S.E.2d 542 (1968).

98. See City of Merrill v. Wenzel Bros., 277 N.W.2d 799, 802 (Wis. 1979), where an award contingent on EPA approval was held to be binding on both parties from the point when the approval, received after the award, was communicated to the bidder.

99. G.S. 143-129(b).

It is not clear how the time limitations in specifications relate to the ten-day limit in the statute or whether the ten-day limit operates as a limitation on the time within which the local government, as opposed to the bidder, must be ready to execute the contract. In practice, local governments usually extend the ten-day period voluntarily since it usually takes longer than ten days to prepare the contract documents and get them to the successful bidder. It is more likely that a court will enforce the time limitations the local government has placed in its own specifications. Even if there are no limitations in the specifications, a court could invalidate a contract or bidding process—with the effect of letting the bidder out of his or her bid without forfeiting the bid bond—if the local government takes too long to execute a contract or issue a notice to proceed. Such a ruling would be based on notions of fairness to the bidders and on a recognition that the prices and assumptions contained in the bids may expire or become so out-of-date that the original bid process is no longer valid and that to force the bidder to perform would work an unreasonable financial burden on him or her. The reasonableness of the time from bid opening to award and from award to contract issuance will depend on the nature of the contract. Local governments should be careful, however, to exercise due diligence in preparing paperwork and expediting the contract award and issuance to avoid hardship and possible liability due to unjustifiable delay.

128. How long must a local government retain bid and contract documents?

The state's public records law requires local governments to comply with the rules and schedules for records retention and destruction promulgated by the state Department of Cultural Resources through its Division of Archives and History (the Division).[100] Records retention and disposition schedules are issued by the Division and must be agreed to by each local government in order for that unit to have authority to dispose of public records. Custodians of public records should consult the most recent records retention schedule and the Division to ensure that they are complying with current record disposal requirements.

Performance and Payment Bonds

129. When and why are performance and payment bonds required?

The formal bidding statute requires local governments to obtain performance and payment bonds from the successful bidder for construction or repair contracts, as required under Chapter 44A, Article 3 of the General Statutes. For the current dollar thresholds, see the "Dollar Thresholds" chart in Appendix 1. In lieu of bonds, bidders may submit a deposit of cash, certified check, or government securities in the full amount of the contract. The statute does not require performance and payment bonds for purchase contracts, but they may be

100. *See* G.S. 121-5, 132-3, *and* David M. Lawrence, *Public Records Law for North Carolina Local Governments* (Chapel Hill, N.C.: Institute of Government at The University of North Carolina at Chapel Hill, 1997), 51–52.

required in the discretion of the unit. Although the bonds or other security are not legally required until after the contract is awarded, many units require bidders to submit bonds or proof that they can provide adequate security along with their bids to ensure that the successful bidder can satisfy this requirement.

Performance bonds, or the monetary substitute permitted under the statute, are designed to secure the performance of the contract. In the event of a default by the contractor, the local government can look to a third party (in the case of a surety bond) or use the funds deposited to complete the project.

Payment bonds, unlike performance bonds, are not for the benefit of the local government. Instead, they provide security to those who contribute labor or materials to the project. (They are also referred to as laborer's and materialmen's bonds.) Since the law prohibits subcontractors from obtaining a lien on public property to secure payment, the statute provides a separate source of security for these participants in the project.[101] Local governments must obtain the security from the successful bidder, hold the bond or funds for the benefit of those who provide labor and materials, and release the bonds only under circumstances and procedures set forth in the statutes.[102]

It is apparent from these descriptions that there is rarely a need for performance or payment bonds on simple purchase contracts. Typically, there are no subcontractors, and performance does not occur over an extended period of time during which mid-performance default might create a hardship to the local government. For this reason, local governments generally do not require performance and payment bonds for purchase contracts. Bidders incur costs to obtain performance and payment bonds, and these costs are generally passed along to the local government. In some cases, bonding requirements may prevent small or new businesses from bidding, since it is sometimes difficult or cost-prohibitive for them to obtain bonds or deposit other security. While the ability to obtain bonds generally reflects the financial stability and responsibility of a contractor, the inability to do so does not necessarily indicate that the contractor is not responsible. A local government should weigh these factors in deciding whether to require bonds under circumstances where the statute provides a choice.

Informal Bidding Procedures (Requirements Found in G.S. 143-131)

130. What is the dollar threshold for contracts that are subject to the informal bidding procedure?

The dollar thresholds for informal bidding are set forth in the "Dollar Thresholds" chart in Appendix 1. G.S. 143-133 provides that contracts may not be divided for the sole purpose of avoiding statutory bidding requirements.

---

101. *See* A. Fleming Bell, II, *Construction Contracts with North Carolina Local Governments,* 3d ed. (Chapel Hill, N.C.: Institute of Government at The University of North Carolina at Chapel Hill, 1996), 62–63.

102. G.S. 44A-27, 44A-28; 143-134.1.

131. What if the estimated cost of a contract is within the informal range but one or more of the bids actually received is within the formal range?

Because of the particular wording of the informal bidding statute, if all the bids exceed the informal limit, the bids must be rejected and resolicited using the formal procedure. The formal bidding statute is based on the *estimated* cost of the contract. The informal procedures may be used, on the other hand, only if the *actual* cost of the contract is within the informal range. If some of the bids exceed the informal threshold, but there is at least one acceptable bid that is within the informal range, the local government may award the contract since, as noted in Question 135, there is no minimum number of bids that must be received in order to award a contract in the informal range.

132. What does the informal procedure require?

The statute requires that informal bids be secured and that contracts be awarded to the "lowest responsible, responsive bidder, taking into consideration quality, performance, and the time specified in the bids for performance of the contract." Finally, the contracting agency must keep a record of all bids received, and this record is available for public inspection after the contract has been awarded.

133. What methods may be used to secure informal bids for contracts in the informal range?

The statute does not specify any particular method for securing informal bids, so any otherwise legal method is acceptable. Common methods include written bids (preferably on bid forms provided by the requesting unit), telephone quotes, and faxed bids. A record must be kept of all bids received. For telephone quotes, this is usually done using a log sheet upon which the person receiving the quotes can record the date, item, source, price, and any other pertinent information.

Some local governments use some or all aspects of the formal bid process for contracts in the informal range. This is appropriate especially for purchases at the high end of the informal limit, which may involve complicated specifications that are best communicated in writing. It is important to recognize that local governments have the option of using some but not all of the formal procedures for contracts in the informal range. For example, the unit may decide to require sealed bids but not to advertise for bids. This is acceptable and may be decided on a case-by-case basis by the local government. Specifications should clearly identify the procedure to be used in each case.

134. During the process of soliciting informal bids, is the person obtaining the bids required to tell a vendor the prices he or she has already received?

No. The statute specifically provides that bids received under the informal procedure are not subject to public inspection until after the contract has been awarded. Furthermore, nothing in the statute requires a public official to provide this information verbally. To do so would seem both inconsistent with the statutory directive to maintain confidentiality until after award and detrimental to a fair, competitive process. The statute does not appear, however, to *prohibit* the unit from disclosing the bids after they have all been received and prior to the award of the contract, and this may be desirable for evaluation and approval after all bids have been received.

135. How many bids are required under the informal procedure?

The statutes do not establish a minimum number of bids that must be received under the informal procedure. The intent and underlying purpose of the statute would seem to require that more than one source be solicited whenever multiple sources are available. It is common practice to strive for three bids. Some local governments may have local policies requiring three bids, and these policies are binding within that local government, even though they are not mandated by state law. Nonetheless, after good faith efforts to obtain competition, contracts in the informal range may legally be awarded even if only one bid is received.

136. What is the standard for awarding contracts in the informal range?

According to the statute, G.S. 143-131, informal contracts must be awarded to the "lowest responsible, responsive bidder, taking into consideration quality, performance, and the time specified in the bids for the performance of the contract." This is the same standard of award as applies to formal bids. (See Questions 115 through 118.) The statute does not require informal contracts to be awarded by the governing body.

137. What procedures are required for contracts costing less than the informal threshold amount?

There are no mandatory procedures for contracts below the informal threshold, so a local government is free to establish any or no procedures, as it sees fit. Most local governments use the informal procedures for small contracts. It is also common for the unit to establish a lower limit, below which no procedures are required. This practice is advisable, since for very small contracts, any cost saving generated by informal bidding may be outweighed by the administrative cost of completing the procedure. As discussed further in Chapter III of this *Legal Guide to Purchasing and Contracting,* many local governments have developed cost-saving strategies, such as procurement cards and term contracts, to increase efficiency and reduce administrative costs for small purchases. (See Questions 148 through 149.)

Contract Issuance

138. What are the legal requirements that apply when a local government issues a contract?

As discussed in Chapter I of this *Legal Guide to Purchasing and Contracting,* there are a number of requirements that affect whether a contract is legal. The subject of the contract must be within the unit's legal authority to act, and the governing body or an individual with authority to contract must be responsible for approving the contract. Local governments vary in the amount of centralized control they exercise over the contracting process, and the extent of approval required generally depends upon the size of the contract. (See Question 148.) Among the legal prerequisites that must be satisfied at the time the contract is issued, probably the most important is the preaudit certification discussed in Question 11, since this statutorily imposed control of funds provides a built-in check on unauthorized contracts.

139. Is a purchase order a contract, and what information should it contain?

Purchase orders are contracts, and most local governments use them for both purchases and small service and construction contracts. Purchase orders are typically preprinted or computer generated, with standard terms and conditions on the reverse side, and are prenumbered to ensure proper accounting and internal control and to prevent unauthorized use. Purchase orders should contain blanks for all of the essential terms of the contract, including items or services ordered, catalog or item numbers, quantity, price, shipping location and terms, payment terms, and identification of the local government and the individual to whom inquiries should be directed. For purchases involving formal bids or other cases where detailed specifications are used, the purchase order generally incorporates the specifications and bid documents into the contract and should contain specific standard language to accomplish this. As noted in Question 11, the purchase order also generally contains the preaudit certificate to be executed by the finance officer or his or her deputy prior to issuance. Some purchase orders also contain space for departmental or other approvals, which may be required under the unit's local procedures.

Optional Procedures

140. How should local governments go about letting contracts that are not subject to the competitive bidding requirements?

Contracts that are not subject to the competitive bidding laws, such as service contracts or contracts costing less than the informal bidding threshold amount, can be entered into following whatever procedures the local government deems appropriate. Indeed, where the competitive procedures are not mandatory, the unit need not follow any procedure and may simply negotiate a contract. Local governments are free, however, to use competitive bidding procedures even when they are not required to do so. Given the underlying purposes of the bidding laws, it is not surprising that many units choose to obtain some kind of competition for many contracts where the law does not require it. Common examples include solid waste collection, janitorial, and maintenance contracts, which are clearly service contracts and are not subject to bidding requirements. Nonetheless, many local governments successfully use competitive bidding for selecting providers of these services, since there is ample competition in the marketplace and the criteria for performance are susceptible to the objective description and comparison necessary for proper bid specifications.

141. Must a local government adhere to a bidding procedure it has undertaken even when the law didn't require bids in the first place?

A local government must either adhere to its own procedure or terminate the procedure and use whatever method the governing board deems appropriate.[103] For example, if the local government has advertised and received bids and then decides that simply negotiating a contract is in its best interest, it should reject all the bids and begin negotiations. The fact that the unit was not required to receive bids in the first place does not justify a failure to adhere to the process once it is begun. In light of this, local governments should be cautious about the optional procedures they adopt and should carefully draft the language contained in specifications to describe the procedures to be used for contracts that are not subject to competitive bidding. Bidding or proposal documents in these situations can be designed to generate adequate competition but can also provide the flexibility appropriate to the needs of the particular contract.

142. Does the local government have to award contracts to the lowest responsible bidder when contracts are not subject to the competitive bidding statutes?

When the bidding laws do not apply, the governing board is free to establish any award standard it deems appropriate and is subject only to constitutional restrictions that prevent government from discriminating against contractors on the basis of race, sex, disability, or their expressed opinions or political affiliations. (See Question 145.) For example, contracts that are not subject to the competitive bidding statutes could be awarded to the bidder that best meets the needs of the unit or to the lowest and best bid, or they may be made in the best interest of the local government. Whenever a local government engages in a locally designed procedure to award a contract, the solicitation documents should specify the basis on which the contract will be awarded. Although a dissatisfied bidder cannot rely on failure to comply with the statute, he or she could argue that failure to articulate or adhere to some standard of award constitutes arbitrariness on the part of the local government.

---

103. *See* 10 McQuillin Mun. Corps. § 29.38 (3d ed. 1990).

Legal Challenges and Protests

143. What are the legal and practical consequences of failing to comply with the competitive bidding statutes?

The North Carolina courts have held that if a contract is covered by mandatory bidding requirements and those requirements are not met, the resulting contract is void.[104] Sometimes failure to comply with the bidding statutes is not discovered until the contract has already been performed by both the contractor and the local government. When this happens, there is not likely to be any legal remedy available to either party. (For a discussion of recovery under the equitable doctrine of *quantum meruit,* see Question 4.) In cases involving extreme abuses of contracting authority by public officials, a taxpayer might be able to sue for return of the public funds that were illegally spent. The bases for legal claims are discussed in Question 145.

A more likely consequence of a failure to comply with the bidding requirements is that it may be noted during the annual independent audit that local governments are required to obtain.[105] Failure to establish and maintain procedures designed to ensure compliance with laws governing the contracting function could result in a negative report in the auditor's management letter and may be noted in the audit. In addition, an individual employee's intentional evasion of bidding requirements has been upheld as a basis for termination.[106]

There are two other sources from which concerns about contracting compliance are likely to emanate: the press and the bidders. Newspapers usually become interested in contracting when there are large dollar contracts at stake or when a conflict of interest is present. Public relations can be an issue even when the competitive bidding laws are not involved, since the public often has an expectation that contracting will be open and competitive for major contracts whether or not the law requires it.

Bidders are the most likely source of challenges about things that directly affect their interests, such as overly narrow specifications, awards to other than the low bidder, or failure to reject bids that contain deviations from specifications. Using pre-bid conferences and maintaining good communications with vendors before, during, and after the bid opening can help reduce these types of complaints.

---

104. Styers v. Gastonia, 252 N.C. 572, 114 S.E.2d 348 (1960); Hawkins v. Town of Dallas, 229 N.C. 561, 50 S.E.2d 561 (1948); Raynor v. Commissioners of Louisburg, 220 N.C. 348, 17 S.E.2d 495 (1941); Abbott Realty Co. v. City of Charlotte, 198 N.C. 564, 152 S.E.2d 686 (1930).

105. *See* G.S. 159-34, *and* David M. Lawrence, *Local Government Finance in North Carolina,* 2d ed. (Chapel Hill, N.C.: Institute of Government, The University of North Carolina at Chapel Hill, 1990), § 1203.

106. *See* Fuqua v. Rockingham County Bd. of Soc. Servs., 125 N.C. App. 66, 479 S.E.2d 273 (1997).

144. What are the procedures for protesting a local government bidding process or contract award decision?

North Carolina state statutes do not contain any protest or claims procedures for local government bidding or contract award decisions. Although local governments could establish their own procedures, most have not done so. In contrast, North Carolina's state government and the federal government have detailed claims procedures which must be pursued by any aggrieved party seeking to challenge a contract award or bidding process. Without specified protest procedures set out by statute, complaints are usually dealt with informally by the local government in roughly the manner described below.

Complaints about bid documents are usually raised with the department issuing the documents—either the purchasing department, a contract architect or engineer, or a specific department if purchasing is not centralized. If the employee or official handling the bid feels the complaint has merit, an adjustment can be made to the specifications or other bid documents and communicated to the other bidders by addendum if necessary. Similarly, if a complaint relates to a bid-opening practice or to the recommendation for award, it is usually raised in person or in writing with the local government employee handling the opening or making the recommendation, or with that person's supervisor. If the complainant is not satisfied, he or she will generally pursue the issue with a supervisor or manager and ultimately with the governing board. Of course, in some cases complaints are taken directly to the governing board; but it is preferable to see if they can be resolved at the staff level first. If the complainant is not satisfied with the decision of the governing body, the only legal recourse is to file an action in court. There are no administrative or other preliminary procedures that must be completed before such an action may be filed.

145. What would be the basis of a legal claim arising out of a competitive bidding process?[107]

There are several legal claims that could be made in the context of a competitive bidding process.

Failure to comply with mandated procedures. A legal challenge could be based on the local government's failure to comply with statutory procedures, such as advertisement, public bid opening, or the award to the lowest responsible bidder. Such a claim might also be based on overly narrow specifications or award of a contract to a bidder who failed to comply with specifications (that is, on the failure of the unit to reject a nonresponsive bid—see Question 101). Since the courts have clearly held that failure to comply with these requirements renders the contract void, a claimant could seek a court order (an injunction) directing the local government to refrain from going forward with an illegal contract and to comply with the applicable statutory requirements.

---

107. For a comprehensive discussion of this issue *see* Frayda S. Bluestein, "Disappointed Bidder Claims Against North Carolina Local Governments," *Local Government Law Bulletin*, No. 98 (May 2001) (Chapel Hill, N.C.: Institute of Government, The University of North Carolina at Chapel Hill).

An injunction is probably the only remedy available for this type of action. As discussed more fully below, except in extraordinary cases, monetary damages are generally not available in legal challenges in the competitive bidding area. Courts have also been reluctant to order a local government to award a contract to a particular bidder who claims to be entitled to the contract. The court's reluctance stems from the extent of discretion accorded to local governments in awarding contracts and their authority to reject any or all bids.[108]

Illegal expenditure of tax dollars. In one North Carolina case, taxpayers were successful in recovering funds from local government officials who had fraudulently abused the competitive bidding process to enter into illegal contracts.[109] The court's findings in this case indicated that there was more than simply a failure to comply with the procedures. Rather there was an intentional abuse resulting in an unauthorized payment to a contractor of funds that greatly exceeded the value of the work. The case was brought as a taxpayer's derivative suit, making demand first on the government entity and then upon the individuals involved. Although this remedy exists, it is likely to be awarded only in cases of extreme abuse of authority.

Violations of constitutional rights: due process, equal protection, free speech. The United States Supreme Court has held that when the government awards contracts, it may not discriminate against potential contractors on the basis of their race, sex, or any other immutable characteristics, nor may it refuse to award a contract to someone because of that person's opinions (even if they are directly critical of the government or its representatives) or because of the contractor's political affiliation.[110] Several federal statutes provide remedies, including monetary damages and attorney's fees in some cases, for violations of constitutional rights. The most commonly used statutes are 42 U.S.C. § 1983, which provides a remedy for violations of civil rights, and § 1988, which allows the court to award attorney's fees to a party who prevails on a claim under § 1983. A challenge on one of the discrimination grounds mentioned above must show that the local government acted intentionally in a discriminatory manner and that there was no nondiscriminatory justification for the challenged decision.

In some cases, a challenge is not based on discrimination but, rather, on the governing board's failure to adhere to statutory or local procedural requirements in bidding and awarding contracts. Such cases might involve allegations of favoritism, arbitrariness, or abuse of authority. As noted above, these allegations would provide a basis for seeking an injunction under state law. A claimant might also want to recover damages, such as expenses incurred in bid preparation, lost profit from losing a contract, or attorney's fees incurred in

108. See G.S. 143-129(b); General Elec. Co. v. Turner, 275 N.C. 493, 168 S.E.2d 385 (1969).

109. Moore v. Lambeth, 207 N.C. 23, 175 S.E. 714 (1934).

110. *See* Adarand Constructors, Inc. v. Pena, 515 U.S. 200 (1995) (race-based contract award subject to the highest level of scrutiny); Board of County Comm'rs, Wabaunsee County v. Umbehr, 518 U.S. 668 (1996) (contractor criticism of government is invalid basis for terminating contract); O'Hare Truck Serv., Inc. v. City of Northlake, 518 U.S. 712 (1996) (political affiliation is invalid basis for denying opportunity to contract).

bringing a challenge. The only way to recover these damages would be to claim a violation of due process—a constitutional claim—for which damages may be awarded under § 1983. The success of such a challenge is somewhat uncertain. The courts are divided about whether a failure to comply with bidding requirements can form the basis of a constitutional claim and, if so, who has standing to bring such a claim.[111] (See Question 147.)

In order to state a claim for a violation of due process, the claimant must demonstrate that he or she had a legally recognized interest, referred to as a property interest, in the benefit to be conferred by the government. Due process requires that persons not be arbitrarily deprived of such benefits or property interests. The courts look to state law to determine whether the property interest exists. In the case of competitively bid contracts, an argument may be made that the board has discretion in awarding contracts and, in any event, has the discretion to reject all the bids and either readvertise or abandon the project. Under this argument, a bidder is not entitled to a contract award even if he or she is the low bidder; therefore, no property interest capable of constitutional protection exists. Some cases have held, however, that even though the governing board has some discretion, the statutory competitive bidding procedures, together with those the local government might adopt, impose enough limitations on the board's discretion in awarding contracts that a bidder has a recognizable property interest in being treated fairly and in accordance with those procedures. Even under this argument, a local government would be liable for a violation of due process only if its actions were deemed by a court to be arbitrary. Courts are unlikely to apply this remedy to technical or insignificant deviations from statutory or local procedures.

146. Can a purchasing agent or other official be personally liable for failure to comply with a competitive bidding requirement?

Individual employees or elected officials are not likely to be held personally liable for errors or omissions in the bidding and contracting process. As noted in Question 11, an individual can be held personally liable for incurring an obligation or disbursing funds without complying with the preaudit requirements or for falsely completing the certification requirements under that statute. Similarly, if an individual purports to enter into a contract on behalf of a local government but does not have the authority to do so, a court might find that the contract was made on behalf of the individual and hold him or her personally liable, although it is more likely that a court would simply rule that the contract is invalid. In addition, intentional abuse or fraudulent use of the contracting process could be the basis for personnel actions, including termination in appropriate cases.[112] The courts have recognized claims for monetary

---

111. *Compare* Independent Enter., Inc. v. Pittsburgh Water & Sewer Auth., 103 F.3d 1165 (3d Cir. 1997); Kim Constr. v. Mundelein, 14 F.3d 1243 (11th Cir. 1994), *with* Pataula Elec. Membership Corp. v. Whitworth, 951 F.2d 1238 (11th Cir. 1992), *cert. denied,* 506 U.S. 907 (1992); Flint Elec. Membership Corp. v. Whitworth, 68 F.3d 1309 (11th Cir. 1995), *modified,* 77 F.3d 1321 (11th Cir. 1996).

112. *See* Fuqua v. Rockingham County Bd. of Soc. Servs., 125 N.C. App. 66, 479 S.E.2d 273 (1997).

damages against individuals, however, only in cases of fraud or intentional misallocation of public funds. (See Question 145.)

147. Who may bring a legal claim arising out of a competitive bidding process?

The issue of who has the legal ability to raise a claim in court is called "standing." Courts establish rules about standing to make sure that those involved in bringing actions have enough of a stake in the matter that they will properly and seriously pursue it and to make sure that the court's time is not wasted by hearing a matter raised by someone who is not affected by its outcome. In many early cases, courts ruled that only taxpayers could bring actions to challenge a contract award or other aspect of a competitive bidding process. The logic behind this rule was that the bidding laws do not exist for the benefit of the bidders. They exist for the benefit of the taxpayers, so only taxpayers (including bidders who are also taxpayers) were afforded standing to challenge bidding procedures or contract award decisions.[113]

More recent cases have recognized that bidders have a sufficient stake in the competitive bidding process to warrant a day in court, and some courts have allowed disappointed bidders to raise both federal and state law claims arising out of competitive bidding procedures. The court's recognition of the bidder's interest in the contracting process for purposes of standing is often confused with the recognition of an interest in a contract for the purpose of raising a claim for violation of due process under the Constitution. (See Question 145.)

North Carolina courts have not directly addressed the issue of who has standing to bring challenges under either federal or state law arising out of a local government's conduct in a competitive bidding process. Several lawsuits brought by disappointed bidders have been decided by the appellate courts, however, but the issue of standing was not discussed in any of these cases.[114] Bidders challenging local government contracting decisions might assume that the courts have implicitly recognized bidder standing, but it is still possible for a local government to raise the issue since no North Carolina court has ruled directly on it.

---

113. *See* 10 McQuillin Mun. Corp. § 29.86 (3d ed. 1990).

114. CB & I Constructors, Inc. v. Wake Forest, 157 N.C. App. 545, 579 S.E.2d 502 (2003); City-Wide Asphalt Paving, Inc. v. Alamance County, 132 N.C. App. 522, 513 S.E.2d 335, *disc. review denied,* 350 N.C. 826 (1999); Kinsey Contracting Co. v. City of Fayetteville, 106 N.C. App. 383, 416 S.E.2d 607, *disc. review denied,* 332 N.C. 345, 421 S.E.2d 149 (1992).

Chapter III
Purchasing Organization and Policies

148. How should the purchasing function be organized in a local government?

The statutes leave the organization of the purchasing function completely within the discretion of the governing board.[1] In most local governments, purchasing is organized using a combination of centralized and decentralized procedures. The arrangement in each organization is usually determined by the local government's size and management philosophy.

A centralized purchasing department, usually headed by a purchasing director or purchasing agent, can schedule purchases for the entire unit, maximize the opportunity to realize savings from buying in large quantities, and ensure that proper accounting and bidding procedures are complied with. A centralized purchasing staff develops expertise in writing specifications, identifying sources, handling bid openings, and evaluating bids, along with other aspects of the purchasing process. A good centralized purchasing department should view itself as providing a service to the other departments, working with them to find out what they need and developing a schedule so that items are acquired when they are needed. From a management perspective, centralized purchasing is efficient because it keeps everyone in the organization from having to become a purchasing expert. Even under a centralized system, flexibility is provided by allowing departments to make small purchases up to an established dollar limit. (See Question 149.)

In smaller units, centralized purchasing may not be practical due to insufficient staff. In these units, each department is responsible for purchasing and for complying with the bidding requirements and the finance officer or manager typically provides final oversight and approval, usually through the preaudit or other fiscal controls.

Decentralization has also become popular in larger units under recent management trends that emphasize localized responsibility within the departments and flexibility for frontline workers. Centralized purchasing can add time and paperwork to the purchasing process. The balance between centralized and decentralized purchasing must be set by each unit, considering the staff resources and management philosophy.

---

1. N.C. Gen. Stat. § 160-146; 153A-76, 115C-40 (hereinafter G.S.).

149. What is the best way to deal with small purchases?

Even in a centralized purchasing system there are some purchases that are simply too small to justify centralized handling. Each local government must determine at what point the cost of administration outweighs the savings from obtaining quotes or processing requisitions for very small items. As noted above, one strategy is for a centralized purchasing department to identify commonly used items, purchase them in bulk, and make them available from warehouses or internal stores. For less commonly used items, however, or in units that are too small or whose facilities are too dispersed to make use of storage facilities, procedures should be developed to allow for efficient purchase of items involving low dollar cost.

There are two major considerations in developing procedures for small purchases: accountability and preaudit compliance. The paperwork associated with purchasing in larger amounts provides accountability, through requisitions and receiving reports, which show that the buyer has approval to purchase and that the goods purchased were actually received. In addition, the preaudit certificate signed by the finance officer, usually as part of the purchase order issuance, guarantees that funds from the appropriate account are available for the purchase. (See Question 11.) Procedures for small purchases often eliminate these steps, so other mechanisms may be necessary to satisfy the underlying concerns.

Many local governments adopt a minimum dollar threshold under which competition is not required. This may also be the threshold below which centralized procedures do not apply, although in some units these may be different amounts. For example, a partially centralized system may provide that departments may, without going through the central purchasing department, make purchases up to $2,000 but that they may be required to obtain quotes for those purchases costing more than $500, while no quotes are required for purchases costing less than $500. As noted earlier, state law does not require competition below the informal threshold (see the "Dollar Thresholds" chart in Appendix 1), but most local governments continue to require quotes below that amount. The minimum dollar threshold for obtaining quotes is often the same as the dollar value the unit has adopted for identifying capital items in the fixed asset list. Although it may be convenient to link these two thresholds, there is no legal or accounting requirement to do so.

For purchases under the minimum dollar amount, units may issue blanket or blank purchase orders. These are preaudited up to a specified amount, and departments may use them either for general purposes or at a particular business up to the dollar amount authorized. The amounts can be set based on historical usage so that they are issued monthly, quarterly, or at whatever interval is most efficient. Depending upon the organizational structure, it will be up to the individual, the department, or a centralized purchasing or finance office to ensure that purchases made are authorized and that goods received are accounted for. Most local governments make a source of petty cash available for very small or emergency purchases. As with blanket or blank purchase orders, procedures should be established for documenting petty cash purchases.

Procurement cards can also be used as an efficient and very accountable way to deal with small purchases. Employees can be given procurement cards issued in the name of the local government but bearing the employee's name. The cards can be limited in various ways, including the businesses at which they may be used and the amount that may be charged in any one transaction or time period. The preaudit certification is usually taken care of in advance, much like the blanket purchase order approach, by preauditing and releasing a set amount of funds to each department or user in advance for a month, a quarter, or other appropriate time period. Procurement cards save time in accounts payable, since all charges are paid under a monthly bill. It is still up to the local government to address accountability and purchasing authority. Although the itemized charge statement provides detailed information about purchases, charges must still be assigned to accounts and the receipts from the purchase must be used to itemize and account for what was purchased.

Whatever method a local government uses for small purchases, it is also important to guard against abuse of the small-purchase authority. Small purchases should be monitored to make sure that items available in an internal store or warehouse are not being purchased elsewhere and that the bidding requirements are not being circumvented. Abuse of the small-purchase procedures may indicate that employees are uninformed about or dissatisfied with the regular procedures or requirements, suggesting a need for training or for revision of policies.

150. Are local governments required to have a purchasing policy or procedures manual?

State law does not require local governments to adopt any kind of purchasing policy or procedures manual although many units have developed them on their own for reasons discussed in the answer to Question 151.

151. What is the purpose of a purchasing policy or procedures manual?

A purchasing policy or procedures manual can serve many different purposes. Some units may distinguish between a policy, which may be more general in nature, and a manual, which may be more detailed and intended for internal use. Some purchasing professionals suggest that three separate documents are needed: a policy manual, an operations manual, and a vendor manual.[2] Although the first two may be combined, a vendor manual should be a separate document since it contains less detailed and different kinds of information than the policy intended for internal use. (See Question 153.) Local governments may also call these documents purchasing handbooks or vendor guides. The names for these documents have no legal significance—that is governed by how they are adopted. (See Question 152.)

2. The Council of State Governments, *State and Local Government Purchasing,* 4th ed. (Lexington, KY: CSG, 1994), 111.

Purchasing policies can (1) describe purchasing goals and principles, (2) delineate the organization of purchasing responsibility, (3) summarize statutory requirements, (4) establish local requirements, (5) distribute current forms and standard contract terms, and (6) establish and describe ethics and conflict of interest rules.

152. Does the governing board have to adopt or approve the purchasing manual or policy?

Since there is no legal requirement that units have a purchasing policy, there are no requirements about how policies may be established. However, a policy will be more practically useful and legally enforceable if it is adopted by the governing board.

From a legal standpoint, a policy that has been adopted by the governing board can serve several important functions. First, it can constitute an explicit delegation of authority to contract. This is accomplished if the policy describes the organization of the contracting process within the unit in specific detail, identifying those people within the unit (purchasing agents, department heads, or others) who have final authority to obligate the unit and at what expenditure level. If this is done, the unit is protected from being bound by contracts made by those within the unit who do not have contracting authority. This protection may be undermined if the unit regularly pays obligations incurred by employees without such authority. (See Question 7.)

A second legal effect of board approval is that the policy can incorporate provisions which state law authorizes the unit to establish through governing board action. Examples include

- delegation of authority to the manager or chief purchasing official for awarding contracts and related actions [Section 143-129(a) of the North Carolina General Statutes (hereinafter G.S.)];
- authorization to use electronic advertisement of bids [G.S. 143-129(b)];
- establishment of M/WBE percentage participation goals and good faith efforts policies [G.S. 143-128.2];
- delegation of authority to dispose of surplus property [G.S. 160A-266(c)];
- establishment of rules regarding confidentiality of cost estimates and identity of contractors who have obtained proposals [G.S. 133-33]; and
- establishment of dollar value for advertising items or souvenirs of nominal value that may legally be accepted [G.S. 133-32].

When the board adopts the policy, the statutory requirements for board action on these matters are satisfied. Note that where the statutes allow for discretion, the policy can also delegate authority to a purchasing official to exercise that discretion in any case where he or she deems it to be in the best interest of the unit. For example, a policy that includes authority to advertise for bids electronically can include a delegation of authority to decide on a case-by-case basis when to use electronic advertisement, newspaper advertisement, or both.

Finally, as a practical matter, board adoption sends a message to all those within the unit that the policy has the approval and support of the board. This is particularly important if the policy incorporates a change in procedures to which there may be some resistance.

Board adoption of the policy also has significance for those outside the unit. Once the policy is adopted by the board, a vendor or taxpayer may argue that compliance with its provisions is mandatory and may seek to enforce the policy either by informal appeal to the unit or in the courts. It is not clear that a court would invalidate a contract for failure to follow local procedures, but such failure could be viewed as evidence of arbitrariness on the part of the local government.

A final consideration is that when the governing board approves purchasing policies, it could be argued that any amendments to those policies must also be approved by the board. While it may be important and even legally necessary for some aspects of the policy to be approved by the board, it may be desirable to have flexibility to change other parts of the policy without board approval. To address this concern, the policy can identify those portions that may be amended by the manager or chief purchasing official without board approval. As noted earlier, governing board approvals that are mandated by statute cannot be delegated. (See Question 113.)

153. Is there a difference between a vendor manual and a purchasing manual?

A vendor manual is usually a less detailed document than a purchasing manual and is directed to vendors rather than to employees within the unit. Purposes of vendor manuals include (1) describing purchasing goals and principles; (2) identifying contact points (names, numbers, and locations) for doing business with the unit; (3) providing an overview of purchasing procedures; (4) listing items and services commonly purchased by the unit; (5) summarizing minority/women business programs; and (6) describing limitations on vendor activity, such as giving gifts to and contacting departmental employees rather than the centralized purchasing staff. Information contained in a vendor manual can also be summarized in a brochure or included in a computer Internet site for easy accessibility. Whether through a vendor manual or some other form, it is important for local governments to provide information to vendors about how they can do business with the unit.

Like purchasing policies, vendor manuals are not required by law; but they can improve relations with vendors and help the purchasing process by developing an informed vendor base. Since the vendor manual summarizes information already contained in a purchasing manual or otherwise established and approved by the board, it is probably not necessary for the governing board to separately approve or adopt a vendor manual.

154. What should be included in a purchasing policy or manual?

The following is a list of some of the subjects that may be addressed in a purchasing policy or procedures manual. This list is not exhaustive and will not necessarily apply to all jurisdictions. Some of these provisions may also be contained in other policies or manuals (such as the personnel policy), in which case a cross-reference may be appropriate. A purchasing policy or manual may cover

- requisition procedures and forms;
- bidding and quotation procedures and forms (both statutory and locally established), including
  - formal, informal, and small purchases,
  - emergency purchases, and
  - service, construction, and design contracts;
- receiving, inspection, and payment procedures and forms;
- vendor listing and evaluation procedures and forms;
- procedures for bid protests or vendor complaints;
- procedures and forms for bid mistakes;
- purchase order/contract procedures and forms;
- procurement schedules;
- bond forms (bid, performance, payment);
- guidelines for preparing specifications;
- procedures and lead-time requirements for specifications;
- standard specifications available;
- state contracts to which the unit is a party;
- requirements and forms for purchasing from warehouses or storehouses;
- guidelines for handling proprietary information;
- guidelines for handling and return of samples;
- M/WBE goal and good-faith effort requirements and forms;
- fixed-asset listing procedures and forms;
- surplus property disposal procedures and forms;
- records retention requirements;
- information about identifying and reporting anticompetitive practices;
- ethics, conflicts of interest, and gift and favor provisions (including local rules and forms for reporting gifts and business interests); and
- purchasing department officials to contact for help (buyer responsibility areas, purchasing office organization).

155. How should a local government or purchasing agent develop a purchasing policy?

A policy must be practical and realistic if it is to be used. The person or group developing the policy should consult those who will use the policy to provide input on substantive provisions and to ensure that the policy will be workable once it is adopted. All existing written and unwritten policies should be collected and evaluated to determine whether they should be incorporated into the new policy, revised, or abandoned. If existing policies are superseded by the new policy, this should be noted to avoid confusion. In addition, any local acts affecting purchasing that are in effect within the jurisdiction should be reviewed and incorporated into the policy.

For overall organization and approach, it might be useful to look at policies from other jurisdictions. However, the drafter should be sensitive to differences in the size, organization, or legal requirements of another unit which may make it inappropriate to import entire provisions from another policy. In addition, the drafter should consult with the users of other policies to avoid duplicating provisions that have not worked well.

The format for the policy should maximize at least two important principles: the policy should be easy to read and use, and it should be easy to update. The latter goal is best accomplished by using a loose-leaf or electronic format and marking each page clearly with identifying dates, headings, and section numbers. Policies may be made available on computer disk or in online formats that are easy to access and update.

Several formatting approaches can be used to make the policy easy to read. A detailed table of contents and an index help direct the readers to policies affecting their areas of concern. A policy can begin with a short summary or overview of basic procedures or an easy-to-read chart identifying procedures with references to places within the policy that contain more detailed descriptions. Signposts in the margins or at the top of each page can help guide the reader through the policy. Cross-references can help direct the reader to related provisions and avoid incomplete understanding of required procedures.

Finally, it may be helpful to include citations to statutes or local acts from which the text or authority for key policy provisions derives. This reemphasizes the legal nature of the document and also directs the reader to the source of the requirement which may be consulted to determine whether or how it applies to a particular situation. These references may also be helpful in tracking provisions that are affected by changes in state law.

Additional resources to consult when developing a purchasing policy include *State and Local Government Purchasing*, published by the National Association of State Purchasing Officials and the Council of State Government, and the "Purchasing Policy" chapter of the North Carolina Department of State Treasurer *Policies Manual*.

156. Can local governments engage in cooperative or joint purchasing with other units of government?

Local governments may team up with each other under the interlocal cooperation authority contained in Chapter 160A, Article 20, Part 1 of the North Carolina General Statutes. Under this authority, local governments can accumulate their requirements and obtain lower prices or jointly acquire expensive equipment that would not be affordable for one unit acting alone. The details of the arrangement should be worked out and must be approved by the governing boards of each participating unit in advance. Examples of such details include whether both boards will have authority to award the contract; whether there will be two separate contracts, and if there are separate contracts, who will be responsible for handling the bid opening (or whether there will be separate bid openings); what will happen if the units disagree about how to proceed at any point; and, in the case of joint ownership, where the equipment will be physically housed and who will be responsible for maintenance and insurance.

The interlocal cooperation statutes also provide authority for merged purchasing departments. For example, a city and county or two cities might realize efficiencies by combining the administration of purchasing and increase savings by combining requirements for commonly used items.[3] Regional cooperation, often through efforts of regional councils of government, can provide opportunities for group purchasing among local governments or of particular items, such as recycled products, where bulk purchases can significantly affect pricing.

3. Winston-Salem and Forsyth County and Charlotte and Mecklenberg County have merged purchasing departments.

Chapter IV
Ethics and Conflicts of Interest

157. What are the sources of law that govern ethics and conflicts of interest in purchasing?

Ethics in purchasing is a broad topic[1] that is mostly addressed by professional codes rather than statutes. These codes describe what is considered to be proper behavior within the purchasing profession and are directed to the members of the organization that adopts the code. They are generally used for guidance and do not typically carry penalties or mechanisms for enforcement. Codes of ethics in public purchasing focus on principles of fairness, avoiding favoritism or personal gain, and avoiding even the appearance of a conflict of interest.[2]

The term "conflict of interest" has a broad meaning and is often used generically to denote any situation in which public officials have an interest, whether financial or personal, in a matter that comes before them in their official capacity. State laws and locally adopted policies governing conflicts of interest establish legal limitations on activity in which individuals may have a financial interest. These are discussed in the answer to Question 158.

Legal restrictions in this area do not address all conflict of interest situations in the broader sense described above. If the law does not address a particular situation, that is, if it does not make illegal what appears to be a conflict of interest in the broader sense of the term, a professional ethics policy or one's personal ethics may provide guidance. The public nature of local government activity dictates that the press and public opinion may be the ultimate judges of the appropriateness of individual decisions in matters of conflict of interest.

158. What does state law prohibit in the area of conflict of interest?

Three major statutes deal with contracting and public officials' interest.

Contracting for own benefit [Section 14-234 of the North Carolina General Statutes (hereinafter G.S.)]. This statute prohibits any public officer or employee who is involved in making or administering a contract from deriving

---

1. For a comprehensive treatment of ethics and conflicts of interest in local government, *see* A. Fleming Bell, II, *Ethics, Conflicts, and Offices: A Guide for Local Officials* (Chapel Hill: Institute of Government, The University of North Carolina at Chapel Hill, 1997).

2. The Code of Ethics and Guidelines to Code of Ethics for the National Institute of Governmental Purchasing (NIGP) can be viewed at the following Web site: www.nigp.org/genlinfo/2001CodeofEthics.pdf.

a direct benefit from the contract.[3] If a public officer or employee is not involved in making or administering a contract but would derive a direct benefit from the contract, he or she is prohibited from influencing or attempting to influence any person who is involved in making or administering the contract.[4] Finally, a public officer or employee is prohibited from soliciting or receiving any gift, reward, or promise of reward in exchange for recommending, influencing, or attempting to influence the award of a contract by the public agency he or she serves.[5] Violation of this statute is a Class 1 misdemeanor.

There are two key elements of this restriction: a person must derive a "direct benefit" and must be "involved in making or administering the contract." A person has a direct benefit if the person or his or her spouse (1) has more than a 10 percent ownership or other interest in an entity that is a party to the contract, (2) derives any income directly from the contract, or (3) acquires property under the contract.[6] An interest in a contract that does not fall within any of these categories does not violate the statute, though such an interest may still raise ethical concerns or an appearance of a conflict.

A person is involved in making a contract if he or she participates in the development of specifications or terms or in the preparation or award of the contract.[7] A person is involved in administering a contract if he or she oversees the performance of the contract or has authority to make decisions regarding the contract or to interpret the contract.[8]

Several types of contracts are exempt from the statute. Whenever a local government enters into a contract that is covered by one of the exceptions, a board member who will derive a direct benefit from the contract is prohibited from deliberating or voting on the contract and may not attempt to influence any other person who is involved in making or administering the contract.[9] The statute specifically exempts contracts with banks, savings and loans, and utilities regulated under Chapter 62 of the North Carolina General Statutes.[10] The statute also exempts reimbursement to board members under public assistance programs, provided that the program involved is (1) open to other providers, (2) beneficiaries may freely choose among the available providers, (3) reimbursement to the board member is at the same rate as to the other available providers, and (4) the board member does not participate in approving his or her own bill.[11] A local government may acquire property from an officer or employee without violating the statute if the transaction is undertaken under a judgment in a condemnation proceeding, including a consent judgment entered by a superior court judge in such a proceeding.[12] Another exception, discussed further in

3. G.S. 14-234(a)(1) N.C. Gen. Stat. 14-234(a)(1) (hereinafter G.S.).
4. G.S. 14-234(a)(2).
5. G.S. 14-234(a)(3).
6. G.S. 14-234(a1)(4).
7. G.S. 14-234(a1)(3).
8. G.S. 14-234(a1)(2).
9. G.S. 14-234(b1).
10. G.S. 14-234(b)(1).
11. G.S. 14-234(b)(4).
12. G.S. 14-234(b)(2).

Question 159, allows the spouse of a public officer to be an employee of the local government the officer serves.[13] This exception only applies to spouses of officers, not to spouses of employees.

There is also an exception that allows board members in small jurisdictions to have a limited financial interest in contracts with their own units, subject to some additional restrictions. The exception, set forth in subparagraph (d1) of G.S. 14-234, applies to cities with a population of 15,000 or less; counties with no incorporated municipality of more than 15,000; city boards of education in cities with a population of 15,000 or less; county boards of education in counties with no incorporated municipality of more than 15,000; local health or area mental health boards serving one or more counties in which there is no incorporated municipality of more than 15,000; and any member of a public hospital board of directors. Population figures are determined by the most recent federal census. This exception authorizes elected officials to contract with their own units of government for certain contracts and for limited amounts. A contract entered into may not exceed $12,500 for medically related goods and services and $25,000 for other goods and services within a twelve-month period. In addition, any contract covered by Article 8 of Chapter 143—that is, any contract that is subject to either formal or informal bidding—is not eligible under this exception.[14] Finally, the statute sets forth additional approval, public notice, and reporting requirements for contracts entered into under this exception.[15]

Gifts and favors [G.S. 133-32]. This statute makes it a Class 1 misdemeanor to give or to receive gifts and favors in the context of contracting. The statute applies to current contractors, those who have performed under a contract within the past year, or those who "anticipate bidding on such a contract in the future."[16] The prohibition on receiving gifts and favors applies to any officer or employee who prepares plans, specifications, or estimates; awards or administers contracts; or inspects or supervises construction. Although the placement of this statute in an article of the General Statutes entitled "Regulation of Contractors for Public Works"[17] might suggest that it only applies to construction contracts, the language of the statute contains no such limitation and it has been interpreted to apply to *any* type of local government contract.[18] This interpretation is also supported by the definition of the term "governmental agency" as used in the statute, which includes all agencies and authorities (including local governments) that are "authorized to enter into public contracts for construction or repair *or for procurement of goods or services.*"[19]

The statute does not define what constitutes a gift or a favor. It does, however, establish some exceptions. It is prudent to interpret the statute,

---

13. G.S. 14-234(b)(3).
14. G.S. 14-234(d2).
15. *See* G.S. 14-234(d1)(2)–(4).
16. G.S. 133-32(a).
17. Article 3 of Chapter 133 of the North Carolina General Statutes.
18. *See* Letter from Attorney General to L.W. Lamar, attorney for the Nash–Rocky Mount Board of Education (May 13, 1993).
19. G.S. 133-23(a) (emphasis added).

therefore, as prohibiting the giving or receiving of anything of value that is not covered by one of the exceptions. The statute allows the gift and receipt of

- honoraria for participating in meetings;
- advertising items or souvenirs of *nominal* value;
- meals furnished at banquets;
- contractor donations to professional organizations to which local government officials or employees may belong, including participation in all scheduled functions of such organizations; and
- customary gifts from friends and family members, as long as the family or friendship relationship, not the desire to do business with the local government, is the motivating factor for the gift.

There is a provision in the statute that requires such gifts to be reported to the head of the agency.[20] It is not clear whether this requirement applies to all of the gifts permitted or only to the category immediately preceding the reporting requirement—"customary gifts from friends and family members." The safest practice is to report all gifts or favors received under any of the categories of exceptions.

Benefit from confidential information [G.S. 14-234.1]. This statute does not directly relate to contracting, but it does prohibit any officer or employee from acquiring a financial benefit using information he or she obtains by virtue of his or her position. The statute also prohibits such a person from using that information to help someone else gain a financial benefit. Violation of the statute is a Class 1 misdemeanor.

159. Is it illegal for the spouse or relative of a public official to benefit from a contract?

The conflict of interest statute specifically includes the interest of a spouse in the definition of "direct benefit."[21] (See Question 158.) This means that a contract that creates a direct benefit to the spouse of a public officer or employee is prohibited under the statute, if the public officer or employee is involved in making or administering a contract, unless an exception applies. A separate exception does allow the spouse of a public officer to work as an employee of the public agency the officer represents.[22] As for other family relations, the statute does not limit contracts with any family member of a public officer or employee. The public official's own financial interest in a contract involving a relative may be sufficient, however, to constitute a conflict. For example, a conflict might exist if the local government contracts with the child of a public officer or employee who is supported by the public official or with a family business in which the public official has an interest. In cases involving family relationships, it is the potential financial gain to the *public officer or employee,* not the family relationship, that is key in determining whether G.S. 14-234 is violated.

20. G.S. 133-32(d).
21. G.S. 14-234(a1)(4).
22. G.S. 14-234(b)(3).

The foregoing discussion, of course, focuses on the legal issues. Public officials should also consider the ethical and practical issues raised by contracts that benefit spouses or close relatives. For example, would there be a negative appearance from such a contract and would it be difficult for the public official and the other board members or employees if disputes with a contractor who is married or related to a board member arise or develop into litigation? These questions must be resolved by the public official in consultation with his or her colleagues, supervisors, or attorney.

It is unclear whether a local government has the authority to prohibit a spouse or relative from competing for contracts where the criminal laws do not clearly make it illegal. For contracts subject to the competitive bidding laws, it does not appear that any qualified contractor could be prohibited from competing without specific statutory authority. Since there is no statutory obligation to provide competition for other types of contracts, local governments may have more flexibility in restricting eligibility (for example, through a locally adopted policy prohibiting contracts with spouses or relatives), but even this approach is untested in the courts and could be subject to challenge.

160. Does a contract create a conflict of interest if a governing board member who stands to benefit was not involved in making or voting on the contract?

As noted in Question 158, the main prohibition under the conflict of interest statute applies when a person who derives a direct benefit is involved in making or administering the contract. Under the statute's definition, a person is involved in "making a contract" if he or she "participates in the development of specifications or terms or in the preparation or award of the contract."[23] A person is involved in "administering" a contract if he or she "oversees the performance of the contract or has authority to make decisions regarding the contract or to interpret the contract."[24]

Interpretations vary as to whether the governing board, by virtue of its general authority over contracting, is *always* involved in making or administering a contract. It could be argued that since others award contracts only under a delegation from the board, that the board members have some sort of legal responsibility for the contract even when they do not actually participate in the award. It could also be argued that the board always has authority to "interpret a contract," based again on its statutory authority over contracts, such that board members are always involved in administering contracts as defined in the statute. On the other hand, the statute seems to contemplate situations where a board member is not involved in making or administering the contract, as indicated by the separate prohibition in the statute for influencing those who are involved under G.S. 14-2349(a)(2). Board members and other public officials should consider the practical and ethical consequences of board members contracting with the public agency, even when the statute is interpreted not to prohibit it.

---

23. G.S. 14-234(a1)(3).
24. G.S. 14-234(a1)(2).

161. Can a board member avoid liability under the statute by not voting on the contract?

No. If an exception in the statute applies to a particular contract, the statute provides that the interested person shall not vote on the contract. In this situation, the exception is what allows the contract, not the simple fact that the board member did not vote. In cases where there is no exception, a violation of the statute occurs even if the interested board member doesn't vote. As expressed in the statute "A public officer is also involved in making a contract if the board, commission, or other body of which he or she is a member takes action on the contract, *whether or not the public officer actually participates in that action*, unless the contract is approved under an exception under which the public officer is allowed to benefit and is prohibited from voting."[25]

162. What is the legal effect of a contract that violates G.S. 14-234?

The contract is void and unenforceable. In addition, the courts have held that no *quantum meruit* recovery (see Question 4) can be awarded for contracts that are void for this reason, since to do so would violate public policy. Essentially, both parties are deemed to have been acting in bad faith, and neither is entitled to any recovery from the courts, even if this results in an unfair situation.

The statute provides limited authority to continue a contract that is void under the statute in circumstances where it is necessary to protect the public health, safety, and welfare while alternative arrangements are made.[26] Continuation of a local government contract under this authority must be approved by the Local Government Commission.[27]

163. Can the governing board ratify a contract that was made in violation of G.S. 14-234?

No. The governing board can only ratify contracts it has the legal authority to make in the first place. (See Question 10.) The courts have held that a contract that is void for public policy reasons is not one the board is legally authorized to make.

164. Is there a dollar figure that is used to determine when a gift is considered of nominal value?

The statute does not establish a dollar amount, and there are no cases that provide any guidance. Some local governments have adopted local policies

25. *See* 14-234(a1)(3) (emphasis added). This is consistent with case law decided under the previous version of the statute. *See* State v. Williams, 153 N.C. 595, 68 S.E. 900 (1910), where a board member was convicted of a misdemeanor under G.S. 14-234 for a purchase made at his hardware store even though he abstained from voting when the contract came before the board for approval.

26. *See* G.S. 14-234(f).

27. G.S. 14-234(f)(1).

on gifts and favors that establish a dollar limit for gifts that may be accepted. The intent and language of the statute suggest that any such limit should be low.[28]

165. Does a gift to the local government or to a department violate the gifts and favors statute?

No. The statute prohibits a gift to an individual, presumably one that is of personal benefit to the receiver. The law does not, however, prohibit a contractor from making a donation to the organization as a whole or to a department for the benefit of the organization as opposed to one or more individuals. For example, a company may want to donate a piece of its equipment for a department to use as a way of introducing it to a potential customer or simply as an act of charity. In addition, some local governments accept donations of gifts for employee appreciation events or professional conferences and raffle them off to individual employees. Although the latter example is somewhat less clear, it seems reasonable to consider this a gift to the organization as a whole, even though the organization then gives it to an individual for personal use. Similarly, gifts of food and other items which are often made to particular individuals or departments probably do not violate the statute if they are shared among the members of the organization. Sharing makes them gifts to the organization, and the amount received by any one individual becomes nominal.

The local government's management must decide whether it is *appropriate*, assuming it is also legal, to allow the giving and receiving of these types of gifts. If a local policy is established, it should be well-publicized both within the organization and to contractors.

166. Can local government officials or employees legally accept an invitation to a site visit to be paid for by a contractor or potential contractor?

The answer to this question is somewhat unclear, particularly since there is no case interpreting the gifts and favors statute that provides guidance. As noted in Question 165, it seems reasonable to distinguish between a gift that is a benefit to the unit of government and one that benefits one or more individuals. In many cases, the benefit of visiting a site in anticipation of contracting is primarily to the unit of government in that it provides useful information for the contracting process. The contractor's willingness to pay the expenses of this type of trip benefits the unit of government, which would otherwise bear this expense. Local governments must exercise great care, however, to make sure that activities that are not related to the business purpose, such as entertainment or golf, are not included in the expenses paid for by the contractor. In

---

28. For a humorous interpretation of the gifts and favors statute, here is the advice given for many years by School of Government faculty member, Warren Jake Wicker: Gifts of "nominal value" include anything you can eat or drink in one sitting and anything valued at less than $10.00—anything that comes in a bottle is automatically valued at $9.99.

addition, public officials should carefully consider whether accepting this type of invitation creates an unfair advantage to a potential contractor in a competitive process or creates an appearance of favoritism or other inappropriate conduct on the part of the public officials.

167. Is it illegal for employees to purchase items for their personal use through local government contracts?

If a contractor with a local government wishes to contract with an individual at the same price as was offered to the local government and the individual pays for the items using his or her own money, the arrangement is perfectly legal. The arrangement is *not legal*, on the other hand, if the local government pays for the item using public funds, even if the person receiving the item reimburses the local government for the total cost. The reason for this limitation is that a local government does not generally have the authority to act as a retailer of goods, nor does it generally have the authority to use the public purchasing power for private use.

There is at least one possible exception to this general rule. Some local governments purchase items that are given to employees to use on the job, such as automobiles, uniforms, or specialized clothing required for their work. In addition, a few local governments have experimented with the purchase of computers for employees to use at home for personal or work-related tasks in order to improve skills they will use at work. These limited uses of the purchasing authority for personal benefit are probably legal since the local government derives a benefit from the employee's use of the equipment and has broad discretion in structuring fringe benefits and other nonmonetary compensation for its employees.

Dollar Thresholds in North Carolina Public Contracting Statutes

UNC SCHOOL OF GOVERNMENT

Dollar limits and statutory authority current as of September 1, 2013

Requirement	Threshold	Statute
Formal bidding	*(estimated cost of contract)*	
Construction or repair contracts	$500,000 *and above*	G.S. 143-129
Purchase of apparatus, supplies, materials, and equipment	$90,000 *and above*	G.S. 143-129
Informal bidding	*(actual cost of contract)*	
Construction or repair contracts	$30,000 to formal limit	G.S. 143-131
Purchase of apparatus, supplies, materials, and equipment	$30,000 to formal limit	G.S. 143-131
Construction methods authorized for building projects	*Over* $300,000	G.S. 143-128(a1)
Separate Prime	*(estimated cost of project)*	
Single Prime		
Dual Bidding		
Construction Management at Risk *(G.S. 143-128.1)*		
Design-Build and Design-Build Bridging *(G.S. 143-128.1A; G.S. 143-128.1B)*		
Public Private Partnership (P3) *(G.S. 143-128.1C)*		
Historically Underutilized Business (HUB) requirements		
Building construction or repair projects		
– Projects with state funding *(verifiable 10% goal required)*	$100,000 *or more*	G.S. 143-128.2(a)
– Locally funded projects *(formal HUB requirements)*	$300,000 *or more*	G.S. 143-128.2(j)
– Projects in informal bidding range *(informal HUB requirements)*	$30,000 to $500,000*	G.S. 143-131(b)
**Note: Formal HUB requirements should be used for informally bid projects costing between $300,000 and $500,000*		
Limit on use of own forces (force account work)	*(not to exceed)*	G.S. 143-135
Construction or repair projects	$125,000 *(total project cost)* <u>or</u> $50,000 *(labor only cost)*	
Bid bond or deposit		
Construction or repair contracts *(at least 5% of bid amount)*	Formal bids *($500,000 and above)*	G.S.143-129(b)
Purchase contracts	Not required	
Performance/Payment bonds		
Construction or repair contracts *(100% of contract amount)*	Each contract *over* $50,000 of project costing *over* $300,000	G.S. 143-129(c); G.S. 44A-26
Purchase contracts	Not required	
General contractor's license required	$30,000 *and above*	G.S. 87-1
Exemption	Force account work *(see above)*	
Owner-builder affidavit required	Force account work *(see above)*	G.S. 87-14(a)(1)
Use of licensed architect or engineer required		
Nonstructural work	$300,000 *and above*	G.S. 133-1.1(a)
Structural repair, additions, or new construction	$135,000 *and above*	
Repair work affecting life safety systems	$100,000 *and above*	
Selection of architect, engineer, surveyor, construction manager at risk, or design-build contractor		
"Qualification-Based Selection" procedure (QBS)	All contracts unless exempted	G.S. 143-64.31
Exemption authorized	Only projects where estimated fee is *less than* $50,000	G.S. 143-64.32

From *A Legal Guide to Purchasing and Contracting for North Carolina Local Governments*, 2nd ed., by Frayda S. Bluestein,

Appendix 2
Selected Statutes

Current through the end of the 2003 session of the North Carolina General Assembly.

General Statutes of North Carolina

Chapter 14. Criminal Law.

Subchapter VIII. Offenses against Public Justice.

Article 31. Misconduct in Public Office.

§ 14-234. Public officers or employees benefiting from public contracts; exceptions.

(a) (1) No public officer or employee who is involved in making or administering a contract on behalf of a public agency may derive a direct benefit from the contract except as provided in this section, or as otherwise allowed by law.

(2) A public officer or employee who will derive a direct benefit from a contract with the public agency he or she serves, but who is not involved in making or administering the contract, shall not attempt to influence any other person who is involved in making or administering the contract.

(3) No public officer or employee may solicit or receive any gift, reward, or promise of reward in exchange for recommending, influencing, or attempting to influence the award of a contract by the public agency he or she serves.

(a1) For purposes of this section:

(1) As used in this section, the term "public officer" means an individual who is elected or appointed to serve or represent a public agency, other than an employee or independent contractor of a public agency.

(2) A public officer or employee is involved in administering a contract if he or she oversees the performance of the contract or has authority to make decisions regarding the contract or to interpret the contract.

(3) A public officer or employee is involved in making a contract if he or she participates in the development of specifications or terms or in the preparation or award of the contract. A public officer is also involved in making a contract if the board, commission, or other body of which he or she is a member takes action on the contract, whether or not the public officer actually participates in that action, unless the contract is approved under an exception to this section under which the public officer is allowed to benefit and is prohibited from voting.

(4) A public officer or employee derives a direct benefit from a contract if the person or his or her spouse: (i) has more than a ten percent (10%) ownership

or other interest in an entity that is a party to the contract; (ii) derives any income or commission directly from the contract; or (iii) acquires property under the contract.

(5) A public officer or employee is not involved in making or administering a contract solely because of the performance of ministerial duties related to the contract.

(b) Subdivision (a)(1) of this section does not apply to any of the following:

(1) Any contract between a public agency and a bank, banking institution, savings and loan association, or with a public utility regulated under the provisions of Chapter 62 of the General Statutes.

(2) An interest in property conveyed by an officer or employee of a public agency under a judgment, including a consent judgment, entered by a superior court judge in a condemnation proceeding initiated by the public agency.

(3) Any employment relationship between a public agency and the spouse of a public officer of the agency.

(4) Remuneration from a public agency for services, facilities, or supplies furnished directly to needy individuals by a public officer or employee of the agency under any program of direct public assistance being rendered under the laws of this State or the United States to needy persons administered in whole or in part by the agency if: (i) the programs of public assistance to needy persons are open to general participation on a nondiscriminatory basis to the practitioners of any given profession, professions or occupation; (ii) neither the agency nor any of its employees or agents, have control over who, among licensed or qualified providers, shall be selected by the beneficiaries of the assistance; (iii) the remuneration for the services, facilities or supplies are in the same amount as would be paid to any other provider; and (iv) although the public officer or employee may participate in making determinations of eligibility of needy persons to receive the assistance, he or she takes no part in approving his or her own bill or claim for remuneration.

(b1) No public officer who will derive a direct benefit from a contract entered into under subsection (b) of this section may deliberate or vote on the contract or attempt to influence any other person who is involved in making or administering the contract.

(c) through (d) Repealed by Session Laws 2001-409, s. 1, effective July 1, 2002.

(d1) Subdivision (a)(1) of this section does not apply to (i) any elected official or person appointed to fill an elective office of a village, town, or city having a population of no more than 15,000 according to the most recent official federal census, (ii) any elected official or person appointed to fill an elective office of a county within which there is located no village, town, or city with a population of more than 15,000 according to the most recent official federal census, (iii) any elected official or person appointed to fill an elective office on a city board of education in a city having a population of no more than 15,000 according to the most recent official federal census, (iv) any elected official or person appointed to fill an elective office as a member of a county board of education in a county within which there is located no village, town or city with a population of more than 15,000 according to the most recent official federal census, (v) any physician, pharmacist, dentist, optometrist, veterinarian, or nurse appointed to a county social services board, local health board, or area mental health, developmental disabilities, and substance abuse board serving one or more counties within which there is located no village, town, or city with a population of more than 15,000 according to the most recent official federal census, and (vi) any member of the board of directors of a public hospital if all of the following apply:

(1) The undertaking or contract or series of undertakings or contracts between the village, town, city, county, county social services board, county or city board of education, local health board or area mental health, developmental disabilities, and substance abuse board, or public hospital and one of its officials is approved by specific resolution of the governing body adopted

in an open and public meeting, and recorded in its minutes and the amount does not exceed twelve thousand five hundred dollars ($12,500) for medically related services and twenty-five thousand dollars ($25,000) for other goods or services within a 12-month period.

(2) The official entering into the contract with the unit or agency does not participate in any way or vote.

(3) The total annual amount of contracts with each official, shall be specifically noted in the audited annual financial statement of the village, town, city, or county.

(4) The governing board of any village, town, city, county, county social services board, county or city board of education, local health board, area mental health, developmental disabilities, and substance abuse board, or public hospital which contracts with any of the officials of their governmental unit shall post in a conspicuous place in its village, town, or city hall, or courthouse, as the case may be, a list of all such officials with whom such contracts have been made, briefly describing the subject matter of the undertakings or contracts and showing their total amounts; this list shall cover the preceding 12 months and shall be brought up-to-date at least quarterly.

(d2) Subsection (d1) of this section does not apply to contracts that are subject to Article 8 of Chapter 143 of the General Statutes, Public Building Contracts.

(d3) Subsection (a) of this section does not apply to an application for or the receipt of a grant under the Agriculture Cost Share Program for Nonpoint Source Pollution Control created pursuant to G.S. 143-215.74 by a member of the Soil and Water Conservation Commission if the requirements of G.S. 139-4(e) are met, and does not apply to a district supervisor of a soil and water conservation district if the requirements of G.S. 139-8(b) are met.

(d4) Subsection (a) of this section does not apply to an application for, or the receipt of a grant or other financial assistance from, the Tobacco Trust Fund created under Article 75 of Chapter 143 of the General Statutes by a member of the Tobacco Trust Fund Commission or an entity in which a member of the Commission has an interest provided that the requirements of G.S. 143-717(h) are met.

(d5) This section does not apply to a public hospital subject to G.S. 131E-14.2 or a public hospital authority subject to G.S. 131E-21.

(e) Anyone violating this section shall be guilty of a Class 1 misdemeanor.

(f) A contract entered into in violation of this section is void. A contract that is void under this section may continue in effect until an alternative can be arranged when: (i) immediate termination would result in harm to the public health or welfare, and (ii) the continuation is approved as provided in this subsection. A public agency that is a party to the contract may request approval to continue contracts under this subsection as follows:

(1) Local governments, as defined in G.S. 159-7(15), public authorities, as defined in G.S. 159-7(10), local school administrative units, and community colleges may request approval from the chair of the Local Government Commission.

(2) All other public agencies may request approval from the State Director of the Budget.

Approval of continuation of contracts under this subsection shall be given for the minimum period necessary to protect the public health or welfare.

§ 14-234.1. Misuse of confidential information.

(a) It is unlawful for any officer or employee of the State or an officer or an employee of any of its political subdivisions, in contemplation of official action by himself or by a governmental unit with which he is associated, or in reliance on information which was made known to him in his official capacity and which has not been made public, to commit any of the following acts:

(1) Acquire a pecuniary interest in any property, transaction, or enterprise or gain any pecuniary benefit which may be affected by such information or official action; or

(2) Intentionally aid another to do any of the above acts.

(b) Violation of this section is a Class 1 misdemeanor.

General Statutes of North Carolina

Chapter 115C. Elementary and Secondary Education.

Subchapter VII. Fiscal Affairs.

Article 31. The School Budget and Fiscal Control Act.

Part 3. Fiscal Control.

§ 115C-441. Budgetary accounting for appropriations.

(a) Incurring Obligations.—Except as set forth below, no obligation may be incurred by a local school administrative unit unless the budget resolution includes an appropriation authorizing the obligation and an unencumbered balance remains in the appropriation sufficient to pay in the current fiscal year the sums obligated by the transaction for the current fiscal year. If an obligation is evidenced by a contract or agreement requiring the payment of money or by a purchase order for supplies and materials, the contract, agreement, or purchase order shall include on its face a certificate stating that the instrument has been preaudited to assure compliance with this section. The certificate, which shall be signed by the finance officer, shall take substantially the following form:

> "This instrument has been preaudited in the manner required by the School Budget and Fiscal Control Act.
>
> ______________________________
>
> (Date)
>
> ______________________________
>
> (Signature of finance officer)"

An obligation incurred in violation of this section is invalid and may not be enforced. The finance officer shall establish procedures to assure compliance with this section.

(b) Disbursements.—When a bill, invoice, or other claim against a local school administrative unit is presented, the finance officer shall either approve or disapprove the necessary disbursement. The finance officer may approve the claim only if he determines the amount to be payable, the budget resolution includes an appropriation authorizing the expenditure and either (i) an encumbrance has been previously created for the transaction or (ii) an unencumbered balance remains in the appropriation sufficient to pay the amount to be disbursed. A bill, invoice, or other claim may not be paid unless it has been approved by the finance officer or, under subsection (c) of this section, by the board of education.

(c) Board of Education Approval of Bills, Invoices, or Claims.—The board of education may, as permitted by this subsection, approve a bill, invoice, or other claim against the local school administrative unit that has been disapproved by the finance officer. It may not approve a claim for which no appropriation appears in the budget resolution, or for which the appropriation contains no encumbrance and the unencumbered balance is less than the amount to be paid. The board of education shall approve payment by formal resolution stating the board's reasons for allowing the bill, invoice, or other claim. The resolution shall be entered in the minutes together with the names of those voting in the affirmative. The chairman of the board or some other member designated for this purpose shall sign the certificate on the check or draft given in payment of the bill, invoice, or other claim. If payment results in a violation of law, each member of the board voting to allow payment is jointly and severally liable for the full amount of the check or draft given in payment.

(c1) Continuing Contracts for Capital Outlay.—An administrative unit may enter into a contract for capital outlay expenditures, some portion or all of which is to be performed and/or paid in ensuing fiscal years, without the budget resolution including an appropriation for the entire obligation, provided:

a. The budget resolution includes an appropriation authorizing the current fiscal year's portion of the obligation;

b. An unencumbered balance remains in the appropriation sufficient to pay in the current fiscal year the sums obligated by the transaction for the current fiscal year; and

c. Contracts for capital outlay expenditures are approved by a resolution adopted by the board of county commissioners, which resolution when adopted shall bind the board of county commissioners to appropriate sufficient funds in ensuing fiscal years to meet the amounts to be paid under the contract in those years.

(d) Payment.—A local school administrative unit may not pay a bill, invoice, salary, or other claim except by a check or draft on an official depository, by a bank wire transfer from an official depository, or by a warrant on the State Treasurer. Except as provided in this subsection each check or draft on an official depository shall bear on its face a certificate signed by the finance officer or signed by the chairman or some other member of the board pursuant to subsection (c) of this section. The certificate shall take substantially the following form:

> "This disbursement has been approved as required by the School Budget and Fiscal Control Act.
>
> ______________________________
>
> (Signature of finance officer)"

No certificate is required on payroll checks or drafts or on State warrants.

(e) Penalties.—If an officer or employee of a local school administrative unit incurs an obligation or pays out or causes to be paid out any funds in violation of this section, he and the sureties on his official bond are liable for any sums so committed or disbursed. If the finance officer gives a false certificate to any contract, agreement, purchase order, check, draft, or other document, he and the sureties on his official bond are liable for any sums illegally committed or disbursed thereby.

Subchapter IX. Property.

Article 37. School Sites and Property.

§ 115C-522. Provision of equipment for buildings.

(a) Except as provided in G.S. 115C-522.1, it shall be the duty of local boards of education to purchase or exchange all supplies, equipment and materials in accordance with contracts made by or with the approval of the Department of Administration. Title to instructional supplies, office supplies, fuel and janitorial supplies, enumerated in the current expense fund budget and purchased out of State funds, shall be taken in the name of the local board of education which shall be responsible for the custody and replacement: Provided, that no contracts shall be made by any local school administrative unit for purchases unless provision has been made in the budget of the unit to pay for the purchases, unless surplus funds are on hand to pay for the purchases, or unless the contracts are made pursuant to G.S. 115C-47(28) and G.S. 115C-528 and adequate funds are available to pay in the current fiscal year the sums obligated for the current fiscal year, and in order to protect the State purchase contractor, it is made the duty of the governing authorities of the local units to pay for these purchases promptly and in accordance with the terms of the contract of purchase.

(b) It shall be the duty of the local boards of education to provide suitable school furniture and apparatus, as provided in G.S. 115C-521(b).

(c) It shall be the duty of local boards of education and tax-levying authorities to provide suitable supplies for the school buildings under their jurisdictions. These shall include, in addition to the necessary instructional supplies, proper window shades, blackboards, reference books, library equipment, maps, and equipment for teaching the sciences.

Likewise, it shall be the duty of said boards of education and boards of county commissioners to provide every school with a good supply of water, approved by the Department of Environment and Natural Resources, and where such school cannot be connected to water-carried sewerage facilities, there shall be provided sanitary privies for the boys and for the girls according to specifications of the Commission for Health Services. Such water supply and sanitary privies shall be considered an essential and necessary part of the equipment of each public school and may be paid for in the same manner as desks and other essential equipment of the school are paid for.

§ 115C-528. Lease purchase and installment purchase contracts for certain equipment.

(a) Local boards of education may purchase or finance the purchase of automobiles; school buses; mobile classroom units; photocopiers; and computers, computer hardware, computer software, and related support services by lease purchase contracts and installment purchase contracts as provided in this section. Computers, computer hardware, computer software, and related support services purchased under this section shall meet the technical standards specified in the North Carolina Instructional Technology Plan as developed and approved under G.S. 115C-102.6A and G.S. 115C-102.6B.

(b) A lease purchase contract under this section creates in the local board the right to possess and use the property for a specified period of time in exchange for periodic payments and shall include either an obligation or an option to purchase the property during the term of the contract. The contract may include an option to upgrade the property during the term. A local board may exercise an option to upgrade without rebidding the contract.

(c) An installment purchase contract under this section creates in the property purchased a security interest to secure payment of the purchase price to the seller or to an individual or entity advancing moneys or supplying financing for the purchase transaction.

(d) The term of a contract entered into under this section shall not exceed the useful life of the property purchased. An option to upgrade shall be considered in determining the useful life of the property.

(e) A contract entered into under this section shall be considered a continuing contract for capital outlay and subject to G.S. 115C-441(c1).

(f) A contract entered into under this section is subject to Article 8 of Chapter 159 of the General Statutes, except for G.S. 159-148(a)(4) and (b)(2). For purposes of determining whether the standards set out in G.S. 159-148(a)(3) have been met, only the five hundred thousand dollar ($500,000) threshold shall apply.

(g) Subsections (e) and (f) of this section shall not apply to contracts entered into under this section so long as the term of each contract does not exceed three years and the total amount financed during any three-year period is no greater than two hundred fifty thousand dollars ($250,000) or is no greater than three times the local board's annual State allocation for classroom materials, equipment, and instructional supplies, whichever is less. The local board shall submit information, including the principal and interest paid and the amount of outstanding obligation, concerning these contracts as part of the annual budget it submits to its board of county commissioners under Article 31 of this Chapter.

(h) No contract entered into under this section may contain a nonsubstitution clause that restricts the right of a local board to:

(1) Continue to provide a service or activity; or

(2) Replace or provide a substitute for any property financed or purchased by the contract.

(i) No deficiency judgment may be rendered against any local board of education or any unit of local government, as defined in G.S. 160A-20(h), in any action for breach of a contractual obligation authorized by this section, and the taxing power of a unit of local government is not and may not be pledged directly or indirectly to secure any moneys due under a contract authorized by this section.

General Statutes of North Carolina

Chapter 133. Public Works.

Article 3. Regulation of Contractors for Public Works.

§ 133-32. Gifts and favors regulated.

(a) It shall be unlawful for any contractor, subcontractor, or supplier who:

(1) Has a contract with a governmental agency; or

(2) Has performed under such a contract within the past year; or

(3) Anticipates bidding on such a contract in the future

to make gifts or to give favors to any officer or employee of a governmental agency who is charged with the duty of:

(1) Preparing plans, specifications, or estimates for public contract; or

(2) Awarding or administering public contracts; or

(3) Inspecting or supervising construction.

It shall also be unlawful for any officer or employee of a governmental agency who is charged with the duty of:

(1) Preparing plans, specifications, or estimates for public contracts; or

(2) Awarding or administering public contracts; or

(3) Inspecting or supervising construction

willfully to receive or accept any such gift or favor.

(b) A violation of subsection (a) shall be a Class 1 misdemeanor.

(c) Gifts or favors made unlawful by this section shall not be allowed as a deduction for North Carolina tax purposes by any contractor, subcontractor or supplier or officers or employees thereof.

(d) This section is not intended to prevent the gift and receipt of honorariums for participating in meetings, advertising items or souvenirs of nominal value, or meals furnished at banquets. This section is not intended to prevent any contractor, subcontractor, or supplier from making donations to professional organizations to defray meeting expenses where governmental employees are members of such professional organizations, nor is it intended to prevent governmental employees who are members of professional organizations from participation in all scheduled meeting functions available to all members of the professional organization attending the meeting. This section is also not intended to prohibit customary gifts or favors between employees or officers and their friends and relatives or the friends and relatives of their spouses, minor children, or members of their household where it is clear that it is that relationship rather than the business of the individual concerned which is the motivating factor for the gift or favor. However, all such gifts knowingly made or received are required to be reported by the donee to the agency head if the gifts are made by a contractor, subcontractor, or supplier doing business directly or indirectly with the governmental agency employing the recipient of such a gift.

§ 133-33. Cost estimates; bidders' lists.

Any governmental agency responsible for letting public contracts may promulgate rules concerning the confidentiality of:

(1) The agency's cost estimate for any public contracts prior to bidding; and

(2) The identity of contractors who have obtained proposals for bid purposes for a public contract.

If the agency's rules require that such information be kept confidential, an employee or officer of the agency who divulges such information to any unauthorized person shall be subject to disciplinary action. This section shall not be construed to require that cost estimates or bidders' lists be kept confidential.

General Statutes of North Carolina

Chapter 143. State Departments, Institutions, and Commissions.

Article 8. Public Contracts.

§ 143-128. Requirements for certain building contracts.

(a) Preparation of specifications.—Every officer, board, department, commission or commissions charged with responsibility of preparation of specifications or awarding or entering into contracts for the erection, construction, alteration or repair of any buildings for the State, or for any county, municipality, or other public body, shall have prepared separate specifications for each of the following subdivisions or branches of work to be performed:

(1) Heating, ventilating, air conditioning and accessories (separately or combined into one conductive system), refrigeration for cold storage (where the cold storage cooling load is 15 tons or more of refrigeration), and all related work.

(2) Plumbing and gas fittings and accessories, and all related work.

(3) Electrical wiring and installations, and all related work.

(4) General work not included in subdivisions (1), (2), and (3) of this subsection relating to the erection, construction, alteration, or repair of any building.

Specifications for contracts that will be bid under the separate-prime system or dual bidding system shall be drawn as to permit separate and independent bidding upon each of the subdivisions of work enumerated in this subsection. The above enumeration of subdivisions or branches of work shall not be construed to prevent any officer, board, department, commission or commissions from preparing additional separate specifications for any other category of work.

(a1) Construction methods.—The State, a county, municipality, or other public body shall award contracts to erect, construct, alter, or repair buildings pursuant to any of the following methods:

(1) Separate-prime bidding.

(2) Single-prime bidding.

(3) Dual bidding pursuant to subsection (d1) of this section.

(4) Construction management at risk contracts pursuant to G.S. 143-128.1.

(5) Alternative contracting methods authorized pursuant to G.S. 143-135.26(9).

(a2) Annually, on or before April 1st, beginning April 1, 2003, The University of North Carolina and all other public entities shall report to the Secretary of the Department of Administration on the effectiveness and cost-benefit of utilization of each of the construction methods authorized in G.S. 143-128(a1) that are used by the public entity. The reports, which shall be initially filed in the year in which the project is completed, shall be in the format and contain the data prescribed by the Secretary of Administration and shall include at least the following:

(1) The type of construction method used on the project.

(2) The total dollar value of building projects by specific project with costs.

(3) The bid costs and relevant post-bid costs.

(4) A detailed listing of all contractors and subcontractors used on the project indicating whether the contractor or subcontractor was an out-of-state contractor or subcontractor.

(5) If any contractor or subcontractor was an out-of-state contractor or subcontractor, the reasons why the contractor or subcontractor was selected.

The Secretary of the Department of Administration shall report to the General Assembly on or before May 1st each year on the information collected pursuant to this subsection.

(b) Separate-prime contracts.—When the State, county, municipality, or other public body uses the separate-prime contract system, it shall accept bids for each subdivision of work for which specifications are required to be prepared under subsection (a) of this section and shall award the respective work specified separately to responsible and reliable persons, firms or corporations regularly engaged in their respective lines of work. When the estimated cost of work to be performed in any single subdivision or branch for which separate bids are required by this subsection is less than twenty-five thousand dollars ($25,000), the same may be included in the contract for one of the other subdivisions or branches of the work, irrespective of total project cost. The contracts shall be awarded to the lowest responsible, responsive bidders, taking into consideration quality, performance, the time specified in the bids for performance of the contract, and compliance with G.S. 143-128.2. Bids may also be accepted from and awards made to separate contractors for other categories of work.

Each separate contractor shall be directly liable to the State of North Carolina, or to the county, municipality, or other public body and to the other separate contractors for the full performance of all duties and obligations due respectively under the terms of the separate contracts and in accordance with the plans and specifications, which shall specifically set forth the duties and obligations of each separate contractor. For the purpose of this section, "separate contractor" means any person, firm or corporation who shall enter into a contract with the State, or with any county, municipality, or other public entity to erect, construct, alter or repair any building or buildings, or parts of any building or buildings.

(c) Repealed by Session Laws 2001-496, s. 3, effective January 1, 2001.

(d) Single-prime contracts.—All bidders in a single-prime project shall identify on their bid the contractors they have selected for the subdivisions or branches of work for:

(1) Heating, ventilating, and air conditioning;

(2) Plumbing;

(3) Electrical; and

(4) General.

The contract shall be awarded to the lowest responsible, responsive bidder, taking into consideration quality, performance, the time specified in the bids for performance of the contract, and compliance with G.S. 143-128.2. A contractor whose bid is accepted shall not substitute any person as subcontractor in the place of the subcontractor listed in the original bid, except (i) if the listed subcontractor's bid is later determined by the contractor to be nonresponsible or nonresponsive or the listed subcontractor refuses to enter into a contract for the complete performance of the bid work, or (ii) with the approval of the awarding authority for good cause shown by the contractor. The terms, conditions, and requirements of each contract between the contractor and a subcontractor performing work under a subdivision or branch of work listed in this subsection shall incorporate by reference the terms, conditions, and requirements of the contract between the contractor and the State, county, municipality, or other public body.

When contracts are awarded pursuant to this section, the public body shall make available to subcontractors the dispute resolution process as provided for in subsection (f1) of this section.

(d1) Dual bidding.—The State, a county, municipality, or other public entity may accept bids to erect, construct, alter, or repair a building under both the single-prime and separate-prime contracting systems and shall award the contract to the lowest responsible, responsive bidder under the single-prime system or to the lowest responsible, responsive bidder under the separate-prime system, taking into consideration quality, performance, compliance with G.S. 143-128.2, and time specified in the bids to perform the contract. In determining the system under which the contract will be awarded to the lowest responsible, responsive bidder, the public entity may consider cost of construction oversight, time for completion, and other factors it considers appropriate. The bids received as separate-prime bids shall be received, but not opened, one hour prior to the deadline for the submission of single-prime bids. The amount of a bid submitted by a subcontractor to the general contractor under the single-prime system shall not exceed the amount bid, if any, for the same work by that subcontractor to the public entity under the separate-prime system. The provisions of subsection (b) of this section shall apply to separate-prime contracts awarded pursuant to this section and the provisions of subsection (d) of this section shall apply to single-prime contracts awarded pursuant to this section.

(e) Project expediter; scheduling; public body to resolve project disputes.—The State, county, municipality, or other public body may, if specified in the bid documents, provide for assignment of responsibility for expediting the work on a project to a single responsible and reliable person, firm or corporation, which may be a prime contractor. In executing this responsibility, the designated project expediter may recommend to the State, county, municipality, or other public body whether payment to a contractor should be approved. The project expediter, if required by the contract documents, shall be responsible for preparing the project schedule and shall allow all contractors and subcontractors performing any of the branches of work listed in subsection (d) of this section equal input into the preparation of the initial schedule. Whenever separate contracts are awarded and separate contractors engaged for a project pursuant to this section, the public body may provide in the contract documents for resolution of project disputes through alternative dispute resolution processes as provided for in subsection (f1) of this section.

(f) Repealed by Session Laws 2001-496, s. 3, effective January 1, 2001.

(f1) Dispute resolution.—A public entity shall use the dispute resolution process adopted by the State Building Commission pursuant to G.S. 143-135.26(11), or shall adopt another dispute resolution process, which shall include mediation, to be used as an alterative to the dispute resolution process adopted by the State Building Commission. This dispute resolution process will be available to all the parties involved in the public entity's construction project including the public entity, the architect, the construction manager, the contractors, and the first-tier and lower-tier subcontractors and shall be available for any issues arising out of the contract or construction process. The public entity may set a reasonable threshold, not to exceed fifteen thousand dollars

($15,000), concerning the amount in controversy that must be at issue before a party may require other parties to participate in the dispute resolution process. The public entity may require that the costs of the process be divided between the parties to the dispute with at least one-third of the cost to be paid by the public entity, if the public entity is a party to the dispute. The public entity may require in its contracts that a party participate in mediation concerning a dispute as a precondition to initiating litigation concerning the dispute.

(g) Exceptions.—This section shall not apply to:

(1) The purchase and erection of prefabricated or relocatable buildings or portions thereof, except that portion of the work which must be performed at the construction site.

(2) The erection, construction, alteration, or repair of a building when the cost thereof is three hundred thousand dollars ($300,000) or less.

Notwithstanding the other provisions of this subsection, subsection (f1) of this section shall apply to any erection, construction, alteration, or repair of a building by a public entity.

§ 143-129. Procedure for letting of public contracts.

(a) Bidding Required.—No construction or repair work requiring the estimated expenditure of public money in an amount equal to or more than three hundred thousand dollars ($300,000) or purchase of apparatus, supplies, materials, or equipment requiring an estimated expenditure of public money in an amount equal to or more than ninety thousand dollars ($90,000) may be performed, nor may any contract be awarded therefor, by any board or governing body of the State, or of any institution of the State government, or of any political subdivision of the State, unless the provisions of this section are complied with.

For purchases of apparatus, supplies, materials, or equipment, the governing body of any political subdivision of the State may, subject to any restriction as to dollar amount, or other conditions that the governing body elects to impose, delegate to the manager or the chief purchasing official, or both, the authority to award contracts, reject bids, or readvertise to receive bids on behalf of the unit. Any person to whom authority is delegated under this subsection shall comply with the requirements of this Article that would otherwise apply to the governing body.

(b) Advertisement and Letting of Contracts.—Where the contract is to be let by a board or governing body of the State government or of a State institution, proposals shall be invited by advertisement in a newspaper having general circulation in the State of North Carolina. Where the contract is to be let by a political subdivision of the State, proposals shall be invited by advertisement in a newspaper having general circulation in the political subdivision or by electronic means, or both. A decision to advertise solely by electronic means, whether for particular contracts or generally for all contracts that are subject to this Article, shall be approved by the governing board of the political subdivision of the State at a regular meeting of the board.

The advertisements for bidders required by this section shall appear at a time where at least seven full days shall lapse between the date on which the notice appears and the date of the opening of bids. The advertisement shall: (i) state the time and place where plans and specifications of proposed work or a complete description of the apparatus, supplies, materials, or equipment may be had; (ii) state the time and place for opening of the proposals; and (iii) reserve to the board or governing body the right to reject any or all proposals.

Proposals may be rejected for any reason determined by the board or governing body to be in the best interest of the unit. However, the proposal shall not be rejected for the purpose of evading the provisions of this Article. No board or governing body of the State or political subdivision thereof may assume responsibility for construction or purchase contracts, or guarantee the payments of labor or materials therefor except under provisions of this Article.

All proposals shall be opened in public and the board or governing body shall award the contract to the lowest responsible bidder or bidders, taking into consideration quality, performance and the time specified in the proposals for the performance of the contract.

In the event the lowest responsible bids are in excess of the funds available for the project or purchase, the responsible board or governing body is authorized to enter into negotiations with the lowest responsible bidder above mentioned, making reasonable changes in the plans and specifications as may be necessary to bring the contract price within the funds available, and may award a contract to such bidder upon recommendation of the Department of Administration in the case of the State government or of a State institution or agency, or upon recommendation of the responsible commission, council or board in the case of a subdivision of the State, if such bidder will agree to perform the work or provide the apparatus, supplies, materials, or equipment at the negotiated price within the funds available therefor. If a contract cannot be let under the above conditions, the board or governing body is authorized to readvertise, as herein provided, after having made such changes in plans and specifications as may be necessary to bring the cost of the project or purchase within the funds available therefor. The procedure above specified may be repeated if necessary in order to secure an acceptable contract within the funds available therefor.

No proposal for construction or repair work may be considered or accepted by said board or governing body unless at the time of its filing the same shall be accompanied by a deposit with said board or governing body of cash, or a cashier's check, or a certified check on some bank or trust company insured by the Federal Deposit Insurance Corporation in an amount equal to not less than five percent (5%) of the proposal. In lieu of making the cash deposit as above provided, such bidder may file a bid bond executed by a corporate surety licensed under the laws of North Carolina to execute such bonds, conditioned that the surety will upon demand forthwith make payment to the obligee upon said bond if the bidder fails to execute the contract in accordance with the bid bond. This deposit shall be retained if the successful bidder fails to execute the contract within 10 days after the award or fails to give satisfactory surety as required herein.

Bids shall be sealed and the opening of an envelope or package with knowledge that it contains a bid or the disclosure or exhibition of the contents of any bid by anyone without the permission of the bidder prior to the time set for opening in the invitation to bid shall constitute a Class 1 misdemeanor.

(c) Contract Execution and Security.—All contracts to which this section applies shall be executed in writing. The board or governing body shall require the person to whom the award of a contract for construction or repair work is made to furnish bond as required by Article 3 of Chapter 44A; or require a deposit of money, certified check or government securities for the full amount of said contract to secure the faithful performance of the terms of said contract and the payment of all sums due for labor and materials in a manner consistent with Article 3 of Chapter 44A; and the contract shall not be altered except by written agreement of the contractor and the board or governing body. The surety bond or deposit required herein shall be deposited with the board or governing body for which the work is to be performed. When a deposit, other than a surety bond, is made with the board or governing body, the board or governing body assumes all the liabilities, obligations and duties of a surety as provided in Article 3 of Chapter 44A to the extent of said deposit.

The owning agency or the Department of Administration, in contracts involving a State agency, and the owning agency or the governing board, in contracts involving a political subdivision of the State, may reject the bonds of any surety company against which there is pending any unsettled claim or complaint made by a State agency or the owning agency or governing board of any political subdivision of the State arising out of any contract under which State funds, in contracts with the State, or funds of political subdivisions of the State, in contracts with such political subdivision, were expended, provided such claim or complaint has been pending more than 180 days.

(d) Use of Unemployment Relief Labor.—Nothing in this section shall operate so as to require any public agency to enter into a contract which will prevent the use of unemployment relief labor paid for in whole or in part by appropriations or funds furnished by the State or federal government.

(e) Exceptions.—The requirements of this Article do not apply to:

(1) The purchase, lease, or other acquisition of any apparatus, supplies, materials, or equipment from: (i) the United States of America or any agency thereof; or (ii) any other government unit or agency thereof within the United States. The Secretary of Administration or the governing board of any political subdivision of the State may designate any officer or employee of the State or political subdivision to enter a bid or bids in its behalf at any sale of apparatus, supplies, materials, equipment, or other property owned by: (i) the United States of America or any agency thereof; or (ii) any other governmental unit or agency thereof within the United States. The Secretary of Administration or the governing board of any political subdivision of the State may authorize the officer or employee to make any partial or down payment or payment in full that may be required by regulations of the governmental unit or agency disposing of the property.

(2) Cases of special emergency involving the health and safety of the people or their property.

(3) Purchases made through a competitive bidding group purchasing program, which is a formally organized program that offers competitively obtained purchasing services at discount prices to two or more public agencies.

(4) Construction or repair work undertaken during the progress of a construction or repair project initially begun pursuant to this section.

(5) Purchase of gasoline, diesel fuel, alcohol fuel, motor oil, fuel oil, or natural gas. These purchases are subject to G.S. 143-131.

(6) Purchases of apparatus, supplies, materials, or equipment when: (i) performance or price competition for a product are not available; (ii) a needed product is available from only one source of supply; or (iii) standardization or compatibility is the overriding consideration. Notwithstanding any other provision of this section, the governing board of a political subdivision of the State shall approve the purchases listed in the preceding sentence prior to the award of the contract.

In the case of purchases by hospitals, in addition to the other exceptions in this subsection, the provisions of this Article shall not apply when: (i) a particular medical item or prosthetic appliance is needed; (ii) a particular product is ordered by an attending physician for his patients; (iii) additional products are needed to complete an ongoing job or task; (iv) products are purchased for "over-the-counter" resale; (v) a particular product is needed or desired for experimental, developmental, or research work; or (vi) equipment is already installed, connected, and in service under a lease or other agreement and the governing body of the hospital determines that the equipment should be purchased. The governing body of a hospital shall keep a record of all purchases made pursuant to this subdivision. These records are subject to public inspection.

(7) Purchases of information technology through contracts established by the State Office of Information Technology Services as provided in G.S. 147-33.82(b) and G.S. 147-33.92(b).

(8) Guaranteed energy savings contracts, which are governed by Article 3B of Chapter 143 of the General Statutes.

(9) Purchases from contracts established by the State or any agency of the State, if the contractor is willing to extend to a political subdivision of the State the same or more favorable prices, terms, and conditions as established in the State contract.

(10) Purchase of used apparatus, supplies, materials, or equipment. For purposes of this subdivision, remanufactured, refabricated or demo apparatus, supplies, materials, or equipment are not included in the exception. A demo item is one that is used for demonstration and is sold by the manufacturer or retailer at a discount.

(11) Contracts by a public entity with a construction manager at risk executed pursuant to G.S. 143-128.1.

(f) Repealed by Session Laws 2001-328, s. 1, effective August 2, 2001.

(g) Waiver of Bidding for Previously Bid Contracts.—When the governing board of any political subdivision of the State, or the manager or purchasing official delegated authority under subsection (a) of this section, determines that it is in the best interest of the unit, the requirements of this section may be waived for the purchase of apparatus, supplies, materials, or equipment from any person or entity that has, within the previous 12 months, after having completed a public, formal bid process substantially similar to that required by this Article, contracted to furnish the apparatus, supplies, materials, or equipment to:

(1) The United States of America or any federal agency;

(2) The State of North Carolina or any agency or political subdivision of the State; or

(3) Any other state or any agency or political subdivision of that state,

if the person or entity is willing to furnish the items at the same or more favorable prices, terms, and conditions as those provided under the contract with the other unit or agency. Notwithstanding any other provision of this section, any purchase made under this subsection shall be approved by the governing body of the purchasing political subdivision of the State at a regularly scheduled meeting of the governing body no fewer than 10 days after publication of notice, in a newspaper of general circulation in the area served by the governing body, that a waiver of the bid procedure will be considered in order to contract with a qualified supplier pursuant to this section. Rules issued by the Secretary of Administration pursuant to G.S. 143-49(6) shall apply with respect to participation in State term contracts.

(h) Transportation Authority Purchases.—Notwithstanding any other provision of this section, any board or governing body of any regional public transportation authority, hereafter referred to as a "RPTA," created pursuant to Article 26 of Chapter 160A of the General Statutes, or a regional transportation authority, hereafter referred to as a "RTA," created pursuant to Article 27 of Chapter 160A of the General Statutes, may approve the entering into of any contract for the purchase, lease, or other acquisition of any apparatus, supplies, materials, or equipment without competitive bidding and without meeting the requirements of subsection (b) of this section if the following procurement by competitive proposal (Request for Proposal) method is followed.

The competitive proposal method of procurement is normally conducted with more than one source submitting an offer or proposal. Either a fixed price or cost reimbursement type contract is awarded. This method of procurement is generally used when conditions are not appropriate for the use of sealed bids. If this procurement method is used, all of the following requirements apply:

(1) Requests for proposals shall be publicized. All evaluation factors shall be identified along with their relative importance.

(2) Proposals shall be solicited from an adequate number of qualified sources.

(3) RPTAs or RTAs shall have a method in place for conducting technical evaluations of proposals received and selecting awardees, with the goal of promoting fairness and competition without requiring strict adherence to specifications or price in determining the most advantageous proposal.

(4) The award may be based upon initial proposals without further discussion or negotiation or, in the discretion of the evaluators, discussions or negotiations may be conducted either with all offerors or with those offerors determined to be within the competitive range, and one or more revised proposals or a best and final offer may be requested of all remaining offerors. The de-

tails and deficiencies of an offeror's proposal may not be disclosed to other offerors during any period of negotiation or discussion.

(5) The award shall be made to the responsible firm whose proposal is most advantageous to the RPTA's or the RTA's program with price and other factors considered.

The contents of the proposals shall not be public records until 14 days before the award of the contract.

The board or governing body of the RPTA or the RTA shall, at the regularly scheduled meeting, by formal motion make findings of fact that the procurement by competitive proposal (Request for Proposals) method of procuring the particular apparatus, supplies, materials, or equipment is the most appropriate acquisition method prior to the issuance of the requests for proposals and shall by formal motion certify that the requirements of this subsection have been followed before approving the contract.

Nothing in this subsection subjects a procurement by competitive proposal under this subsection to G.S. 143-49, 143-52, or 143-53.

RPTAs and RTAs may adopt regulations to implement this subsection.

§ 143-129.1. Withdrawal of bid.

A public agency may allow a bidder submitting a bid pursuant to G.S. 143-129 for construction or repair work or for the purchase of apparatus, supplies, materials, or equipment to withdraw his bid from consideration after the bid opening without forfeiture of his bid security if the price bid was based upon a mistake, which constituted a substantial error, provided the bid was submitted in good faith, and the bidder submits credible evidence that the mistake was clerical in nature as opposed to a judgment error, and was actually due to an unintentional and substantial arithmetic error or an unintentional omission of a substantial quantity of work, labor, apparatus, supplies, materials, equipment, or services made directly in the compilation of the bid, which unintentional arithmetic error or unintentional omission can be clearly shown by objective evidence drawn from inspection of the original work papers, documents or materials used in the preparation of the bid sought to be withdrawn. A request to withdraw a bid must be made in writing to the public agency which invited the proposals for the work prior to the award of the contract, but not later than 72 hours after the opening of bids, or for a longer period as may be specified in the instructions to bidders provided prior to the opening of bids.

If a request to withdraw a bid has been made in accordance with the provisions of this section, action on the remaining bids shall be considered, in accordance with North Carolina G.S. 143-129, as though said bid had not been received. Notwithstanding the foregoing, such bid shall be deemed to have been received for the purpose of complying with the requirements of G.S. 143-132. If the work or purchase is relet for bids, under no circumstances may the bidder who has filed a request to withdraw be permitted to rebid the work or purchase.

If a bidder files a request to withdraw his bid, the agency shall promptly hold a hearing thereon. The agency shall give to the withdrawing bidder reasonable notice of the time and place of any such hearing. The bidder, either in person or through counsel, may appear at the hearing and present any additional facts and arguments in support of his request to withdraw his bid. The agency shall issue a written ruling allowing or denying the request to withdraw within five days after the hearing. If the agency finds that the price bid was based upon a mistake of the type described in the first paragraph of this section, then the agency shall issue a ruling permitting the bidder to withdraw without forfeiture of the bidder's security. If the agency finds that the price bid was based upon a mistake not of the type described in the first paragraph of this section, then the agency shall issue a ruling denying the request to withdraw and requiring the forfeiture of the bidder's security. A denial by the agency of the request to withdraw a bid shall have the same effect as if an award had been made to the bidder and a refusal by the bidder to accept had been made, or as if there had been a refusal to enter into the contract, and the bidder's bid deposit or bid bond shall be forfeited.

In the event said ruling denies the request to withdraw the bid, the bidder shall have the right, within 20 days after receipt of said ruling, to contest the matter by the filing of a civil action in any court of competent jurisdiction of the State of North Carolina. The procedure shall be the same as in all civil actions except all issues of law and fact and every other issue shall be tried de novo by the judge without jury; provided that the matter may be referred in the instances and in the manner provided for by North Carolina G.S. 1A-1, Rule 53, as amended. Notwithstanding the foregoing, if the public agency involved is the Department of Administration, it may follow its normal rules and regulations with respect to contested matters, as opposed to following the administrative procedures set forth herein. If it is finally determined that the bidder did not have the right to withdraw his bid pursuant to the provisions of this section, the bidder's security shall be forfeited. Every bid bond or bid deposit given by a bidder to a public agency pursuant to G.S. 143-129 shall be conclusively presumed to have been given in accordance with this section, whether or not it be so drawn as to conform to this section. This section shall be conclusively presumed to have been written into every bid bond given pursuant to G.S. 143-129.

Neither the agency nor any elected or appointed official, employee, representative or agent of such agency shall incur any liability or surcharge, in the absence of fraud or collusion, by permitting the withdrawal of a bid pursuant to the provisions of this section.

No withdrawal of the bid which would result in the award of the contract on another bid of the same bidder, his partner, or to a corporation or business venture owned by or in which he has an interest shall be permitted. No bidder who is permitted to withdraw a bid shall supply any material or labor to, or perform any subcontract or work agreement for, any person to whom a contract or subcontract is awarded in the performance of the contract for which the withdrawn bid was submitted, without the prior written approval of the agency. Whoever violates the provisions of the foregoing sentence shall be guilty of a Class 1 misdemeanor.

§ 143-129.7. Purchase with trade-in of apparatus, supplies, materials, and equipment.

Notwithstanding the provisions of Article 12 of Chapter 160A of the General Statutes, municipalities, counties, and other political subdivisions of the State may include in specifications for the purchase of apparatus, supplies, materials, or equipment an opportunity for bidders to purchase as "trade-in" specified personal property owned by the municipality, county, or other political subdivision, and the awarding authority may award a contract for both the purchase of the apparatus, supplies, materials, or equipment and the sale of trade-in property, taking into consideration the amount offered on the trade-in when applying the criteria for award established in this Article.

§ 143-129.8. Purchase of information technology goods and services.

(a) In recognition of the complex and innovative nature of information technology goods and services and of the desirability of a single point of responsibility for contracts that include combinations of purchase of goods, design, installation, training, operation, maintenance, and related services, a political subdivision of the State may contract for information technology, as defined in G.S. 147-33.81(2), using the procedure set forth in this section, in addition to or instead of any other procedure available under North Carolina law.

(b) Contracts for information technology may be entered into under a request for proposals procedure that satisfies the following minimum requirements:

(1) Notice of the request for proposals shall be given in accordance with G.S. 143-129(a).

(2) Contracts shall be awarded to the person or entity that submits the best overall proposal as determined by the awarding authority. Factors to be considered in awarding contracts shall be identified in the request for proposals.

(c) The awarding authority may use procurement methods set forth in G.S. 143-135.9 in developing and evaluating requests for proposals under this section. The awarding authority may negotiate with any proposer in order to obtain a final contract that best meets the needs of the awarding authority. Negotiations allowed under this section shall not alter the contract beyond the scope of the original request for proposals in a manner that: (i) deprives the proposers or potential proposers of a fair opportunity to compete for the contract; and (ii) would have resulted in the award of the contract to a different person or entity if the alterations had been included in the request for proposals.

(d) Proposals submitted under this section shall not be subject to public inspection until a contract is awarded.

§ 143-129.9. Alternative competitive bidding methods.

(a) A political subdivision of the State may use any of the following methods to obtain competitive bids for the purchase of apparatus, supplies, materials, or equipment as an alternative to the otherwise applicable requirements in this Article:

(1) Reverse auction. - For purposes of this section, "reverse auction" means a real-time purchasing process in which bidders compete to provide goods at the lowest selling price in an open and interactive environment. The bidders' prices may be revealed during the reverse auction. A reverse auction may be conducted by the political subdivision or by a third party under contract with the political subdivision. A political subdivision may also conduct a reverse auction through the State electronic procurement system, and compliance with the procedures and requirements of the State's reverse auction process satisfies the political subdivision's obligations under this Article.

(2) Electronic bidding. - A political subdivision may receive bids electronically in addition to or instead of paper bids. Procedures for receipt of electronic bids for contracts that are subject to the requirements of G.S. 143-129 shall be designed to ensure the security, authenticity, and confidentiality of the bids to at least the same extent as is provided for with sealed paper bids.

(b) The requirements for advertisement of bidding opportunities, timeliness of the receipt of bids, the standard for the award of contracts, and all other requirements in this Article that are not inconsistent with the methods authorized in this section shall apply to contracts awarded under this section.

(c) Reverse auctions shall not be utilized for the purchase or acquisition of construction aggregates, including, but not limited to, crushed stone, sand, and gravel.

§ 143-131. When counties, cities, towns and other subdivisions may let contracts on informal bids.

(a) All contracts for construction or repair work or for the purchase of apparatus, supplies, materials, or equipment, involving the expenditure of public money in the amount of five thousand dollars ($5,000) or more, but less than the limits prescribed in G.S. 143-129, made by any officer, department, board, or commission of any county, city, town, or other subdivision of this State shall be made after informal bids have been secured. All such contracts shall be awarded to the lowest responsible, responsive bidder, taking into consideration quality, performance, and the time specified in the bids for the performance of the contract. It shall be the duty of any officer, department, board, or commission entering into such contract to keep a record of all bids submitted, and such record shall not be subject to public inspection until the contract has been awarded.

(b) All public entities shall solicit minority participation in contracts for the erection, construction, alteration or repair of any building awarded pursuant to this section. The public entity shall maintain a record of contractors solicited and shall document efforts to recruit minority business participation in those contracts. Nothing in this section shall be construed to require formal advertisement of bids. All data, including the type of project, total dollar value of the project, dollar value of minority business participation on each project, and documentation of efforts to recruit minority participation shall be reported to the Department of Administration, Office for Historically Underutilized Business, upon the completion of the project.

§ 143-132. Minimum number of bids for public contracts.

(a) No contract to which G.S. 143-129 applies for construction or repairs shall be awarded by any board or governing body of the State, or any subdivision thereof, unless at least three competitive bids have been received from reputable and qualified contractors regularly engaged in their respective lines of endeavor; however, this section shall not apply to contracts which are negotiated as provided for in G.S. 143-129. Provided that if after advertisement for bids as required by G.S. 143-129, not as many as three competitive bids have been received from reputable and qualified contractors regularly engaged in their respective lines of endeavor, said board or governing body of the State agency or of a county, city, town or other subdivision of the State shall again advertise for bids; and if as a result of such second advertisement, not as many as three competitive bids from reputable and qualified contractors are received, such board or governing body may then let the contract to the lowest responsible bidder submitting a bid for such project, even though only one bid is received.

(b) For purposes of contracts bid in the alternative between the separate-prime and single-prime contracts, pursuant to G.S. 143-128(d1) each single-prime bid shall constitute a competitive bid in each of the four subdivisions or branches of work listed in G.S. 143-128(a), and each full set of separate-prime bids shall constitute a competitive single-prime bid in meeting the requirements of subsection (a) of this section. If there are at least three single-prime bids but there is not at least one full set of separate-prime bids, no separate-prime bids shall be opened.

(c) The State Building Commission shall develop guidelines no later than January 1, 1991, governing the opening of bids pursuant to this Article. These guidelines shall be distributed to all public bodies subject to this Article. The guidelines shall not be subject to the provisions of Chapter 150B of the General Statutes.

§ 143-133. No evasion permitted.

No bill or contract shall be divided for the purpose of evading the provisions of this Article.

§ 143-135. Limitation of application of Article.

Except for the provisions of G.S. 143-129 requiring bids for the purchase of apparatus, supplies, materials or equipment, this Article shall not apply to construction or repair work undertaken by the State or by subdivisions of the State of North Carolina (i) when the work is performed by duly elected officers or agents using force account qualified labor on the permanent payroll of the agency concerned and (ii) when either the total cost of the project, including without limitation all direct and indirect costs of labor, services, materials, supplies and equipment, does not exceed one hundred twenty-five thousand dollars ($125,000) or the total cost of labor on the project does not exceed fifty thousand dollars ($50,000). This force account work shall be subject to the approval of the Director of the Budget in the case of State agencies, of the responsible commission, council, or board in the case of subdivisions of the State. Complete and accurate records of the entire cost of such work, including without limitation, all direct and indirect costs of labor, services, materials, supplies and equipment performed and furnished in the prosecution and completion thereof, shall be maintained by such agency, commission, council or board for the inspection by the general public. Construction or repair work undertaken pursuant to this section shall not be divided for the purposes of evading the provisions of this Article.

General Statutes of North Carolina

Chapter 153A. Counties.

Article 2. Corporate Powers.

§ 153A-13. Continuing contracts.

A county may enter into continuing contracts, some portion or all of which are to be performed in ensuing fiscal years. In order to enter into such a contract, the county must have sufficient funds appropriated to meet any amount to be paid under the contract in the fiscal year in which it is made. In each year, the board of commissioners shall appropriate sufficient funds to meet the amounts to be paid during the fiscal year under continuing contracts previously entered into.

Article 23. Miscellaneous Provisions.

§ 153A-449. Contracts with private entities.

A county may contract with and appropriate money to any person, association, or corporation, in order to carry out any public purpose that the county is authorized by law to engage in.

General Statutes of North Carolina

Chapter 159. Local Government Finance.

Subchapter III. Budgets and Fiscal Control.

Article 3. The Local Government Budget and Fiscal Control Act.

Part 3. Fiscal Control.

§ 159-28. Budgetary accounting for appropriations.

(a) Incurring Obligations.—No obligation may be incurred in a program, function, or activity accounted for in a fund included in the budget ordinance unless the budget ordinance includes an appropriation authorizing the obligation and an unencumbered balance remains in the appropriation sufficient to pay in the current fiscal year the sums obligated by the transaction for the current fiscal year. No obligation may be incurred for a capital project or a grant project authorized by a project ordinance unless that project ordinance includes an appropriation authorizing the obligation and an unencumbered balance remains in the appropriation sufficient to pay the sums obligated by the transaction. If an obligation is evidenced by a contract or agreement requiring the payment of money or by a purchase order for supplies and materials, the contract, agreement, or purchase order shall include on its face a certificate stating that the instrument has been preaudited to assure compliance with this subsection. The certificate, which shall be signed by the finance officer or any deputy finance officer approved for this purpose by the governing board, shall take substantially the following form:

> "This instrument has been preaudited in the manner required by the Local Government Budget and Fiscal Control Act.
>
> ______________________________
>
> (Signature of finance officer)."

Certificates in the form prescribed by G.S. 153-130 or 160-411 as those sections read on June 30, 1973, or by G.S. 159-28(b) as that section read on June 30, 1975, are sufficient until supplies of forms in existence on June 30, 1975, are exhausted.

An obligation incurred in violation of this subsection is invalid and may not be enforced. The finance officer shall establish procedures to assure compliance with this subsection.

(b) Disbursements.—When a bill, invoice, or other claim against a local government or public authority is presented, the finance officer shall either approve or disapprove the necessary disbursement. If the claim involves a program, function, or activity accounted for in a fund included in the budget ordinance or a capital project or a grant project authorized by a project ordinance, the finance officer may approve the claim only if

> (1) He determines the amount to be payable and
>
> (2) The budget ordinance or a project ordinance includes an appropriation authorizing the expenditure and either (i) an encumbrance has been previously created for the transaction or (ii) an unencumbered balance remains in the appropriation sufficient to pay the amount to be disbursed.

The finance officer may approve a bill, invoice, or other claim requiring disbursement from an intragovernmental service fund or trust or agency fund not included in the budget ordinance, only if the amount claimed is determined to be payable. A bill, invoice, or other claim may not be paid unless it has been approved by the finance officer or, under subsection (c) of this section, by the governing board. The finance officer shall establish procedures to assure compliance with this subsection.

(c) Governing Board Approval of Bills, Invoices, or Claims.—The governing board may, as permitted by this subsection, approve a bill, invoice, or other claim against the local government or public authority that has been disapproved by the finance officer. It may not approve a claim for which no appropriation appears in the budget ordinance or in a project ordinance, or for which the appropriation contains no encumbrance and the unencumbered balance is less than the amount to be paid. The governing board shall approve payment by formal resolution stating the board's reasons for allowing the bill, invoice, or other claim. The resolution shall be entered in the minutes together with the names of those voting in the affirmative. The chairman of the board or some other member designated for this purpose shall sign the certificate on the check or draft given in payment of the bill, invoice, or other claim. If payment results in a violation of law, each member of the board voting to allow payment is jointly and severally liable for the full amount of the check or draft given in payment.

(d) Payment.—A local government or public authority may not pay a bill, invoice, salary, or other claim except by a check or draft on an official depository or by a bank wire transfer from an official depository. Except as provided in this subsection each check or draft on an official depository shall bear on its face a certificate signed by the finance officer or a deputy finance officer approved for this purpose by the governing board (or signed by the chairman or some other member of the board pursuant to subsection (c) of this section). The certificate shall take substantially the following form:

> "This disbursement has been approved as required by the Local Government Budget and Fiscal Control Act.
>
> ______________________________
>
> (Signature of finance officer)."

Certificates in the form prescribed by G.S. 153-131 or 160-411.1 as those sections read on June 30, 1973, or by G.S. 159-28(a) as that section read on June 30, 1975, are sufficient until supplies in existence on June 30, 1975, are exhausted.

No certificate is required on payroll checks or drafts on an imprest account in an official depository, if the check or draft depositing the funds in the imprest account carried a signed certificate.

(e) Penalties.—If an officer or employee of a local government or public authority incurs an obligation or pays out or causes to be paid out any funds in violation of this section, he and the sureties on his official bond are liable for any sums so committed or disbursed. If the finance officer or any properly designated deputy finance officer gives a false certificate to any contract, agreement, purchase order, check, draft, or other document, he and the sureties on his official bond are liable for any sums illegally committed or disbursed thereby.

General Statutes of North Carolina

Chapter 160A. Cities and Towns.

Article 3. Contracts.

§ 160A-16. Contracts to be in writing; exception.

All contracts made by or on behalf of a city shall be in writing. A contract made in violation of this section shall be void and unenforceable unless it is expressly ratified by the council.

§ 160A-17. Continuing contracts.

A city is authorized to enter into continuing contracts, some portion or all of which are to be performed in ensuing fiscal years. Sufficient funds shall be appropriated to meet any amount to be paid under the contract in the fiscal year in which it is made, and in each ensuing fiscal year, the council shall appropriate sufficient funds to meet the amounts to be paid during the fiscal year under continuing contracts previously entered into.

§ 160A-17.1. Grants from other governments.

The governing body of any city or county is hereby authorized to make contracts for and to accept grants-in-aid and loans from the federal and State governments and their agencies for constructing, expanding, maintaining, and operating any project or facility, or performing any function, which such city or county may be authorized by general law or local act to provide or perform.

In order to exercise the authority granted by this section, the governing body of any city or county may:

(1) Enter into and carry out contracts with the State or federal government or any agency or institution thereof under which such government, agency, or institution grants financial or other assistance to the city or county;

(2) Accept such assistance or funds as may be granted or loaned by the State or federal government with or without such a contract;

(3) Agree to and comply with any lawful and reasonable conditions which are imposed upon such grants or loans;

(3a) Agree to and comply with minimum minority business enterprise participation requirements established by the federal government and its agencies in projects financed by federal grants-in-aid or loans, by including such minimum requirements in the specifications for contracts to perform all or part of such projects and awarding bids pursuant to G.S. 143-129 and 143-131, if applicable, to the lowest responsible bidder or bidders meeting these and any other specifications.

(4) Make expenditures from any funds so granted.

§ 160A-20.1. Contracts with private entities.

A city may contract with and appropriate money to any person, association, or corporation, in order to carry out any public purpose that the city is authorized by law to engage in.

Article 20. Interlocal Cooperation.

Part 1. Joint Exercise of Powers.

§ 160A-461. Interlocal cooperation authorized.

Any unit of local government in this State and any one or more other units of local government in this State or any other state (to the extent permitted by the laws of the other state) may enter into contracts or agreements with each other in order to execute any undertaking. The contracts and agreements shall be of reasonable duration, as determined by the participating units, and shall be ratified by resolution of the governing board of each unit spread upon its minutes.

Appendix 3

Interpretations of the "Piggybacking" Exception to North Carolina's Formal Bidding Requirements

In 1997 the General Assembly added an exception to the competitive bidding laws that is commonly referred to as the "piggybacking" exception. This exception can be found in Section 143-129(g) of the North Carolina General Statutes (hereinafter, G.S.) and is entitled, "Waiver of Bidding for Previously Bid Contracts." The text of the exception, along with questions and answers interpreting it, are set out below.

The exception reads as follows:

> When the governing board of any municipality, county, or other subdivision of the State, or the manager or purchasing official delegated authority under subsection (a) of this section, determines that it is in the best interest of the unit, the requirements of this section may be waived for the purchase of apparatus, supplies, materials, or equipment from any person or entity that has, within the previous 12 months, after having completed a public, formal bid process substantially similar to that required by this Article, contracted to furnish the apparatus, supplies, materials, or equipment to:
>
> (1) The United States of America or any federal agency;
> (2) The State of North Carolina or any agency or political subdivision of the State; or
> (3) Any other state or any agency or political subdivision of that state, if the person or entity is willing to furnish the items at the same or more favorable prices, terms, and conditions as those provided under the contract with the other unit or agency.
>
> Notwithstanding any other provision of this section, any purchase made under this subsection shall be approved by the governing body of the purchasing municipality, county, or other political subdivision of the State at a regularly scheduled meeting of the governing body no fewer than 10 days after publication of notice, in a newspaper of general circulation in the area served by the governing body, that a waiver of the bid procedure will be considered in order to contract with a qualified supplier pursuant to this section. Rules issued by the Secretary of Administration pursuant to G.S. 143-49(6) shall apply with respect to participation in State term contracts.

Note: This material represents a slightly revised version of a *Local Government Law Bulletin* that was published by the School of Government under the same title.

Questions and Answers

1. Does the piggybacking exception apply to construction or repair contracts?

No. It only applies to contracts for the purchase of apparatus, supplies, materials, or equipment.

2. Does the piggybacking exception apply to contracts in the informal range?

No. The exception is contained in the formal bidding statute (G.S. 143-129), and there is no indication of legislative intent to extend it to informal bids, which are governed by G.S. 143-131. More importantly, an exception is not really necessary to piggyback on a contract in the informal range (contracts costing from $5,000 to $90,000). If a seller is willing to extend pricing established in prior contracts, the local government can simply accept the seller's price as an informal bid, seek additional bids (no minimum number is required but competition should be sought), and award to the lowest responsible bidder. No advertisement or governing board action is required for contracts in the informal range.

3. When a local government piggybacks on another contract, does the local government actually become a party to that contract?

No. In this sense, the term "piggybacking" is actually not an accurate description of what the statute allows. The exception allows a local government to enter into a new and separate contract with a vendor who has contracted with another public agency and who is willing to extend the same or more favorable prices and terms to the local government.

4. Are local governments still required to "sign on" in advance in order to participate in state contracts? How should local governments interpret the language in the statute about complying with Department of Administration rules for participating in state term contracts?

The piggybacking exception allows local governments to purchase directly from a state contract vendor without agreeing to be a party to the state contract in advance as long as the state contract was entered into within the past twelve months. Local governments can also purchase directly from a state contract under a separate exception covering these purchases. (See Question 41.i.) When a local government uses the piggybacking exception to purchase from a state contract vendor the local government does not become a party to the state contract and is not "participating" in the state contract. As noted earlier, the piggybacking exception allows a local government to enter into a new and separate contract with a vendor who has contracted with another unit. The vendor is not legally obligated to extend to the local government the state contract prices and terms; but if the vendor is willing to do so, the purchase can be made after the procedures in G.S. 143-129(g) are followed.

To participate in a state contract, on the other hand, local governments must comply with the procedures and regulations established by the Department of Administration through the Division of Purchase and Contract. If a local government takes this route, the vendor is obligated to extend the state contract prices and terms to the participating unit, and the participating unit is obligated during the term of the contract to purchase from the state contract vendor all of its needs for the items covered by the contract. The effect of agreeing to participate in a state contract is that the local government is bound to the same extent as if it had awarded the contract itself.

This means that if the local government wants to be guaranteed the state contract price, it must participate in the contract in accordance with the Division of Purchase and Contract procedures. If the local government does not wish to be bound by the state contract it is free to purchase from a willing state contract vendor without signing on in advance under the state contract exception, or under the piggybacking exception. If a local government uses the piggybacking exception, however, the twelve-month limitation and the requirement of notice and board approval in G.S. 143-129(g) must be met. As noted earlier, if a contract is in the informal range, the local government can purchase from the state contract vendor without going through the piggybacking procedure and without signing on in advance as long as it complies with the informal bidding procedures. A listing of state term contracts is available through the Internet at the State Purchase and Contract Web site: www.doa.state.nc.us/PandC/stdhp.htm.

5. What information should be contained in the notice that must be published under the piggybacking exception?

The statute does not specify, but I recommend that the notice contain at least the following information: (1) a general description of the item(s) to be purchased (the anticipated quantity probably does not need to be included, but could be if the unit feels the information would be useful); (2) the identity of the supplier; (3) the city, state, or other agency with whom the supplier has contracted within the past twelve months (the date the contract was entered into might be useful, but probably is not essential); and (4) the date of the regular board meeting at which the board will consider the waiver of bidding.

A local government may also want to list the name and phone number of a person within the unit to contact for more information. This would allow interested competitors to contact the appropriate person to present an alternative offer prior to the board's award of a contract under the exception (see discussion below about alternate offers).

A sample notice might read (substitute information appropriate to your unit of government for material in brackets):

> "The [Landville Board of Commissioners] will consider a waiver of competitive bidding under G.S. 143-129(g) at its regular meeting on [August 22, 1998] for the purchase of [two front end loaders] from [Heavy Duty Equipment, Inc.], the seller having agreed to extend to [Landville] the same or

more favorable prices and terms set forth in its contract with [Greenleaf County], entered into on [November 12, 1997]. For additional information, contact [Pat Johnson, Landville Purchasing Director] at [phone number, fax number, e-mail address]." Return to List of Questions

6. Is a local government required to accept bids offered by other suppliers during the process of purchasing under the piggybacking exception?

Although the statute does not require this, it seems logical that one purpose of the notice requirement is to let potential competitors know about the board's intent to award a contract without bidding. If an alternative proposal is made that would result in savings to the unit, or if the responsible person otherwise becomes aware that it would be in the best interest of the unit to obtain competition, he or she should abandon the piggybacking option in favor of receiving formal bids. It does not appear that board action would be required to abandon the piggybacking option and initiate a formal bidding process.

7. Does the unit of government that originally contracted with the vendor have to take any action prior to piggybacking by a North Carolina local government?

No. No action is required by the prior contracting agency because, as noted earlier, the North Carolina local government is not becoming a party to the prior contract. Instead, the exception allows the local government to enter into a new and separate contract with the vendor. Some cooperative purchasing contracts have provisions that require the vendor to make its prices available to other local governments, but the exception in the North Carolina statute does not require such a provision to have been included in order for the piggybacking to occur. It may be necessary for the local government to contact the original contracting agency, however, to verify that a public bidding process was undertaken, and to verify the terms and date of the original contract.

8. How must a local government document the existence of the prior contract in order to use the piggybacking exception?

The statute does not require any specific proof of the existence of the prior contract, but local governments should not rely upon the representations of a vendor or other person without verification. If it turns out that there was no contract, or that the contract is more than twelve months old, the local government is not entitled to a waiver of bidding and the resulting contract, if challenged, would be held to be void. The local government could require the vendor to present a certified copy of the contract or a copy of the contract accompanied by a verification letter from the original contracting agency, or the local government could simply contact the agency and verify the information directly. The local government should also obtain information about the bidding process that was used for the contract to make sure it is similar to North Carolina's formal bidding statute, as required under the exception.

9. From what date does the twelve-month period begin to run?

The statute does not provide much guidance on this question. It says that the seller must have "contracted" within the previous twelve months. Although there are several possible interpretations of this language, the most conservative and, therefore, the safest interpretation is that the period begins to run from the date the contract became effective—that is, when the last act necessary to create a mutually binding contract occurred. Where a contract is evidenced by a purchase order, there is some question about when the contract actually comes into being since there is often no separate document signed by the vendor. In such cases, it would be appropriate to use the date of the purchase order as the contract date.

10. What if the original contract was entered into more than twelve months ago, but it has been renewed within the past twelve months?

If a renewal option was a part of the original contract, then the renewal does not amount to a new contract, but is instead a continuation of the original contract. In such a case it appears that a contract would not meet the requirement for piggybacking. If, on the other hand, a renewal was not a part of the original contract, but is a new contract, an argument could be made that the new contract is within the twelve-month limit. A counter argument could be raised, however, that the new contract was not formally bid, but perhaps a court would view the new contract as having resulted from the original bid process.

It is also possible that a court would interpret the statute as not allowing piggybacking on a renewed contract in either case. One interpretation of the intent behind the twelve-month limitation is that it is designed to ensure that the bidding process undertaken for the original contract is recent enough to justify piggybacking without rebidding. The statute may reflect an assumption that a bidding process has occurred just before the contract was issued and, thus, roughly within the past year. If a local government piggybacks on a contract that was bid three years ago but that was renewed within the past year, a court may find that the original bidding process is too old and does not reflect the current competitive market. Under this reasoning, a court might rule that the use of the exception on a renewed contract violates the intent of the statute.

11. What are the key aspects of a "public, formal bid process" that must be present in order for a prior contract to be eligible for piggybacking under the exception?

Again, the statute is not specific on this point. Based on a review of competitive bidding requirements from other jurisdictions, the key aspects of a public competitive bidding process typically include (1) public advertisement or other broadly announced and generally accessible notice of an opportunity to bid and (2) sealed, competitive bids. Most competitive bidding procedures from other jurisdictions probably satisfy this requirement.

12. Can a local government piggyback on its own contract?

Although this probably wasn't how the exception was intended to be used, the statute appears to allow it. The unit would still have to comply with the notice and board approval requirements under the exception even though the prior contract was already approved by the same board. A better way to accomplish this result, however, is to include an "additional quantities" clause in the specifications for the initial contract. This would authorize the local government, at its option, to obtain additional quantities of items under contract at the same price (usually for a specified period) and alleviates the need, when additional quantities are desired, either to conduct a second bidding procedure, or to use the piggybacking procedure to avoid bidding. The specifications for the initial bid should clearly indicate that an additional quantities clause will be a part of the contract.

13. Can a local government piggyback on a contract that was entered into under the piggybacking exception (piggyback on a piggybacked contract)?

Although the statute does not specifically address this issue, it does not appear that this would be legal. The statute requires the original contract to have been entered into following a public, formal bid process substantially similar to that required under G.S. 143-129. Although it could be argued that since the piggybacking exception is contained in G.S. 143-129 the contract complies with that statute's requirements, the better interpretation is that a contract entered into under the piggybacking exception does not satisfy the requirement of formal, public bidding.

14. Can a local government purchasing under the exception make any changes in the terms of the original contract if the vendor will agree to them?

The statute specifically allows the vendor to provide more favorable terms or prices than those offered under the original contract. It is probably also acceptable for the local government to purchase a different quantity of items or to agree to a different duration term for the new contract than in the original contract. Great caution should be exercised, however, in making other types of changes that might place the new contract outside the scope of the exception. Since the statute authorizes the purchase of the same items that were purchased under the original contract, a substantial change in the character of the items to be purchased under the new contract may render the contract void. For example, if the original contract was for two-door vehicles and the local government wishes to purchase a four-door vehicle, such a purchase could not legitimately be made under the piggybacking exception. A closer case would involve a change in the options chosen by the local government. It may be legitimate for the local government to choose options that were not chosen by the original contracting agency without undermining the use of the exception as long as the options are minor and would not have been likely to change the outcome of the original bid had they been included in the solicitation by the other public agency.

There is no way to establish a hard rule on this issue, but local governments should consider whether modifications to the original contract would have been outside the scope of what was originally bid or would substantially increase the price. If so, a separate bidding process should be undertaken instead of using the piggybacking exception, even if the contractor has offered competitive prices. The exception does not authorize simply entering into negotiations with a vendor who has contracted with another public agency. Local governments should be cautious when purchasing under the exception to stay within the limits of its scope.

Appendix 4
Understanding the Responsiveness Requirement in Competitive Bidding

Public contracts are subject to competitive bidding requirements for several reasons. One is to secure goods and services at competitive (low) prices. Another is to provide a contracting process that is open and visible to the public. Yet a third is to guarantee fairness in the contracting process, particularly to those who seek contracting opportunities: the bidders. These goals do not always work in harmony with each other. In some cases, for example, the best interest of the public agency might appear to favor accepting a bid despite a defect that it might contain. For some kinds of defects, however, the law limits the agency's discretion to take that action.

The legal concept at issue in this situation is the requirement of "responsiveness." This legal limitation, in effect, elevates the interest of fairness to the bidders over the agency's interest in expediency or in obtaining a low price. Because the process of determining when bids are responsive often presents a conflict between the agency's interest and that of the bidders, it is important for public officials to understand the limitations the law imposes on their discretion in this area.

This bulletin discusses the legal standard for determining when bids are responsive, and summarizes rulings in cases evaluating a variety of commonly encountered bid irregularities. The analysis presented draws substantially on cases from jurisdictions outside North Carolina. Though there is relatively little case law on this subject from the North Carolina courts, the legal standard on this issue is sufficiently consistent across the country that cases from other jurisdictions provide useful and reliable guidance.

Defining Responsiveness

In order for a bidder to be eligible for the award of a contract, his or her bid must be responsive. Put simply, a responsive bid is one that meets the

---

Note: This material represents a slightly revised version of a *Local Government Law Bulletin* that was published by the School of Government under the same title.

requirements established in the specifications and under the applicable law governing the bidding procedure. As described in one case:

> The requirement that a bid be responsive is designed to avoid unfairness to other contractors who submitted a sealed bid on the understanding that they must comply with all of the specifications and conditions in the invitation for bids, and who could have made a better proposal if they imposed conditions upon or variances from the contractual terms the government had specified.[1]

Though it is simple to describe, the concept of responsiveness is often complicated to apply. Public agencies and courts have long recognized that neither bids nor specifications are perfect. Specifications may be purposefully broad in order to avoid limiting competition. Bids in response to these specifications will naturally contain variations in the products or services offered. In addition, bids are often prepared under extreme time pressure due to the bidders' practice of receiving pricing up to the last minute before the bid opening. These conditions result in mistakes, both in the form and in the substance of bids submitted.

In anticipation of this built-in lack of perfection, most bid specifications contain standard language reserving to the public body or its agents the right to "waive minor irregularities," or similar language. Although this statement is intended to provide the agency maximum discretion in evaluating bids, if that evaluation is challenged, a court will protect the interest of fairness in the bidding process and may override the public agency's judgment about what constitutes a "minor irregularity." Cases in this area focus on the question of whether a particular irregularity is so significant that its waiver creates a situation that is unfair to the other bidders. Stated another way, the question in responsiveness cases is: When does the law *require* the public agency to reject a bid and *prohibit* the agency from waiving a deviation from specifications as a minor irregularity?

Despite variation in statutory provisions governing the award of public contracts, the legal standard established by the courts for evaluating responsiveness is remarkably consistent. Although there is only one North Carolina case on this subject, it is consistent with case law elsewhere in the country. In *Professional Food Services Management v. North Carolina Department of Administration*[2] the North Carolina Court of Appeals ruled that a responsive bid is one that conforms substantially to the specifications, and does not contain a "material variance." The court went on to define a material variance as one that gives a bidder "an advantage or benefit not enjoyed by the other bidders."[3]

A similar standard is contained in the Federal Acquisition Regulations (FAR), which govern contracting by federal agencies. Those regulations provide that "to be considered for award, a bid must comply in all material respects with the invitation for bids. Such compliance enables all bidders to stand on an equal footing and maintains the integrity of the sealed bidding system."[4]

---

1. Toyo Menka Kaisha, Ltd. v. U.S., 597 F.2d 1371, 1377 (1979) [citing R. Nash & J. Cibinic, Federal Procurement Law, 260 (3rd ed. 1977)].
2. 109 N.C. App. 265, 426 S.E.2d 447 (1993).
3. Professional Food Serv. Management, 109 N.C. App. at 269, 426 S.E.2d at 450 [citing 64 Am.Jur.2d , Public Works and Contracts, §59 (1972)].
4. 48 C.F.R. § 14.301(a) (1988).

Before discussing the application of this standard to commonly encountered bid defects, it is important to note several preliminary issues: (1) the difference between responsiveness and responsibility; (2) the standard of review courts use when a public agency's decision to waive a bid defect is challenged; and (3) the difference between defects that may be resolved as a matter of responsiveness and defects that allow the bidder to withdraw his or her bid due to a mistake.

Distinguishing between Responsiveness and Responsibility

As noted earlier, a public agency must determine that a bid is responsive before the bid may be eligible for award. As such, responsiveness is a threshold determination in the bid evaluation process that comes before a recommendation can be made on the award of the contract. As a legal matter, a bid that does not substantially meet specifications is not eligible to be the basis for the award of a contract. As one court has stated it, "[r]esponsiveness addresses whether a bidder has promised to perform in the precise manner requested by the government. . . . A responsive bid is one that, if accepted by the government as submitted will obligate the contractor to perform the exact thing called for in the solicitation."[5] In contrast, responsibility relates to the issue of performance by the contractor in terms of the skill, experience, financial resources, and integrity necessary to complete the requirements of the contract.[6] The difference between the two concepts is well stated in the following description by a court:

> In terms of identifying whether a particular requirement is related to responsiveness or responsibility, the distinction is *whether the bidder will conform* to the [invitation for bids], as opposed to *how the bidder will accomplish conformance*. Stated another way, the concept of responsibility specifically concerns the question of a bidder's performance capability, as opposed to its promise to perform the contract, which is a matter of responsiveness.[7]

Thus, while responsibility focuses on the qualifications and characteristics of the bidder, responsiveness is a determination that compares the bid to the specifications. In evaluating responsiveness, the qualifications of the bidder generally are not relevant.

Judicial Review of Responsiveness Determinations

There are several common factual situations that are presented in legal challenges involving the responsiveness issue. One involves a bidder challenging the rejection of his or her bid, arguing that the public agency erroneously

---

5. Bean Dredging Corp. v. U.S., 22 Cl. Ct. 519, 522–23 (1991) (internal citations omitted).

6. Kinsey Contracting Co. v. City of Fayetteville, 106 N.C. App. 383, 385, 416 S.E.2d 607, 609, *disc. review denied,* 332 N.C. 345, 421 S.E.2d 149 (1992).

7. Okada Trucking Co. v. Board of Water Supply, 40 P.3d 946, 958–59 (Haw. Ct. App, 2001) (emphasis added), *vacated and remanded on other grounds,* 40 P.3d 73 (2002).

determined that the bid was nonresponsive. A second involves a challenge by one or more bidders who argue that the bid of another bidder *should* have been rejected as nonresponsive. Stated another way, the second scenario involves a situation where the public agency is alleged to have unlawfully waived a material deviation from specifications. A third type of challenge, alleging that the public agency was *obligated* to waive a deviation from specifications but failed to do so, is the most difficult to sustain, for reasons discussed below. The result of a successful claim under any of these theories would likely be a court order invalidating the award of the contract.[8]

It is notable that all of the potential plaintiffs discussed above would be bidders. It is beyond the scope of this bulletin to fully discuss the legal standing of a disappointed bidder to challenge decisions in a public bidding process.[9] In some jurisdictions, courts have denied standing to bidders on the rationale that bidding statutes are designed to benefit the public in general rather than individual bidders.[10] The majority of cases, however, recognize bidder standing because, among other reasons, they have a sufficient interest to bring the action and are thus more likely to ensure the integrity of the process than would reliance on citizen lawsuits.[11] This would seem particularly persuasive in cases involving the question of responsiveness, as opposed to decisions more directly related to the final award of the contract. Responsiveness issues are technical in nature and are rarely presented to or understood by the public at large. Furthermore, the legal issue in the responsiveness determination is based on the issue of fairness to the bidders, as opposed to the broader interests of the public at large. Although the North Carolina courts have not addressed this issue, it is reasonable to assume that bidders will be allowed to bring cases involving the responsiveness determination where they can demonstrate that they will be harmed by the action of the public agency at issue.

A significant factor in the outcome of cases involving responsiveness is the degree of deference the court gives to the agency in reviewing the challenged action. When evaluating responsiveness decisions, courts use a deferential standard of review, similar or identical to the standard used in reviewing the award of a contract. Under this standard, the court will not interfere with the agency's decision unless it is arbitrary, illegal, corrupt, or fraudulent.[12] This means that even if there is support for more than one outcome, a court will

---

8. For a more detailed discussion of specific remedies that might be sought, *see* Frayda S. Bluestein, Disappointed Bidder Claims Against North Carolina Local Governments, *Local Government Law Bulletin*, No. 98, May 2001, Institute of Government, The University of North Carolina at Chapel Hill.

9. For such a discussion, *see* Bluestein, Disappointed Bidder Claims, *supra* note 8.

10. *See* H & W Contracting v. City of Watertown, 633 N.W.2d 167, 171–74 (S.D. 2001)(bidders do not have standing to challenge responsiveness determination except in cases of favoritism, improvidence, extravagance, fraud, or corruption).

11. H & W Contracting, 633 N.W.2d at 172 (citing cases).

12. Kinsey Contracting Co. v. City of Fayetteville, 106 N.C. App. at 384; 416 S.E. 2d at 608. *See also* Power Systems Analysis, Inc. v. City of Bloomer, 541 N.W.2d 214, 216 (Wis. Ct. App. 1995), Schindler Elevator Corp. v. Metro Development Comm'n, 641 N.E. 2d 653, 656–67 (Ind. App. 1994).

defer to the discretion of the agency in interpreting the legal requirement and sustain its decision unless it was arbitrary or unreasonable.[13]

Similarly, courts have declined to *require* the agency to waive a defect in a bid, even upon a finding that the deviation lawfully could have been waived.[14] In these cases, the courts support the right of the agency to insist upon strict compliance with the specifications and recognize that the determination of responsiveness is an action that involves discretion to which the courts must defer.[15]

An abuse of this discretion would occur, however, if the agency waives a defect that is material under the legal standard discussed in the rest of this article. There are also cases, including the only North Carolina decision on this issue, in which a court overrode the agency's decision to *reject* a bid. These cases are based on the court's conclusion either that the agency's determination that the bid was nonresponsive was erroneous as a factual matter,[16] or that the rejection of a bid that contained only technical defects constituted an abuse of discretion.[17]

The North Carolina case provides a good example of the fact-specific nature of some of these cases. That case involved a bidder on a food service contract with the State Department of Administration. The bidder completed the form, but instead of using the categories provided on the bid form for certain foods and beverages ("small, medium, and large"), the bidder listed the salad price "per ounce," and the beverages with a single price "all you can drink." The court held that the State's rejection of the bid as nonresponsive was not supported by the evidence, since the bid was clearly understandable on its face and was in fact more specific than bids listed as "small, medium, and large" that did not identify the volume or weight.[18]

There are relatively few cases, however, setting aside the decision of the agency to insist on strict compliance. More often, courts must grapple with whether a deviation that the agency chose to waive is in fact a "material" deviation requiring the rejection of the bid as a matter of law. In these cases, especially where there are reasonable interpretations supporting both sides of the issue, a court's deference to the agency may make the difference in the outcome of litigation.

---

13. Williams Brothers v. Kane County, 612 N.E.2d 890, 895 (Ill. App. Ct.), *appeal denied,* 622 N.E.2d 1229 (1993).

14. Barriere Construction Co., LLC v. Terrebonne Parish Consolidated Govt., 754 So.2d 1123 (La. Ct. App. 2000) (agency not required to waive bidder's failure to note project name and number on bid envelope); Miami Valley Contractors. Oak Hill, 671 N.E.2d 646, 650 (Ohio Ct. App. 1996) (upholding rejection of bid for failure to submit data sheet form); Serenity Contracting Group, Inc. v. Borough of Fort Lee, 703 A.2d 352, 354 (N.J. Super. Ct. App. Div. 1997), *cert. denied,* 708 A.2d 65 (N.J. 1998) (hand-written changes on a bid could have been accepted, but unit's decision to reject was not arbitrary).

15. *See* Martel v. Montana State Board of Examiners, 668 P.2d 222 (Montana 1983), and State v. Bowers, 621 P. 2d 11, 13–14 (Alaska 1980), upholding agencies' decisions to reject bids for failure to acknowledge addenda.

16. Professional Food Serv. Management, 109 N.C. App. at 269, 426 S.E.2d at 450.

17. Chris Berg, Inc. v. State Dept. of Transp., 680 P.2d 93 (Alaska 1984).

18. Professional Food Serv. Management, 109 N.C. App. at 269–70, 426 S.E.2d at 450–51.

Errors That Justify Bid Withdrawal

Under North Carolina's competitive bidding statute, like many such statutes in other states, a bidder has a limited period of time following the bid opening within which to request that his or her bid be withdrawn without penalty due to an error in the bid.[19] In North Carolina, the statute allows withdrawal only if the bidder can document that the error is clerical in nature, as opposed to a judgment error, and that it was due to "an unintentional and substantial arithmetic error or an unintentional omission of a substantial quantity of work, labor, apparatus, supplies, materials, equipment, or services made directly in the compilation of the bid."[20] If a bidder becomes aware of a defect in his or her bid that is clerical in nature and the bidder is not willing to enter into a contract based upon the bid as submitted, the bidder's only option is to request withdrawal. Under the statutory scheme, this decision is the bidder's to make. The determination of responsiveness, on the other hand, is made by the public entity or its agents. It is unlikely that an error that is substantial enough to justify withdrawal would be minor enough to be waived. It is possible, however, that in a particular circumstance the bidder will need to know quickly whether the unit will waive a defect before the bidder can decide whether to seek withdrawal of the bid. An example of how this may occur is helpful in illustrating the potential overlap between these issues.

A bidder may discover, after bids are opened, that he or she has neglected to include in the bid the cost of the plumbing work. This might have been because a price supplied by a subcontractor was omitted erroneously from the bidder's lump sum bid. The error might not be obvious from the face of the bid, other than through the fact that the bid is significantly lower than the rest of the bids received. The public agency staff may notice the price difference, but if there is nothing on the face of the bid that would constitute a deviation from specifications, the agency must accept the bid as submitted. The most the agency could do is notify the bidder either directly or by means of a bid tabulation, which public agencies commonly prepare and make available to the bidders shortly after bids are opened. After becoming aware of his or her low bid, the bidder might recheck the documentation and discover the error. It would be up to the bidder, in this situation, to decide whether the error warrants withdrawal and, if so, to request withdrawal in writing.

A variation of this scenario might involve an error that is evident from the face of the bid. For example, a bid might be submitted containing a price for the wrong piece of equipment. In this case the unit would be in a position to reject the bid as nonresponsive, and the bidder might also be able to justify a request to withdraw. From a practical standpoint, it would be best for the agency expeditiously to make a decision about whether the bid will be rejected

---

19. N.C. Gen. Stat. (hereinafter G.S.) §143-129.1 (1999). Requests to withdraw must be in writing and must be submitted within seventy-two hours after the bid opening (or a longer period as specified in the instructions to bidders). A bidder who does not meet the criteria for withdrawal forfeits the 5 percent bid bond, which must be submitted with the bid.

20. *Id.*

as nonresponsive so that the bidder will know whether he or she needs to request withdrawal. In this type of situation, it is simpler for the agency to reject the bid than it is to comply with the procedures for withdrawal.

It is important to recognize that in no event may the bidder alter or correct the bid. The competitive bidding process requires that bids be evaluated as submitted. Errors in bids may be the basis for rejection or for withdrawal, but they may not be corrected, even when it would suit the agency to do so. Correction of a material error in a bid creates an unfair advantage and creates the potential for collusion and abuse of the competitive bidding process.[21] As noted below, courts have upheld an agency's discretion to *interpret* bids, where the intent of the bidder is clear, and when doing so does not give the bidder an unfair advantage.

Situations Requiring Rejection of Bids

When considering the application of the legal standard for responsiveness to specific situations, there are several obvious cases in which the agency's obligation to reject bids is clear. First, bids must be rejected when they do not meet statutory requirements.[22] In North Carolina, for bids that are subject to the formal bidding requirements,[23] these cases would include late bids,[24] bids that are not sealed, and bids that are not accompanied at the time of their filing by the requisite bid bond or deposit.[25] Each of these things is required in the formal bidding statute. An agency receiving bids under a bidding requirement that is mandated by state law simply has no authority to alter the statutory requirement by waiving it.[26]

---

21. Davis/HRGM Jt. Venture v. U.S., 50 Fed. Cl. Ct. 539, 542 (2001); Missouri v. Stricker, 858 S.W.2d 771, 776 (Mo. Ct. App. 1993); Rosetti Contracting Co., Inc. v. Brennan, 508 F.2d 1039 (7th Cir. 1974).

22. Contracts that are subject to competitive bidding requirements are void if those requirements are not met. Styers v. Gastonia, 252 N.C. 572, 114 S.E.2d 348 (1960); Raynor v. Commissioners of Louisburg, 220 N.C. 348, 17 S.E.2d 495 (1941); Phipps Prod. Corp. v. Massachusetts Bay Transp. Auth., 443 N.E. 2d 115 (Mass. 1982).

23. Bids on contracts for construction or repair work estimated to cost $300,000 or more, or for the purchase of apparatus, supplies, materials, or equipment estimated to cost $90,000 or more. G.S. 143-129.

24. In jurisdictions in which the time for filing bids is not governed by statute, courts have gone both ways in deciding whether lateness of bids is material or waivable. *Compare* Power Systems, Inc. v. City of Bloomer, 541 N.W.2d 214 (Wis. Ct. App. 1995) (where statute did not establish requirement for bid opening time, court deferred to discretion of agency in waiving a bid that was late due to a delivery truck breakdown) *with* Holly's Inc. v. County of Greensville, 458 S.E.2d 454 (1995) (lateness of bids material and not waivable). *See* SANDRA M. STEVENSON, ANTIEAU ON LOCAL GOVERNMENT LAW, 2d ed., § 34.04 [4] (2001), *and* Robert M. Ey, J.D., *Authority of State, Municipal, or Other Governmental Entity to Accept Late Bids for Public Works Contract*, 49 A.L.R. 5th 747 (1997).

25. Bid bonds or deposits are mandatory for bids on construction or repair work estimated to cost more than $300,000 under G.S. 143-129(b).

26. *See* Neilsen & Co. v. Cassia and Twin Falls School Dist., 536 P.2d 1113, 1116 (Idaho 1975).

A second clear case for rejection of bids is when the bidder simply fails to offer what the unit seeks to acquire in the contract. In some jurisdictions, this element forms the first part of a two-part test for determining when bids must be rejected. As stated in these cases, the test of materiality includes "first, whether the effect of a wavier would be to deprive the municipality of its assurance that the contract will be entered into, performed and guaranteed according to its specified requirements."[27] (The second part of the test is whether the waiver gives the bidder an advantage over the other bidders.) The agency has the right to insist upon absolute compliance with specifications and clearly may reject a bid that fails to offer what the specifications require. More importantly, even if the agency is willing to accept the different materials or services offered in a particular bid, it would be unfair to the other bidders to accept an offer that does not meet the minimum specified requirement. It may even be unlawful to accept an offer that exceeds the minimum requirement, if the effect of doing so is to award a contract on which the other bidders were not given the opportunity to compete.[28] If the bid is simply beyond the scope of the solicitation, it must be rejected.

Understanding Materiality: What Types of Advantages Make Waiver Inappropriate

As noted earlier, courts evaluate materiality of defects in bids by reference to the principle of fairness. Specifically, agencies may not waive defects in bids when to do so would give the beneficiary of the waiver an unfair advantage in the competitive process. One could argue that the bidder gains an advantage simply by virtue of the fact that his or her bid has not been rejected. The courts do not approach the issue this way. The case law supports the idea that some defects are waivable, recognizing that substantial compliance with bid specifications, rather than perfection, is to be expected.

There are several types of advantage that courts identify when analyzing responsiveness cases. These interpretations of the basic legal standard are applied in a variety of recurrent scenarios and provide useful guidance in resolving specific cases.

Types of advantages that make waiver of defects inappropriate include:

1. The bidder saves money. Since the competition in the bidding process centers substantially around money, the failure of a bidder to meet a specification that allows that bidder to reduce his or her cost and thus to submit a lower bid clearly creates an unfair advantage in a bidding process.
2. The bidder saves time. In many cases, bids are prepared in a hectic, time-sensitive environment. This is especially true in construction

27. L. Pucillo & Sons, Inc. v. Township of Belleville, 592 A.2d 1218, 1225 (N.J. Super. Ct. App. 1991), *cert. denied*, 606 A.2d 364 (1991).

28. *See* Owensboro Grain Co. v. Owensboro Riverport Auth., 818 S.W.2d 605 (Kentucky 1991) (acceptance of bidder's alternate proposals prevented fair evaluation of bids and was invalid).

bids, where subcontractor prices are obtained up to the last minute before bids are submitted and the most competitive price offered before bids are due will be used. A bidder who fails to comply with a specification may gain an advantage by using the time saved to pursue better bids.

3. A defect in the bid gives the bidder the legal ability to back out. Some types of defects create an ambiguity about whether the bidder is actually bound by the bid. The best example of this is a bid that is not signed (see cases discussed below). Even if the bidder decides to honor the bid, the point here is that it is unfair for the bidder to be in a position to choose, after all the bids are exposed, whether or not to go forward with his or her bid. On the other hand, if the agency concludes that, as a matter of contract law, the bidder would be bound by the bid even with the defect, the defect may be waivable since the bidder does not have the advantage of being able to back out.
4. A defect in the bid gives the bidder an opportunity to improve the bid. A variation on the previous example, this situation occurs when there is an ambiguity in a bid that must be resolved after bids are opened. It is not fair to the other bidders for the agency to allow a bidder to clarify or interpret the bid if this gives the bidder an opportunity to improve his or her standing in comparison to the other bids received.
5. The waiver creates the potential for collusion or abuse of the competitive bidding process. A court may require rejection of bids in cases where the action by either an owner (in waiving a defect or interpreting a bid) or a bidder (such as bid shopping, discussed below) may threaten the fairness or other purposes of the bidding process.[29] While this may not always constitute an advantage to the bidder, a court may invoke this rationale to invalidate the action in the context of applying the basic responsiveness standard.

Application of Legal Standard to Specific Bid Defects

Failure to sign bids or related bid documents

The main issue regarding signatures on bids or bid documents is whether, taken as whole, the bid submission would constitute a binding offer by the bidder as a matter of contract law.[30] If the bidder would not be bound by the documents submitted due to the lack of signature, it would be unfair to waive this defect even if the bidder has agreed to be bound by his or her bid.

---

29. *See* San Jose Const. Group v. Loudoun County School Board, 47 Va. Cir. 487 (Va. Cir. Ct.1998) (interpretation and use of alternate bids creates opportunity for favoritism).

30. As noted in a later section, the lack of a signature on a document that is statutorily mandated, such as a bid bond or performance bond, may be a separate basis for rejection of a bid.

The fact that the bidder, who may have had the opportunity to review all the bids submitted, chooses to stand by his or her bid, does not cure the unfair advantage the bidder gains by leaving open the option of refusing to do so based on his or her incomplete bid. The question of whether a bidder would be bound by a particular bid that lacks signatures depends entirely upon the documents involved and is governed by case law within the jurisdiction. As such, cases that seem to have similar facts may have different outcomes. Examples of cases are discussed below.[31]

Some cases involve situations in which the bidder has signed one or more bid documents but has not signed all the documents in the proper places.[32] In these cases, courts rely on general contract law to determine whether the documents are sufficient to indicate an intention by the bidder to make an offer to contract. If the bidder would be bound by the bid as submitted, he or she gains no competitive advantage from the waiver of the defect. For example, in a case from Ohio in which the bidder did not sign the cover page of the bid but did sign an addendum, the court looked at the entire package of documents and concluded that they were sufficient to constitute a binding offer.[33] Based on this conclusion, the court held that the failure to sign the cover page was not material and could be waived. A similar result was reached in a case involving an unsigned bid accompanied by a signed bid bond,[34] and in another involving a signed bid containing an unsigned affirmative action form.[35]

Cases in which the court concluded that the bidder would not be bound by the bid as submitted have held that the defect is not waivable.[36] A case in which the bid was not signed anywhere resulted in a ruling that the bid must be rejected.[37] The bidder argued that the bid bond would protect the agency, but the court correctly noted that the surety would be entitled to any defense the bidder had and would not be liable on the bid bond if the bidder were not bound by the bid.[38] Similar results have been reached in cases where the bid was signed but the signature was invalid. An example is a bid signed by someone without legal authority to bind the bidding entity.[39]

---

31. There is no reported North Carolina case directly addressing this issue in the public bidding context.

32. *See, e.g.,* Spawglass v. Houston, 974 S.W.2d 876, 881–87 (Texas App. 1998) (summarizing cases).

33. Leaseway Distribution Centers v. Dept. of Administrative Services, 550 N.E.2d 955 (Ohio Ct. App. 1988). *See also,* Menefee v. County of Fresno, 210 Cal. Rptr. 99 (Cal. App. 1985).

34. Eastside Disposal Co. v. Mercer Island, 513 P.2d 1047 (Wash. Ct. App. 1973). *See also* Farmer Construction Ltd. V. State, 656 P.2d 1086 (Wa. 1983).

35. Kokosky v. Dixon, 594 N.E.2d 675 (Ohio Ct. App. 1991).

36. Kennedy Construction v. Chicago, 481 N.E.2d 913 (Ill.Ct. App. 1985) *vacated on other grounds,* 491 N.E.2d 1160 (1986).

37. A.A.B. Elec., Inc. v. Stevenson Public School Dist., 491 P.2d 684 (Wash. Ct. App. 1971).

38. A.A.B. Elec., 491 P.2d at 687. Note that under the Uniform Commercial Code, a bidder on a contract for the sale of goods may be bound by a bid that does not contain a signature as long as there is other evidence of an intent to authenticate the contract, such as a letterhead or other symbol representing the party to be charged. *See* G.S. 25-1-201(39).

39. Intercontinental Properties, Inc. v. State, 606 So. 2d (Fla. Ct. App. 1992); Davis/HRGM Joint Venture.v. U.S., 50 Fed. Cl. 539 (Fed. Cl. 2001).

Finally, several cases have held that the agency must reject an unsigned bid if the signature requirement is a matter of statute or regulation.[40] This is consistent with the rule, discussed above, that the agency has no authority to waive statutory requirements.

Failure to use proper bid form

Many bid specifications require that bids be submitted on the form supplied by the agency. There are several important reasons for this requirement. First, it is designed to encourage prospective bidders to obtain complete bid specifications directly from the agency (rather than submitting a bid using specifications borrowed from another bidder). The agency encourages this in order to maintain a list of bidders who may intend to submit bids so they can be notified of changes in specifications or other important information about the bid process. In addition, complications in interpreting bids can arise if the bids are not submitted in the common format set out in the bid form supplied by the agency. Ideally, the bid form, if properly completed, will minimize confusion in interpreting alternate bids, unit price extensions, and other aspects of the pricing requested in the solicitation. Despite the best efforts of the agency, however, bidders sometimes fail to obtain or to properly complete bid forms.

A reliable rule of interpretation in cases involving a bidder's failure to use the proper form is that if the bid amount and other terms of the offer are clear from the face of the document as submitted, the failure to use the form is a waivable defect.[41] Where all of the information necessary to understand and evaluate the bid is contained on the document, the failure to complete the proper form is purely a technicality and does not provide any benefit or advantage to the bidder. It is important to note, however, that if the failure to use the proper form results in a need to clarify the bid, this may give the bidder an opportunity to improve his or her position after bids are opened. Such clarification should be avoided and the bid, in these circumstances, must be rejected.[42]

Numerical errors

Certainly the most important aspect of most bids is the price offered. Errors in bid amounts are common and may, as noted earlier, cause a bidder to seek withdrawal of a bid. In other cases, however, the agency may be tempted to interpret the prices offered in a way that preserves its ability to award the contract. A general rule in cases involving unclear or ambiguous bid amounts

---

40. *See* Whitmarsh Township Auth. v. Finelli Brothers, Inc., 184 A.2d 512 (Pa. 1962); Thigpen Const. Co., Inc. v. Parish of Jefferson, 560 So.2d 947 (La. Ct. App. Cir. 1990). There is no specific signature requirement in the North Carolina bidding statutes.

41. State *ex rel.* KNC, Inc. v. New Mexico Dept. of Finance and Adm., 704 P.2d 79 (N.M. Ct. App. 1985) *cert. denied,* 702 P.2d 1007 (failure to acknowledge addenda); McCloskey v. Independence Cablevision Corp, 460 A.2d 1205 (Pa. Commw. Ct. 1983); Bryan Construction Co. v. Montclair, 106 A.2d 303 (N.J. Super. Ct. App. Div.1954).

42. *See* Fratello Construction Corp., v. Tuxedo Union Free School Dist., 726 N.Y.S.2d 705, 706 (N.Y. App. Div. 2001).

is that unless the bid amount can be determined by reference to the face of the bid document, or by applying objective rules for interpretation of bids, the bid must be rejected.

A common rule of interpretation, for example, is that in the case of a discrepancy between a unit price and the extension (the unit price multiplied by the number of units), the unit price governs. Another common rule is that where numerical bids are stated both in numbers and in words, the words govern. While these rules of interpretation are widely used and generally accepted, it is unclear whether they may be used if they are not contained in the specifications or in laws governing the solicitation. Public agencies should include these rules of interpretation in their standard specifications for bids, or in local regulations, so that they will have stronger authority to rely on them to resolve ambiguous bids. Without such authority, it could be argued that the unit must reject bids that contain these types of ambiguities.

Some numerical errors can be resolved from the face of the bid document without reference to a rule of interpretation. For example, consider a bid specification that requests a base bid and an additive alternate. The bid document requires the alternate to be stated as the base bid amount plus the alternate. One bidder offers a base bid of $250,000 and an alternate bid of $35,000. Obviously, the bidder has stated the alternate as a separate amount, rather than adding it to the base bid amount. The intent of the bidder is obvious and can be resolved without consultation with, or other advantage to the bidder.

Even when a rule of interpretation, like the ones described above, would dictate a different outcome, courts have allowed agencies to make practical interpretations of bids when the intent of the bidder is clear from the face of the bid.[43] In a case, for example, where the numbers clearly indicated that a bidder put the extended price in the unit price line on the bid form, a court approved the agency's evaluation based on division of the lump sum bid by the number of units, which resulted in a unit price in line with those of the other bidders.[44] In this type of case, courts have upheld an agency's decision *not* to use a standard rule of interpretation where the intent of the bidder was clear from the bid and the application of the rule would be inconsistent with that intent.[45]

A more difficult case, however, is presented by a bidder's failure to include a price for a listed item or portion of work. This may be interpreted two ways: One is that the bidder intended to provide the item or work at no additional cost, and the other is that the bidder made an error and failed to complete the bid. (Note that a bid of zero does not present this ambiguous scenario.) Asking the bidder to clarify his or her intent after bids are opened is not an option, since this would clearly give the bidder an advantage by allow-

---

43. *See* H & W Contracting, LLC v. City of Watertown, 633 N.W.2d 167 (S.D. 2001); Spina Asphalt Paving Excavating Contractors, Inc. v. Fairview, 701 A.2d 441 (N.J. Super. Ct. App. Div. 1997); Sciaba Construction Corp. v. City of Boston, 617 N.E.2d 1023 (Mass. App. Ct. 1993), *review denied,* 621 N.E.2d 685 (Mass. 1983).

44. *H & W Contracting,* 633 N.W.2d at 175.

45. *See also,* Jensen & Reynolds Construction Co., v. Dept. of Transportation, 717 P.2d 844 (Alaska 1986) (rule providing that written bid governs over numerical bid rejected where the intent of the bidder was clearly the opposite).

ing him or her to decide, after seeing the competitors' bids, which interpretation was more advantageous to use.[46] The agency could quickly notify the bidder that the agency will interpret the incomplete bid as an offer to do the work at no cost and give the bidder an opportunity to withdraw the bid if this was an error. Otherwise, it is probably best, and may be legally necessary, to reject the bid.[47]

Failure to acknowledge receipt of addenda

Bidders are not the only ones in the bidding process who make mistakes. It is common to discover errors or changes in specifications that require correction or modification prior to the receipt of bids. These changes are made by "addenda," which are simply changes in or additions to the specifications that are added after the initial release of specifications to the bidders. Addenda are distributed to each bidder who has received specifications or who the agency is otherwise aware intends to submit a bid. A standard practice is to require the bidders to acknowledge receipt of addenda in order to assure that the bids reflect the changes they contain.

If it is clear from the face of a bid that the bid incorporates the changes called for in an addendum, the failure to acknowledge receipt of the addendum is a waivable defect.[48] The rationale for this interpretation is the same as in the cases discussed above regarding failure to use the proper bid form: that is, that the failure is of a technical nature and does create an advantage for the bidder. Waiver has also been approved in situations where the bidder provided an oral acknowledgment of receipt *prior* to the opening of bids, or where the substance of the addendum at issue has negligible or no effect on the essential terms or prices in the bid.[49]

The more difficult case is one in which it cannot be determined from the face of the bid whether the bid amount incorporates a change made by addendum. In this situation, the bidder gains an advantage from having the ability after bids are exposed to provide an interpretation of his or her bid. In the second situation, the bid must be rejected.[50]

---

46. *See* Fratello Construction Corporation v. Tuxedo Union Free School Dist., 726 N.Y.S. 2d 705 (N.Y. App. 2001), *and* Lovering-Johnson v. Prior Lake, 558 N.W.2d 499 (Minn. Ct. App. 1997).

47. *Compare* Turner Construction Co. v. New Jersey Transit, 687 A.2d 323 (N.J.Super. Ct. App. 1997) (zero bid acceptable) *with* Hall Construction v. New Jersey Sports Authority, 685 A.2d 983 (N.J. Super.Ct. App.Div. 1996) (bid must be rejected where alternate was left blank).

48. Martel v. Montana State Board of Examiners, 668 P.2d 222 (Mont. 1983); State ex rel. KNC, Inc. v. New Mexico, 704 P.2d 79 (N.M. Ct. App. 1985), *cert. denied,* 702 P.2d 1007.

49. *See* Charles N. White Construction v. Dept. of Labor, 476 F. Supp. 862, 866 (D.C. Miss. 1972).

50. *See id.*; Lovering-Johnson v. Prior Lake, 558 N.W.2d 499 (Minn. Ct. App. 1997).

Failure to list subcontractors

In some jurisdictions and for some types of contracts, the failure to list subcontractors is a violation of state law and must, as noted earlier, be rejected.[51] In North Carolina, for example, when bids on building projects are received using the single-prime or dual-bidding methods, the law requires the single prime bids to identify the subcontractors that will be used in specified categories of work.[52] The purpose of a subcontractor listing requirement is to prevent "bid shopping." Once a bidder is the apparent low bidder or has received a contract, he or she may attempt to improve profits or favor particular subcontractors by soliciting new bids from subcontractors and substituting those who are willing to underbid the subcontractors whose bids were used in the original bid. Preventing bid shopping is a sufficiently important goal that courts have been hesitant to allow waiver of a failure to list subcontractors, even when the listing is not required by statute.[53] Indeed, even when not required by statute, the failure to list subcontractors probably gives the bidder an advantage not enjoyed by other bidders and may be sufficient to constitute a material deviation under the legal standard for responsiveness.

Failure to provide minority-utilization information

Responsiveness issues also arise with public contracting requirements that are designed to promote the use of minority contractors. In some jurisdictions contractors are required by statute or regulation to list or otherwise document the efforts they have made to solicit bids from minority contractors, or to list minority contractors who will be used on the project. These things are required in North Carolina for most building construction or repair projects.[54] As noted earlier, the general rule is that the failure to comply with a statutory requirement cannot be waived. Courts in other jurisdictions have also held the failure to provide minority-contracting documentation to be a material defect in bids.[55]

A question of interpretation sometimes arises when a bidder who has failed to submit documentation of good faith efforts indicates that he or she in fact made the required effort to recruit and use minority businesses but simply failed to enclose the form or affidavit, and the bidder offers to provide it immediately or shortly after the bids are opened. Cases are unclear on whether

---

51. Ray Bell Construction Co., Inc. v. School Dist. Of Greenville County, 501 S.E. 2d 725 (S.C. 1998); George & Lynch, Inc. v. Division of Parks and Recreation, 465 A.2d 345 (Del. 1983).

52. G.S. 143-128(d), (d1).

53. *See* Conduit and Foundation Corp. v. City of Philadelphia, 401 A.2d 376 (Pa. Commw. Ct. 1979).

54. *See* G.S. 143-128.2(c); 143-131(b).

55. *See* Carl Bolander & Sons v. Minneapolis, 451 N.W.2d 204 (Minn. 1990); Leo Michuda & Sons v. Metro Sanitation Dist., 422 N.E.2d 1078, 1083 (Ill. App. 1981); Rossetti Contracting Co. v. Brennan, 508 F.2d 1039 (7th Cir. 1975). *But see* James Luterback Const. Co. Inc. v. Adamkus, 577 F. Supp. 869 (D.C. Wisc. 1984), *vacated for mootness,* 781 F.2d 599 (7th Cir. 1986).

this type of defect is material. If a bidder can demonstrate that the efforts were made prior to the bid opening, perhaps it could be argued that the failure to include the form does not provide an advantage.[56]

The better approach, however, is probably to reject bids in this circumstance. It is difficult to establish what efforts were made prior to the bid and to verify the accuracy of material provided after the bid opening. Furthermore, even a small amount of time gained by failing to prepare the affidavit or documentation of good faith efforts may be a material advantage in the bid preparation process. Refusal to accept late submission may also promote better compliance with the minority outreach program.[57] Finally, if state law requires affidavits to be submitted with the bid, as is the case for some contracts under North Carolina law,[58] a bid that fails to meet that requirement must be rejected.

Failure to submit technical materials or other documentation

It is impossible to catalogue the various types of documentation that an agency might require bidders to submit as part of a bid. Examples include technical material describing the performance capability or characteristics of material to be purchased, schedules for performance, and information about the bidder's experience or financial resources. There is no clear rule of interpretation for cases involving the failure to include this type of material, other than the general rule of determining whether the failure to include the material gives the bidder a competitive advantage. In most cases, the failure to include documentation does not create an advantage and may therefore be waived and cured by the later submission of the information.

The fact-specific nature of these types of situations, however, is illustrated by comparing two cases. In one case, a bidder failed to supply a graphic representation of a construction progress schedule that was required in the bidding documents.[59] The court held that this was a waivable defect since it did not alter the bidder's obligation to finish the work by a certain date and because the schedule was not required by statute.[60] In contrast, another case held that the failure to include appropriate data, sketches, drawings, sales specifications, and other information to be used for complete evaluation of the bids required rejection.[61] Similarly, the failure to specify a time for completion of the project was a material deviation requiring rejection of the bid.[62] Resolution of these cases will necessarily depend entirely upon the nature of

---

56. *See* Schindler Elevator Corp. v. Metro Dev. Comm'n, 641 N.E.2d 653 (Ind. Ct. App. 1994); Kokosing Construction Co. v. Dixon, 594 N.E.2d 675, 680 (Ohio Ct. App. 1991).

57. *See* Rossetti Contracting, 508 F.2d at 1082–83.

58. G.S. 143-128.2(c)(applies to building construction and repair projects costing $300,000 or more).

59. Gil-Bern Constr. Corp. v. Brockton, 233 N.E.2d 197 (Mass. 1968).

60. *Id.* at 199–200.

61. National Engineering & Contracting Co. v. City of Cleveland, 146 N.E.2d 340 (Ohio 1957).

62. Bale Contracting, Inc. v. City of Westerville, 455 N.E.2d 517 (Ohio Ct. App. 1982).

the documentation at issue, its importance in the bid evaluation process, and the advantage, if any, gained by a delay in submission.

Errors in bid bonds

Public agencies often require each bidder to submit a bid bond, which secures the obligation of the bidder to enter into a contract if he or she is the successful bidder. When a bond is submitted, errors in the form or content of the bid bond raise issues of responsiveness. A defect in a bid bond that renders the bond invalid constitutes a failure to supply a bond. Where a bond is required by statute, this type of defect requires rejection of the bid. In North Carolina, bid bonds are required for construction or repair contracts in the formal bidding range.[63] The statute prohibits the consideration of a bid in this category unless it is accompanied "at the time of its filing" by a bid bond or deposit in an amount equal to not less than five percent of the total bid amount.[64] This requirement is sufficiently specific that many questions about improper bid bonds are easily resolved. A bid that is accompanied by a bond that is not valid due to improper signatures or amount must be rejected. A bid that is not accompanied by a bond at all must be rejected, even if the bidder can supply it shortly after the bid opening, since the statute requires the bid bond to accompany the bid *at the time of its filing.*

Another question that sometimes arises in this area is whether an alternate form of security, such as a letter of credit, is acceptable. The North Carolina statute allows three specific alternatives to a bid bond: cash, cashier's check, or a certified check on a federally insured bank or trust company.[65] Though there is no North Carolina case or other interpretation of the statute on this question, since the statute is so specific as to the forms of security permitted, it appears that alternatives other than those specifically listed are not acceptable.[66]

Another common issue involving bid bonds is whether a bid accompanied by a faxed bid bond is acceptable. The legal issue is whether the faxed document as submitted is valid: that is, whether the surety is bound by the document as submitted by the bidder. Although there does not appear to be case law directly on this subject, the law increasingly recognizes the validity of contractual obligations evidenced by electronic documents.[67] A court would be likely to uphold the obligation of the surety under a faxed bid, assuming that the document is otherwise valid. Public agencies may choose to insist upon

---

63. G.S. 143-129(b). Formal bidding is required when the estimated amount is $300,000 or more.

64. *Id.*

65. *Id.*

66. *See* Kennedy Temporaries v. Comptroller, 468 A.2d 1026, 1033–34 (Md. Ct. Spec. App. 1984).

67. *See, e.g.,* G.S. 66-317, a key provision of the North Carolina Uniform Electronic Transactions Act, which recognizes the validity of electronic contracts and electronic signatures.

original bid bonds, however, in order to reduce the chances of receiving a falsified document or to otherwise insure authenticity. The ability to use a faxed document makes a big difference to contractors when submitting bids, since it takes more time to obtain and submit an original document from the surety. Public agencies should specify in their bid documents whether they will accept faxed bid bonds so that the bidders are in an equal position with regard to the submission of bid bonds. If there is nothing in the specifications indicating that faxed bid bonds will be accepted, bidders may assume they are not acceptable. In this circumstance, acceptance of a faxed bid bond would be unfair to those who took the time to obtain original documents.

Conclusion

The bid preparation and submission process is fraught with opportunities for error. Public agencies are often inclined to waive errors in order to avoid additional expense and delay in the contracting process. Courts play a unique role in promoting fairness on behalf of all of the participants in the process, especially the bidders, in cases challenging a public agency's exercise of discretion to waive defects in bids. Cases decided around the country provide guidance to public officials in determining when defects in bids lawfully may be waived. Adherence to the general rules articulated in these cases, supported by the generally deferential standard of review applied in most cases, should promote consistency and legally enforceable results for pubic agencies in North Carolina when they analyze the responsiveness of the public bids they receive.

Index

References are to page numbers.

A

addenda, 45, 51–52, 149
additional quantities provisions, 48–49
advertisement of bid opportunity
  date of bid opening, changing, 51–52
  disqualification of bidders, 53–54
  information in advertisement, 51
  notification of individual bidders, 52–53
  readvertisement and already-received bids, 63
  when and how long to advertise, 50–51
  where to advertise, 49–50
"approved products" list, 43
authority to contract, 5–6
  apparent authority, doctrine of, 7
  awarding contracts, 69, 74–75
  budgetary authority, 8–13, 110–111, 125–127
  delegation of authority, explicit or implicit, 6
  entities other than board, 74
  execution vs. approval authority, 5–6
  lowest possible bidder standard, discretion regarding, 70–73
  ratification, cure of lack of authority by, 6, 7–8
  signatures, 15–16
awarding contracts, 69–70
  authority regarding, 69, 74–75
  binding contract, when created, 74–75
  contingent awards, 76
  entities other than board, 74
  informal bids, 80
  legal claims protesting awards, 84
  length of time taken to award or execute contract, 76–77
  lowest responsible bidder standard, 70–73, 82
  optional procedures for contracts not subject to competitive bidding requirements, 82
  post-award procedures, 74–77
  preferences in, 73–74
  rescinding awards, 75–76

B

bid bonds or bid deposits, 58–61, 152–153
bid opening, 54–58
  changing date, 51–52
  late bids, acceptance of, 58
  number of bids required for. *See* three-bid requirement
  persons attending, 56–57
  public inspection of bids at, 57
  public meeting requirement, 56
  reverse auctions, 56, 123
  sealed bids, 54–55, 61
bidders. *See also* responsibility of bidder
  disqualification of, 53–54
  length of time taken to award or execute contract, 76–77
  lists of, 52–53, 114
  lowest responsible bidder standard, 70–73, 82
  negotiating with, 67–68
  preferences, 73–74
bids
  advertisement (*see* advertisement of bid opportunity)
  competitiveness of (*see* competitive bidding requirements)
  electronic receipt, 55, 123
  errors (*see* errors in bids)
  evaluating, 64–65
  form of, 61–64, 65
  formal bidding procedures, 19, 49–78
  informal, 40, 78–80
    "piggybacking," 130
    statute law, 123–124
  late bids, acceptance of, 58
  legal claims (*see* legal claims related to competitive bidding requirements)
  number required
    formal bids (*see* three-bid requirement)
    informal bids, 89

bids (*continued*)
- opening (*see* bid opening)
- optional procedures for contracts not subject to competitive bidding requirements, 81–82
- pre-solicitation or pre-bid conferences, 45–46
- rejection of, 65, 143–144
- retention of bid and contract documents, 77
- sealed bids, 54–55, 61
- solicitation practices, 45–49, 79–80 (*see also* advertisement of bid opportunity)
- statute law on procedures, 117–121
- withdrawal of (*see* withdrawal of bids)

binding contract, when created, 74–75

bonds
- bid bonds or bid deposits, 58–61, 152–153
- performance and payment bonds, 77–78

brand names, 42–43

budget year. *See* fiscal year

budgetary authority, 8–13, 110–111, 125–127

building construction contracts. *See* construction/repair contracts

C

change orders, 29–30, 40–41

common law of contracts, 1–3

competitive bidding requirements
- covered agencies, 19
- covered contracts, 21–27 (*see also* specific types of contract)
- dollar thresholds (*see* dollar thresholds)
- donated funds requiring use of specified contractor, 22
- exemptions (*see* exemptions from competitive bidding requirement, and also specific subjects of exemption)
- failure to comply (*see* legal claims related to competitive bidding requirements)
- fairness requirements, 17–18, 144
- legal claims (*see* legal claims related to competitive bidding requirements)
- nonprofit and nongovernmental organizations, 20–21
- optional procedures for contracts not subject to, 81–82
- outside funding, contracts involving, 21
- pre-solicitation or pre-bid conferences, 45–46
- public money, contracts involving expenditure of, 19
- purpose of, 17
- rescinding awards under, 75–76
- responsiveness (*see* responsiveness requirements)
- solicitation practices, 45–49
- specifications (*see* specifications)
- statute law on, 19, 117–121, 123
- value as purpose, 17–18

computer hardware and software contracts, 25–26. *See also* information technology goods and services

conferences, pre-solicitation or pre-bid, 45–46

confidential information, benefiting from, 100, 109–110

conflicts of interest. *See* ethics and conflicts of interest

constitutional violations, legal claims based on, 85–86

construction/repair contracts
- competitive bidding requirements, 23
- construction management at risk method, 33
- demolition work not regarded as, 26
- "piggybacking," 130
- statute law, 114–117
- three-bid requirement, 62, 63–64

contingent awards of contracts, 76

continuing contracts, 9, 12, 125, 127

contracts, 1–16. *See also* specific types, e.g. services contracts
- authorization (*see* authority to contract)
- awarding (*see* awarding contracts)
- binding contract, when created, 74–75
- budgetary authority, 8–13, 110–111, 125–127
- common law, 1–3
- competitive bidding requirements
  - covered contracts, 21–27
  - optional procedures for contracts not subject to, 81–82
- continuing contracts, 9, 12, 125, 127
- deficiency judgments, 13
- defined, 1
- discretion of board bound by, 5
- divided, prohibition on, 39, 124
- electronic documents, 15
- faxed documents, 15
- fiscal year, contracts extending beyond, 9, 12
- issuance of, 81
- length of time taken to award or execute, 76–77
- limitations on, 3–5
- modifications, 40–41
- nonappropriation clause, 12
- nonsubstitution clause, 12–13
- oral vs. written, 13–14
- post-award procedures, 74–77
- ratification
  - cure of lack of authority by, 6, 7–8
  - ethics and conflicts of interest, contract violating laws against, 102
- record of board's actions, 14–15
- renewal or additional quantities provisions, 48–49, 133
- requirements for, 1–2
- retention of bid and contract documents, 77
- seals, 16
- signatures, 15–16
- statute law, 1, 13–14, 117–121
- statute of frauds, 13
- Uniform Commercial Code (UCC), 1, 13–14
- witnesses, 16
- written contract requirement, 13–15, 127

cooperative or joint purchasing with other governmental units, 95–96, 128

Correction Enterprises products, competitive bidding exemptions for, 38–39
cost estimates. *See* estimated cost

D

defective bids. *See* errors in bids
deficiency judgments, 13
demolition contracts, 26
deposits, bid, 58–61
disabled, competitive bidding exemptions for purchases from nonprofit work centers for, 36
discretion of board
  contracts binding, 5
  lowest possible bidder standard, 70–73
disqualification of bidders, 53–54
divided contracts, prohibition on, 39, 124
Division of Purchase and Contract, state contract purchases by, 32–33
documentation. *See* records and reports
dollar figure for nominal gifts, 102–103
dollar thresholds, xii, 39–41
  chart, 105
  informal bids, 78, 80, 105
donated funds requiring use of specified contractor, 22
due process rights, legal claims based on violation of, 85–86

E

electronic bids, 55, 123
electronic contracts, 15
emergencies, competitive bidding exemptions for, 27–28
energy-related projects, competitive bidding exemptions for
  guaranteed energy savings contracts, 32
  joint municipal power agencies, 19
equal protection rights, legal claims based on violation of, 85–86
erroneous opening of bids, 54–55
errors in bids
  addenda, failure to acknowledge receipt of, 149
  advantages making waiver of defects inappropriate, 144–145
  bid bonds, 152–153
  evaluation of bids, 65
  minority utilization information, failure to provide, 150–151
  numerical errors, 65, 147–149
  rejection due to, 65, 143–144
  signature failures, 145–147
  subcontractors, failure to list, 150
  technical materials or other documentation, failure to submit, 151–152
  unit price and extension, discrepancy in bid between, 65
  withdrawal due to, 66–67, 142–143
estimated cost
  determining, 40
  informal bids, 79
  statute law, 114
ethics and conflicts of interest. *See also* gifts and favors
  confidential information, benefiting from, 100, 109–110
  contracting for own benefit, 97–99, 107–109
  legal effect of contracts violating law regarding, 102
  noninvolvement of benefiting party in making of contract, 101
  personal use items purchased through contracts, 104
  professional codes, 97
  ratification of contract violating laws against, 102
  site visit paid for by contractor or potential contractor, 103–104
  spouses benefiting from contracts, 100–101
  statute law, 97–100, 107–110, 113–114
  voting, abstention of benefiting party from, 102
evaluating bids, 64–65
exemptions from competitive bidding requirements
  change order work, 30
  construction management at risk method, 33
  contracts exempted, 27–39
  Correction Enterprises products, 38–39
  demolition work, 26
  emergencies, 28–29
  energy-related projects
    guaranteed energy savings contracts, 32
    joint municipal power agencies, 19
  force account work, 35
  governmental units (*see* governmental units)
  group purchasing programs, 29–30
  information technology goods and services, 31–32
  lease or rental contracts, 36–37
  nonprofit and nongovernmental organizations, 20–21
  nonprofit work centers for disabled, purchases from, 36
  "piggybacking" (*see* "piggybacking")
  purchases from other governmental units, 27–28, 95–96, 128
  school food and food services, 36
  services contracts, 23
  sole-source purchases, 30–31, 37
  solid waste management facilities, 34
  state contract vendors, purchases from, 32–33, 37
  transportation authority purchases, 34–35
  used goods, 33
  volunteer fire organizations, 21
extension and unit price, discrepancy in bid between, 65

F

fairness requirements in competitive bidding, 17–18, 144
favors and gifts. *See* gifts and favors

faxes
acceptance of bid by, 61–62
bid bond or bid deposit, 61
contract documents, 15
federal grants or loans, competitive bidding requirements for contracts involving, 21
fire organizations, volunteer, 21
fiscal year
awarding contracts in one year to be paid in following year, 70
contracts extending beyond (continuing contracts), 9, 12, 125, 127
food and food services
competitive bidding requirements, 27
school food and food services, competitive bidding exemptions for, 36
force account work (use of governmental unit's own permanent work force), competitive bidding exemption for, 35
form of bids, 61–64, 65
formal bids, 19, 49–78
frauds, statute of (contracts), 13
free speech rights, legal claims based on violation of, 85–86
funding, contract awards contingent on, 76

G

gifts and favors
dollar figure for nominal gifts, 102–103
local governments and departments, gifts to, 103
site visit paid for by contractor or potential contractor, 103–104
statute law, 99–100, 113–114
governmental units
competitive bidding exemptions
agencies exempted, 19
force account work, 35
"piggybacking" (*see* "piggybacking")
purchases from other government units, 27–28, 95–96, 128
competitive bidding requirements, agencies covered by, 19
cooperative or joint purchasing between, 95–96, 128
gifts to local governments and departments, 103
grants or loans, competitive bidding requirements for contracts involving, 21, 127–128
group purchasing programs, competitive bidding exemptions for, 29–30

H

hospital authorities, 19, 20
housing authorities, 19
husbands and wives benefiting from contracts, 100–101

I

IFB (invitation for bids), 46
IFQ (invitation for quotes), 47
informal bids, 40, 78–80
"piggybacking," 130
statute law, 123–124
information technology goods and services
competitive bidding exemptions for, 30–31
computer hardware and software contracts, 25–26
request for proposals (RFP) procedure, 37–38
statute law, 122–123
installment-purchase contracts, 9–11, 12, 13, 36, 112–113
invitation or request for bids (IFB or RFB), 46
invitation or request for quotes (IFQ or RFQ), 47
issuance of contracts, 81

J

joint municipal power agencies, 19
joint or cooperative purchasing with other governmental units, 95–96, 128
judicial review of responsiveness determinations, 139–141

L

late bids, acceptance of, 58
lease or rental contracts, 36–37
lease-purchase contracts, 9–11, 12, 23, 36, 112–113
legal claims related to competitive bidding requirements
basis for, 84–86
constitutional violations, 85–86
failure to comply with requirements
basis for claim in, 84–85
legal consequences of, 83
personal liability of official for, 86–87
persons able to bring case, 87
procedures for protesting bid process or contract award, 84
tax dollars, illegal expenditure of, 85
loans or grants, competitive bidding requirements for contracts involving, 21, 127–128
local bidders, preferences for, 73
local government units. *See* governmental units
lowest responsible bidder standard, 70–73, 82

M

manuals. *See* purchasing organization and policies
meetings of board
awarding contracts, 69
bid opening, public meeting requirement for, 56
minority-owned businesses, preferences for, 74
minority-utilization information, failure to provide, 150–151

mistakes. *See* errors in bids
mixed goods and services contracts, 24–25

N

negotiating with bidders, 67–68
nominal gifts, dollar threshold for, 102–103
nonappropriation clause, 12
nonprofit organizations, competitive bidding exemptions and requirements for, 20–21, 36
nonsubstitution clause, 12–13
North Carolina Correction Enterprises products, competitive bidding exemptions for, 38–39
notice
  individual bidders, 52–53
  "piggybacking," 131–132
number of bids required
  formal bids (*see* three-bid requirement)
  informal bids, 80
  statute law, 124
numerical errors in bids, 65, 147–149

O

opening bids. *See* bid opening
organization of purchasing. *See* purchasing organization and policies
outside funding, competitive bidding requirements for contracts involving, 21

P

performance and payment bonds, 77–78
performance specifications, 44
personal liability of official for failure to comply with competitive bidding requirements, 86–87
personal use items purchased through contracts, 104
"piggybacking," 33–34, 39, 129–130
  acceptance of bids from other purchasers, 132
  changes in terms of contract, 134–135
  construction/repair contracts, 130
  informal bids, 130
  notice requirements, 131–132
  original purchaser, actions required of, 132
  own contract, piggybacking on, 134
  participation rules, 130–131
  parties to contract, 130
  piggyback on a piggybacked contract, 134
  procedural requirements, 133
  records and reports, 132–133
  renewed contracts, 133
  twelve-month period, determining, 133
policies on purchasing. *See* purchasing organization and policies
pre-solicitation or pre-bid conferences, 45–46
preaudit requirement, 8–9, 70
predominance approach to mixed goods and services contracts, 24–25
preferences, 73–74
previously contracted persons, competitive bidding exemptions for. *See* "piggybacking"
prison system (Correction Enterprises) products, competitive bidding exemptions for, 38–39
private organizations
  competitive bidding exemption, 20–21
  statute law on contracting with, 125, 128
procedures for purchasing. *See* purchasing organization and policies
professional codes governing ethics and conflicts of interest, 97
public housing authorities, competitive bidding exemptions for, 19
public inspection of bids at bid opening, 57
public meeting requirement for bid opening, 56
public money
  competitive bidding requirements for contracts involving expenditure of, 19
  legal claims based on illegal expenditure of tax dollars, 85
public transportation authority purchases, competitive bidding exemptions for, 34–35
purchase contracts, 23, 36
purchase orders, 81
purchasing organization and policies, 89
  adoption or approval by board, 92–93
  contents of manual, 93–94
  cooperative or joint purchasing with other governmental units, 95–96
  development of, 94–95
  purpose of, 91–92
  requirement to have policy or manual, 91
  small purchases, 90–91
  vendor manual vs. purchasing manual, 93

Q

"qualified products" list, 43
quasi-public organizations and competitive bidding requirements, 20–21

R

racial preferences, 74
ratification of contract
  cure of lack of authority by, 6, 7–8
  ethics and conflicts of interest, contract violating laws against, 102
readvertisement and already-received bids, 63
records and reports
  lowest possible bidder standard, 72–73
  "piggybacking," 132–133
  retention of bid and contract documents, 77

records and reports (*continued*)
technical materials or other documentation, failure to submit, 151–152
written contract requirement, 14–15
recycled, remanufactured, or reused materials requirements, 44
rejection of bids, 65, 143–144
renewal options, 48–49, 133
rental or lease contracts, 36–37
repair contracts. *See* construction/repair contracts
request for proposals (RFP)
defined, 46–47
information technology goods and services, 37–38
request or invitation for bids (RFB or IFB), 46
request or invitation for quotes (RFQ or IFQ), 47
rescinding awarded contracts, 75–76
resources and research materials
purchasing information generally, xi–xii
specifications, 41–42
responsibility of bidder
disqualification for lack of, 53–54
lowest responsible bidder standard, 70–73, 82
performance and payment bonds, 77–78
responsibility distinguished from responsiveness, 139
responsiveness requirement, 18, 64–65, 137
advantages making waiver of defects inappropriate, 144–145
definition, 137–139
judicial review of determinations, 139–141
legal standards applied to specific bid defects, 145–153
responsibility distinguished from, 139
withdrawal of bids, 142–143
reverse auctions, 56, 123
RFB (request for bids), 46
RFP. *See* request for proposals (RFP)
RFQ (request for quotes), 47

S

schools
food and food services, competitive bidding exemptions for, 36
statute law on contracting for, 110–113
sealed bids, 54–55, 61
seals on contracts, 16
services contracts, 23–25
signatures
contracts, 15–16
failure to sign bids or related documents, 145–147
small purchases, 90–91
software contracts, 25–26
soil and water conservation districts, 19
sole-source purchases, competitive bidding exemptions for, 30–31, 37
solicitation of bids, 45–49, 79–80. *See also* advertisement of bid opportunity
solid waste management facilities, competitive bidding exemptions for, 35
specifications, 41–46
"approved products" or "qualified products" list, 43
brand names, 42–43
changes made for second round of bidding, 62–63
defined, 41
evaluation of bids against, 64
limitations on, 42
performance specifications, 44
pre-solicitation or pre-bid conferences, 45–46
recycled, remanufactured, or reused materials, 44
resources and research materials, 41–42
statute law, 41
specified contractor, donated funds requiring use of, 22
speech, legal claims based on violation of freedom of, 85–86
spouses benefiting from contracts, 100–101
standardization and specification of brand names, 43
state contract vendors, competitive bidding exemptions for purchases from, 32–33, 37
state grants or loans, competitive bidding requirements for contracts involving, 21, 127–128
state law governing ethics and conflicts of interest, 97–100
state prison system (Correction Enterprises) products, competitive bidding exemptions for, 38–39
statute law, 107–128
budgetary authority, 110–111, 125–127
cities and towns, 127–128
competitive bidding, 19, 117–121, 123
construction/repair contracts, 114–117
contracts, 1, 13–14, 117–121
cooperation, interlocal, 128
counties, 125
ethics and conflicts of interest, 97–100, 107–110, 113–114
gifts and favors, 99–100, 113–114
public works, 113–114
school contracting, 110–113
specifications, 41
state agencies, 114–124
statute of frauds for contracts, 13
subcontractors, failure to list, 150
surplus property, trading in, 47–48, 122

T

tax dollars (public money)
competitive bidding requirements for contracts involving expenditure of, 19
legal claim based on illegal expenditure of, 85
technical materials or other documentation, failure to submit, 151–152
three-bid requirement, 61, 124
bid bond or bid deposit, lack of, 60–61

construction/repair contracts, 62
errors in bids, 66
unacceptable/nonresponsive bids, 62
trade-in of surplus property, 47–48, 122
transportation authority purchases, competitive bidding exemptions for, 34–35

U

Uniform Commercial Code (UCC) on contracts, 1, 13–14
unit price and extension, discrepancy in bid between, 65
used goods, 33

V

value requirements in competitive bidding, 17–18
vendors
purchasing manual vs. vendor manual, 93
state contract vendors, competitive bidding exemptions for purchases from, 32–33, 37
volunteer fire organizations, 21
voting, abstention of benefiting party from, 102

W

water and soil conservation districts, 19
withdrawal of bids
errors, due to, 66–67, 142–143
responsiveness requirement, 142–143
statute law, 117–121
witnesses to contracts, 16
wives and husbands benefiting from contracts, 100–101
women-owned businesses, preferences for, 74
work force of governmental unit, competitive bidding exemption for (force account work), 35
written contract requirement, 13–15, 127

www.ingramcontent.com/pod-product-compliance
Lightning Source LLC
LaVergne TN
LVHW082337200926
848481LV00012B/3370
* 9 7 8 1 5 6 0 1 1 4 6 4 2 *